BRITISH ROYAL PROCLAMATIONS RELATING TO AMERICA, 1603-1783

LECTOR HOUSE PUBLIC DOMAIN WORKS

BRITISH ROYAL PROCLAMATIONS RELATING TO AMERICA 1603-1783

CLARENCE SAUNDERS BRIGHAM

ISBN: 978-93-5614-063-9

Published: -

LECTOR HOUSE LLP
E-MAIL: lectorpublishing@gmail.com

By the King,

A PROCLAMATION

Prohibiting His Majesties Subjects to Trade within the Limits Assigned to the Governour and Company of Adventurers of *England*, Trading into *Hudson's Bay*, except those of the Company.

JAMES R.

Whereas Our Dearest Brother King *Charles* the Second of blessed Memory, did by His Letters Patents under the Great Seal of *England*, bearing Date the Second day of *May*, in the Two and Twentieth Year of His Reign, Incorporate a Governour and Company for carrying on a Trade in the North West parts of *America* within the Streights and Bay, commonly called *Hudson's Streights* and did Grant unto them and their Successors, the Sole Trade and Commerce of all those Seas, Streights, Bayes, Rivers, Lakes, Creeks and Sounds in whatsoever Latitude they should be, lying within the Entrance of the Streights commonly called *Hudson's Streights*, together with all the Lands, Countreys, and Territories upon the Coasts and Confines of the Seas, Bayes, Lakes, Rivers, Creeks and Sounds aforesaid, which were not then Possessed by, or Granted to any of the Subjects of Our said Royal Brother, or Possessed by the Subjects of any other Christian Prince or State, Thereby Erecting and Constituting the said Governour and Company for the time being, and their Successors, the true and absolute Lords and Proprietors of the same Territories, Limits and Places aforesaid, and of all other the Premisses, with exprels Prohibition to all other the Subjects of Our said Royal Brother to Trade to the Parts aforesaid. And Whereas We are satisfied that the said Company hath for many years with great Industry, and at a very great Charge and Expence, settled several Factories, Erected several Fortifications, and maintained the Trade in the Parts aforesaid, to the great honour and profit of this Our Kingdom, until of late several ill-disposed Persons not being Members of the said Company, nor Licensed by them, preferring their private profit before the publick good, have contrary to the said Royal Grant, in a clandestine and disorderly manner, Traded into those parts, to the apparent prejudice, if not destruction, of the Trade aforesaid, and in manifest Contempt of Our Prerogative Royal; and the better to colour their evil practices, do frame Designs to Hire, or do Hire themselves out in the Service of, or in conjunction with foreigners to Sail to the Parts aforesaid, to undermine and destroy the said Companies Trade. We, taking the Premisses into Our Princely Consideration, do not only (of Grace and Favor, That the Persons who have so contemptuously violated the said Companies Charter, be Prosecuted in Our Name at Law, in order to their condign punishment according to their demerits) But for prevention of the like evil practices for the future, We have thought fit, with the Advice of Our Privy Council, to Publish and Declare Our Royal Will and Pleasure to be, and We do hereby strictly Prohibit and Forbid that none of Our Subjects whatsoever, except the said Governour and Company and their Successors, and such as shall be duly Licensed by them at any time or times hereafter do presume to send or Navigate any Ship or Ships, Vessel or Vessels, or exercise any Trade whatsoever directly or indirectly on their own accounts, or in the Service of, or in conjunction with any foreigner or foreigners whatsoever, to, in or from the said Streights and Bay, called *Hudson's Streights*, or to, in or from any Bayes, Rivers, Creeks or Places whatsoever, by what nature or denominations soever they or any of them have been heretofore, or shall hereafter be called or distinguished, that not are or lie within the Entrance of *Hudson's Streights* aforesaid, in what Latitude or Longitude soever the same or any of them do, both or shall lie, remain or be within the Liberties, Territories, or Priviledges of the said Company, upon pain of Our high Displeasure, and the forfeiture and loss of the Goods, Merchandizes, Ships and Vessels which shall be taken or found Trading in any the place or places aforesaid, or within the Limits aforesaid. And We do hereby strictly Charge and Command all and every Our Subjects of What degree or quality soever, now Trading or Traffiquing, or designing to Trade or Traffique out to or from the Parts aforesaid, or any of them, contrary to the true meaning of the said Companies Charter, That they forthwith do cease and forbear such their Trade and Traffique, and withdraw themselves from the parts aforesaid. And We do further hereby streightly Require and Command all and singular Our Governours, Lieutenant-Governours, Admirals, Vice-Admirals, Generals, Judges of all Our Courts of Admiralty, Commanders of Our Forts and Castles, Captains of Our Royal Ships, Justices of the Peace, Provost Marshals, Marshals, Comptrollers, Collectors of Our Customs, Waiters, Searchers, and all other Our Officers and Ministers Civil and Military by Sea or Land, in all and every of Our Dominions or Plantations, and all other Our Subjects whatsoever and wheresoever, to take effectual care that no person or persons whatsoever (except the said Company and their Successors, and such as shall be duly Licensed) do send or Navigate any Ship or Vessels, or exercise any Trade directly or indirectly from any of Our Kingdoms, Dominions or Plantations whatsoever, contrary to the said Charter granted to the said Company as aforesaid, to any the places or Limits aforesaid, or from thence to any of Our said Kingdoms, Dominions, Plantations, or other places. And if any person or persons shall presume to act or do in any wise contrary to this Our Royal Proclamation, We do Will, Require and streightly Command all and singular Our said Governours, Lieutenant-Governours, Admirals, Vice-Admirals, Generals, Judges of Our Courts of Admiralty, Commanders of Our Forts and Castles, Captains of Our Royal Ships, Justices of the Peace, Provost-Marshals, Marshals, Sheriffs, Comptrollers, Collectors of Our Customs, Waiters, Searchers, and all other Our Officers and Ministers Civil and Military by Sea or Land in every of Our said Dominions and Plantations, and all other Our Officers, Ministers and Subjects whatsoever and wheresoever, that as often as need shall require, they and every of them respectively be Aiding and Assisting to the said Company, their Factors, Deputies, or Assigns, to Attach, Arrest, Take and Seize all such Ship or Ships, Vessel or Vessels, Goods, Wares and Merchandizes of such person or persons as shall be Used, Employed, or Traded in contrary to the Charter Granted to the said Company, wheresoever they shall be found, for Our Use, upon pain of Our high Displeasure, and as they will answer the contrary at their perils.

Given at Our Court at *Whitehall* the One and thirtieth day of *March* 1688. In the Fourth Year of Our Reign.

GOD SAVE THE KING.

London, Printed by Charles Bill, Henry Hills, and Thomas Newcomb, Printers to the Kings most Excellent Majesty, 1688.

Proclamation of 1688 (reduced facsimile).

BRITISH ROYAL PROCLAMATIONS RELATING TO AMERICA 1603-1783

EDITED BY

CLARENCE S. BRIGHAM, A.M.

Burt Franklin: Bibliography and Reference Series # 56

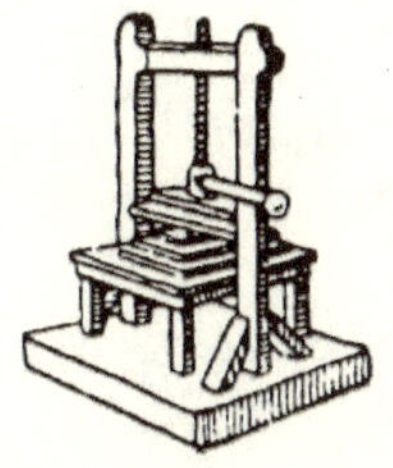

LIST OF PROCLAMATIONS.

Page

LIST OF PROCLAMATIONS.

1638, May 1.	Requiring Licenses for New England
1639, March 25.	Concerning Tobacco
1639, August 19.	Licensing of Tobacconists
1643, November 24.	Requiring Loyalty from America
1655, October 10.	Encouraging Settling in Jamaica
1658, March 9.	Limiting Greenland Trade to Muscovy Company
1660, September 22.	For Apprehension of Whalley and Goffe
1661, March 29.	Prohibiting Planting of Tobacco in England
1661, May 9.	Suppressing Vagrancy
1661, December 14.	Encouraging Settling in Jamaica
1667, August 23.	Recalling Dispensations of Navigation Act
1671, December 22.	Concerning the Planters at St. Christophers
1674, March 11.	Recalling Dispensations of Navigation Act
1674, November 30.	Prohibiting African Trade to Plantations
1675, October 1.	For Apprehending Don Philip Hellen
1675, November 24.	Enforcing Navigation Acts
1676, April 1.	Concerning Passes for Ships
1676, October 27.	Suppressing the Rebellion in Virginia
1681, April 2.	Granting Pennsylvania to William Penn
1685, February 6.	Continuing Officers in the Colonies
1685, April 1.	Prohibiting African Trade to Plantations
1688, January 20.	Suppressing Pirates in America
1688, March 31.	Prohibiting General Trading at Hudson's Bay
1689, February 19.	Continuing Officers in the Colonies
1689, May 7.	Declaration of War against France
1690, July 14.	For Apprehending William Penn
1691, February 5.	For Apprehending William Penn
1700, January 29.	For Apprehending Author of Darien Libel
1701, March 6.	For the Apprehension of Pirates
1702, March 9.	Continuing Officers in the Colonies
1704, June 18.	Rates of Foreign Coins in Plantations
1708, June 26.	Encouraging Trade to Newfoundland
1711, June 23.	Establishing Post Office in America
1714, October 4.	Concerning Passes for Ships
1714, November 22.	Continuing Officers in the Colonies
1717, September 5.	For Suppressing Pirates in West Indies

LIST OF ABBREVIATIONS
OF THE NAMES OF LIBRARIES
POSSESSING PROCLAMATIONS.

Adv.	Advocates' Library, Edinburgh.
Antiq.	Society of Antiquaries, London.
B. M.	British Museum, London.
Bodl.	Bodleian Library, Oxford.
Camb.	Cambridge University Library.
Cant.	Municipal Library, Canterbury.
Ch.	Chetham Library, Manchester.
Crawf.	Lord Crawford's Library, Haigh Hall.
D. H.	Devonshire House, London (Friends' Historical Society).
Dalk.	Dalkeith Palace (Duke of Buccleuch), Scotland.
Dubl.	Dublin Public Record Office.
Guild.	Guildhall Library, London.
Hodg.	J. Eliot Hodgkins' Library, London.
I. T.	Inner Temple, Library, London.
P. C.	Privy Council Office, London.
P. R. O.	Public Record Office, London.
Q. C.	Queen's College, Oxford.
Signet	Signet Library, Edinburgh.
T. C. D.	Trinity College, Dublin.

INTRODUCTION.

This volume is the outgrowth of action taken by the Society at its annual meeting in October, 1906, when a committee consisting of Mr. Waldo Lincoln, Professor William MacDonald, and Dr. J. Franklin Jameson was appointed to arrange for a new volume of the Society's Transactions. At the April meeting, 1907, the committee was given power to proceed with the publication of the British Royal Proclamations relating to America, and in October following appointed the writer to edit the volume. The editor spent the summer of 1908 in England engaged in this undertaking.

The present volume includes all English Royal proclamations which concern North and South America, from 1603 to 1783. Only those proclamations are printed which emanated directly from the King. The numerous declarations and proclamations issued by provincial and colonial governors, the unauthorized proclamations of minor English officials serving in America, the proclamations of the governors-general of Canada and the Thanksgiving and Fast-Day proclamations of the New England governors have all been omitted. They are documents of another class, and exist in such profusion as to be quite beyond the scope of this volume. These colonial proclamations, furthermore, are practically never entered in the English records. As original broadsides, they are very rarely found in English depositories, but are scattered throughout the libraries and archives of America. Enough of these exist to form the basis of another volume. Limiting the present field to royal proclamations allows the subject to be covered with reasonable completeness.

Proclamations only are included, under which heading would come manifestos and declarations of the King. In a few cases proclamations were issued by the Lords Justices during the King's absence from England. The great mass of orders in council, which were occasionally issued as broadsides, but generally are found only in manuscript entries, are not included. These are now being printed in the "Acts of the Privy Council, Colonial Series," the third volume of which has progressed as far as the year 1745. Another class of proclamations rejected are those of the Lords Lieutenants of Ireland, which repeat verbatim the English orders in council.

From the early days of English history, proclamations were issued by the Crown to make known to the people new acts or regulations or declarations of public importance. Distributed for public view in printed broadside form, they have been familiar to twenty generations of English-speaking people. Yet, in spite of their frequency of issue and in spite of their occasional importance as public documents, there has been scarcely a book upon the forms of English government or upon the history of records, which gives a detailed account of the method of issuing, entering, and publishing proclamations. It remained for Mr. Robert Steele to compile during the past year, "A Bibliography of Royal Proclamations, 1485-1714, with an Historical Essay on their Origin and Use." This work, in two folio volumes, forms volumes five and six of the Earl of Crawford's splendidly published series, the *Bibliotheca Lindesiana*, and in this country can be consulted at most of the large libraries. Mr. Steele so thoroughly treats of the issuing, enforcement, and history of proclamations, that more than a brief allusion to their method of publication is unnecessary in this place.

Proclamations, during the seventeenth and eighteenth centuries at least, usually underwent the following routine. They were drawn up by the Attorney General upon instructions from the Privy Council, then engrossed on vellum and signed by the King. After having been printed as broadsides in an edition of a thousand or more by the King's printer, they were sent by messengers to the sheriffs of the various counties and towns, by whom they were posted. A document of the period of Charles II preserved in the Public Record Office shows the method of issuing a proclamation:

> "Proclamations how passed.—Proclamations are usually drawn by the Attorney Generall and assented to by the Council and brought down to a Secretary of State to be engrossed in vellum and soe signed by the King (without any attestation of the Secretary), then being dated they are sent (sealed in a paper) to the King's Printing House by a messenger, who of course receives for their service 2s. 6d. of the Printer. Then are printed off such a number as is judged convenient, and of them some Copys furnished on the K.'s and to the Secry^s to the Councell, &ca.: and 1250 are carried to the Clerk of the Crown to be distributed under the Great Seal, together with the original Proclamation signed by the King, which is there kept upon a File for the Clerk of the Crown's discharge and warrant. There are made up by the Clerk of the Crown, 66 writs directed to so many Sheriffs; each containing a certain number of proclamations tyed up with a Label, and then sealed. These writs are delivered over to the 4 Riding Messengers, whose office it is to distribute them, and for their pains have among them £40 out of the Hanaper paid by Bill, if it be ye King's business (as generally they are), or else £50 if it be a private man's concern. His fees for the 66 writs are, £22 at 6s. 8d. per writt. The Printer has, by old Rates & Custom, 1d. per sheet for what he prints at the King's charge which comes to £15 for a Proclamation, and upon bills exhibited to the Lord Chancellor is paid in the

Hanaper. His bills for quantitys furnished to the Secretary's office are attested by the Secretaries respectively & those to the Council office by the Clerks there." (S.P.D. Entry Book 72, p. 219, quoted by Steele.)

Another interesting side light upon their method of distribution is shown by a quotation from the records of the Privy Council:

January 10, 1678-79. "Whereas his Majesty did this Day in Council take notice of some Proclamations that have issued whereof no notice has come into severall parts of the Kingdome than what happens to be given by the Gazet, notwithstanding the great charge that is brought unto his Majesties accompt for the sending and Dispatching all Proclamations that issue, therefore to reform this abuse, and to settle for the future a method of lesse expence, and more certainty and expedition in the publique Service, It is this day ordered by his Majesty in Councill that the Right honorable the principall Secretaries of State do call before them Philip Frowde Esq. Governor of the Post office, and settle a method for sending all Proclamations to the respective Sheriffs, so as the next Postmaster to such Sheriff be charged with the Delivery of the same, and send up the Sheriffs receipt for his Discharge. The clerk of the Crowne is also to be summoned, and orders given him, that as soon as Proclamations passe the Seale, he do deliver them the next post day into the Post office and take a receipt thereof for the Discharge of his Duty herein, And the messengers of the Exchequer who have formerly been intrusted with this Service to his Majesties Damage and Expence are to be summoned and acquainted with the Rule that is now to be established, and that they desist hereafter from intermedling with this matter." (Privy Council Register, II Chas., 14:12.)

This new order, however, took away much of the revenue of the messengers and after a formal complaint had been made and duly heard, the Council concluded not to alter

"the ancient Course of Dispersing Proclamations, but leaves the Same to the Execution of the messengers of the Exchequer as formerly and that they take care that no Complaints be brought against them hereafter for not timely delivering of Proclamations. And his Majesty is graciously pleased to Command that the said Order of the 10th Instant be, and the same is hereby Superseded." (Idem, p. 39.)

With the reform of the postal service in 1709, the Privy Council discontinued the use of riding messengers and ordered that in future proclamations should be sent out by post.

Proclamations when signed by the King were termed "signed bills" and most of them are now preserved in the Public Record Office among the Privy Seal bundles. During the period covered by this volume, proclamations were generally copied on the backs of the Patent Rolls, and can be found through the Indexes. The eighteenth century proclamations were furthermore noted in the Crown Office Docquet Books, which are in the Public Record Office. Since proclamations were first ordered in the Privy Council, they were duly entered in its records and are to be found in the Registers in the Privy Council Office. After 1665, proclamations were generally published in the *London Gazette*, and before that date occasionally in London newspapers, such as the *Mercurius Politicus* and the *Kingdomes Intelligencer*.

It would seem as if there would be in England at least one official collection of broadside proclamations, yet no depository—the Public Record Office, the Privy Council Office, or the British Museum—possesses more than a fair share of the total number. Private collections are often the most valuable for certain periods, and as Mr. Steele's work shows, it requires a canvass of all existing collections to insure anything like completeness.

The principal depositories of proclamations have the following distinguishing characteristics:

The British Museum collection, although but sparsely represented for the eighteenth century, is notably full for the seventeenth century issues. Scattered in many different volumes, however, a comprehensive search requires a considerable amount of time. The Museum also has excellent files of the newspapers in which many of the proclamations were printed.

The collection of proclamations in the Public Record Office is contained in eight folio volumes, and is also less strongly represented for the eighteenth century. Here the Indexes to the Patent Rolls and the Crown Office Docquet Books are invaluable.

At the Privy Council Office is the best collection of proclamations for American reference and one which is especially good for the eighteenth century. The long, bulky series of Privy Council Registers, which is full of interest to students of American affairs, contains the entries of most proclamations.

Other London libraries, where the collections of proclamations were examined for this volume, were the Guildhall and the Society of Antiquaries. Each of these depositories had large numbers of the earlier proclamations and possessed certain issues which existed in no other place. At the Bodleian Library, Oxford, the Public Record Office in Dublin, and the Register House in Edinburgh, valuable collections were consulted.

Of the private collections, easily the most comprehensive is that gathered by the Earl of Crawford and described in the Bibliography of Royal Proclamations before referred to, in which volume other collections, both private and public, are noted at length. There is no large collection of broadside proclamations in any one American library, although many of the larger public and historical libraries possess occasional issues, and these, so far as found, have been noted.

There are one hundred and one proclamations entered in this volume. They have been carefully transcribed from the printed broadsides, except in the few instances where the broadside could not be found and some other source had to be used. Above each proclamation the date is given, and also a descriptive heading supplied by the editor and enclosed in brackets. The notes serve chiefly to explain obscure points, or to refer to original sources for certain Acts printed in the text. The bibliographical information entered at the end of each document gives the size of the original broadside, a list of libraries where it is to be found, a reference regarding the entry of the proclamation upon the Patent Roll, Crown Office Docquet Book, or Privy Council Register, and a note of the fact as to whether it is reprinted elsewhere. A list of the libraries referred to as containing the broadsides, and a chronological list of the proclamations precede the body of the text. The frontispiece reproduction of a proclamation of 1688 is from an original broadside owned by the John Carter Brown Library.

The editor's indebtedness to many English officials and librarians for courtesies extended to him in the course of his work is hereby gratefully acknowledged, especially to Mr. Hubert Hall of the Public Record Office and Sir Almeric FitzRoy, Clerk of the Privy Council. Professor W. L. Grant, then editing the "Acts of the Privy Council, Colonial Series," made many helpful suggestions. To Mr. Robert Steele above all others the Society is most deeply indebted. His aid and advice willingly given, his exceptional knowledge of the particular subject constantly placed at the editor's service, and finally his scholarly published work on the Bibliography of Royal Proclamations have all greatly helped to lighten the burden of research.

CLARENCE S. BRIGHAM,
Editor.

August 5, 1911.

ROYAL PROCLAMATIONS

1603, SEPTEMBER 17.

[BANISHING VAGABONDS TO NEWFOUNDLAND AND WEST INDIES.]

BY THE KING.

A Proclamation for the due and speedy execution of the Statute against Rogues, Vagabonds, Idle, and dissolute persons.

Whereas at a Parliament holden at Westminster in the nine and thirtieth yeere of the Reigne of his Majesties late deare Sister deceased Queene Elizabeth, a profitable and necessary Law was made for the repressing of Rogues, Vagabonds, idle and dissolute persons,[1] wherewith this Realme was then much infested, by the due execution of which Lawe, great good ensued to the whole Commonweale of this Realme, but now of late by the remissenesse, negligence, and connivencie of some Justices of the Peace, and other Officers in divers parts of the Realme, they have swarmed and abounded every where more frequently then in times past, which will grow to the great and imminent danger of the whole Realme, if by the goodness of God Almighty, and the due and timely execution of the said Law the same be not prevented.

And where to the end that no impediment might be to the due and full execution of the same Law, his Highnesse Privie Councell, according to the power to them in that behalfe given by the sayd Law, have by their Order assigned places and parts beyond the Seas, unto which such incorrigible or dangerous Rogues should according to the same Lawe be banished and conveyed, as by the Order in that behalfe made, and under this present Proclamation particularly mentioned and set downe, more at large appeareth: His Majestie purposing (for the universall good of the whole Realme) to have the same Law duely and fully executed, doth by advice of his Privie Councell require all Justices of Peace, Maiors, Bayliffes, Hedboroughs, Constables, and other Officers whatsoever to whom it appertaineth, to see that the said Law be in all the parts, and branches of the same carefully, duely and exactly executed, as they and every of them will answere the contrary at their uttermost perils.

---

[1] Printed in *Statutes of the Realm,* iv, 899: "An Acte for punyshment of Rogues Vagabonds and Sturdy Beggars," 39 Eliz. ch. 4.

Given at his Majesties Mannour of Woodstocke the seventeenth day of September, 1603, in the first yeere of his Highnesse Reigne of England, France, and Ireland, and of Scotland the seven and thirtieth.

GOD SAVE THE KING.

THE ORDER.[2]

Forasmuch as it hath appeared unto us aswell by our owne viewes in our travailes in this present Progresse of his Majestie, as also by good and credible information from divers and sundrie partes of the Realme, that Rogues grow againe and increase to bee incorrigible, and dangerous not onely to his Majesties loving Subjects abroad, but also to his Majestie and his Honourable Houshold and attendants in and about his Court, which growing partly through the remissenes of some Justices of the Peace, and other Officers in the Countrey, and partly for that there hath beene no Suite made for assigning some place beyond the Seas, to which such incorrigible or dangerous Rogues might bee banished, according to the Statute in that behalfe made: We therfore of his Majesties privie Councel, whose names are hereunto subscribed, finding it of necessitie to reforme great abuses, and to have the due execution of so good and necessarie a Law, doe according to the power limitted unto us by the same Statute, hereby Assigne and thinke it fit and expedient, that the places and partes beyond the Seas to which any such incorrigible or dangerous Rogues shall bee banished and conveyed according to the said Statute, shall bee these Countries and places following, viz. The New-found Land, the East and West Indies, France, Germanie, Spaine, and the Low-countries, or any of them.

T. Buckhurst.	*Lenox.*	*Nottingham.*
Suffolke.	*Devonshire.*	*Mar.*
Ro. Cecill.	*E. Wotton.*	*Jo. Stanhop.*

Imprinted at London by Robert Barker, Printer to the Kings most Excellent Majestie. Anno 1603.

2 pp. folio. Copies in Antiq., B. M., Crawf., P. R. O., and Q. C. Entered on Patent Rolls. Printed in Rymer's "Fœdera," xvi, 554, and in Barker's "Booke of Proclamations," p. 44.

---

[2] This Order in Council is not to be found among the Records of the Privy Council, which for the period from 1603 to 1613 were burned in a fire at Whitehall in 1618.

1606, AUGUST 23.

[TRANSPORTING OF WOMEN AND CHILDREN TO FOREIGN PARTS.]

BY THE KING.

A PROCLAMATION TOUCHING PASSENGERS.

Whereas in the first Session of our Parliament holden at Westminster the nineteenth day of March in the yeere of our raigne of England, France and Ireland the first, and of Scotland the seven and thirtieth; It was amongst other things Enacted, That no woman nor any childe under the age of one and twenty yeeres (Except Saylers or Shipboyes or Apprentice, or Factor of some Merchant in trade of Merchandize) should bee permitted to passe over the Seas, except the same should be by licence of us, our Heires or Successors, or some sixe or more of our privy Councell, thereunto first had under their handes, upon paine that the Officers of the Port that should willingly or negligently suffer any such to passe, or should not enter the names of such Passengers licenced, should forfeit his Office, and all his goods and Chattels, And upon paine that the owner of any Ship or Vessell, that should wittingly or willingly cary any such over the Seas, without licence as is aforesaid, should forfeit his Ship or Vessell, and all the Tackle, And every Master or Mariner, of or in any such Ship or Vessell, offending as is aforesaid, should forfeit all their goods, and suffer imprisonment by the space of twelve moneths without Baile, or Maineprise, As by the saide Acte of Parliament amongst other things may more at large appeare:[3]

And whereas many such our Subjects, That is to say, Women and persons under the age of twenty and one yeeres, have from time to time just and necessary causes and occasions to goe and passe over the Seas, In which cases for every such women and persons under the age of twenty and one yeeres to obteine such licence, either from our selves, or from sixe of our said Privy Counsel according to the said Law, is very inconvenient, and almost impossible; Wee have therefore thought convenient, for the ease as well of our selfe and our said Counsell, as of such of our Subjects as are of the condition mentioned in the saide Acte of Parliament, to graunt our Commission to persons of trust in certaine Ports of our Realme, lying most apt and convenient for passage, That is to say, London, the <u>Cinque Ports</u>, Harwich, Yarmouth, Hull, and Waymouth, to licence such women

[3] This Act, entitled "An Acte for the due Execution of the Statutes againste Jesuits, Seminarie Priestes Recusants &c.," is printed in *Statutes of the Realm*, iv. 1021, 1 James I, ch. 4, sec. 7.

and persons under the age of twenty and one yeeres, as shall have just cause to passe out of our Realme, upon due examination had of them, to passe without perill to themselves, or the Officers of our said Ports, Notwithstanding the said Statute or anything therein conteined, And we have thought it fit to give publique knowledge hereof to al our Subjects, and to all our Officers whom it may concerne, to the ende they may know what shall bee lawfull for them to doe in those cases.

Given at the Castle of Farneham the xxiii. day of August, in the fourth yeere of our Reigne of Great Britaine, France and Ireland.

God Save the King.

Imprinted at London by Robert Barker, Printer to the Kings most Excellent Majestie. 1606.

1 p. folio. Copies in Antiq., B. M., Crawf., P. R. O., and Q. C. Entered on Patent Rolls. Printed, in Barker's "Booke of Proclamations," p. 133.

1614, SEPTEMBER 11.

[IMPORTATION OF WHALE-FINS FROM GREENLAND.]

BY THE KING.

A Proclamation concerning the bringing in of Whale-Finnes into his Majesties Dominions, etc.

As Wee conceive, it cannot be construed by any Our doings or proceedings, that Wee are caried with any ambitions or unjust appetite, to covet that which appertaineth to others So it shalbe alwayes Our desire and resolution, to nourish and maintaine the happy estate of Our loving Subjects, and the honour of Our Kingdomes; not onely in the same degree, in the which We have received them; but likewise with that increase and advancement, whereof the providence of Almighty God by just occasions shal put meanes and opportunities into Our hands; and in nothing more (next unto the true worship of God, and the administration of Justice) then in the maintenance and increase of Navigation, wherein Our kingdomes both by scituation, strength of shipping, skill of Marriners, valew of Commanders at Sea, and many honourable discoveries and exploits, have for long time, and more and more of late time flourished. And whereas Our Company of Merchants for the discovery of new Trades, commonly called the Muscovia Company,[4] have with their great costs and charges, of late yeeres discovered a Land, which they call by the name of King James his Newland,[5] to the increase of Navigation and Mariners; and have further by their care and industry entred into a trade of fishing for the Whale, and procured Biscainers, skilfull in striking the Whale, to teach and instruct the English Nation therein: And whereas a principall part of the benefit of the Whale-fishing consisteth in the commoditie of Whale-finnes imported into Our

---

[4] The Russia, or Muscovy Company, chartered as a company of Merchant Adventurers in 1554, received from King James in 1613 an additional charter giving them the exclusive rights to the whale fishery of Greenland. For the subsequent career of this Company and their struggles with the Dutch for the possession of the Greenland trade, see Cawston and Keane, *Early Chartered Companies*, pp. 45-52.

[5] In 1613 the Muscovy Company set up the King's arms at Spitzbergen, calling it King James's Newland. (Anderson, *Origin of Commerce,* ii, 343.) In vol. iv of the *Transactions* of the American Antiquarian Society is printed from the original manuscript the Narrative of a Voyage to Spitzbergen, being "A Brief Description of the Country of Greenland, otherwise called King James his New Land." The rise of the Muscovy Company and its participation in the Greenland trade is carefully treated by Dr. S. F. Haven in the introduction to the Narrative. This recently discovered land was Spitzbergen and not Greenland proper.

Kingdomes; And that experience already sheweth, that Our owne subjects in their returne from that Fishing, are able to furnish and serve Our Kingdomes with sufficient quantity for the use of Our loving subjects: it being also a matter of delicacie, and rather to be considered as it may concerne Navigation, then in itselfe: We have therfore thought fit for the better encouragement of the said Company, and other Our Subjects, in services of like nature, to prohibite all Aliens and strangers, and also Our owne subjects, (except the said Muscovia Merchants, and that in their joynt stocke) to bring hereafter into any Our Kingdomes the said commodity.

Wherefore We do by these presents, straitly and expresly forbid and prohibite, all Aliens and strangers whatsoever, and also Our owne Subjects (others then the said Muscovia Merchants, and that in their joynt stocke) to bring into any Our kingdomes, and Dominions any Whale-finnes, upon paine of Confiscation of the same, and of Our high indignation and displeasure, and of such further punishment, as shalbe meet to be inflicted upon the offenders for their contempt in that behalfe: And We do further hereby charge and require all Our Customers, Comptrollers, Searchers and other Officers, and also the Farmors of Our Customes, and their ministers, carefully to attend every one in their severall dueties, the execution of this Our Royall Proclamation, and in no wise to permit or suffer any Whale-finnes, either directly or indirectly, openly or privately, to be brought into the Ports, or other places of any of Our kingdomes: And in case any be brought in, the same to seaze to Our use, and by all other meanes to finde out, and informe of all offences tending to the breach of this Our Royall Proclamation.

Given at Wansted the eleventh day of September, in the twelfth yeere of Our Raigne of Great Britaine, France, and Ireland, 1614.

GOD SAVE THE KING.

Imprinted at London by Robert Barker, Printer to the Kings most Excellent Majestie. Anno Dom. 1614.

1 p. folio. Copies in Antiq., I. T., P. C., P. R. O., and Q. C. Entered on Patent Rolls.

1617, DECEMBER 23.

[BANISHING NOTORIOUS OFFENDERS TO VIRGINIA.]

BY THE KING.

A Proclamation for the better and more peaceable government of the middle Shires of Northumberland, Cumberland, and Westmerland.

[A long proclamation for the prevention of disorders and outrages in certain shires, requiring that no person shall lease lands and tenements without sufficient surety, that all persons shall assist in the pursuit of criminals, that notorious offenders shall not receive bail except in open court, that care shall be exercised in the granting of licenses to "hostler houses and malsters," that known malefactors shall not be countenanced "by wearing of their liveries or any other dependance," that the families of offenders who have been banished shall be sent to join the fugitives, that all outlaws shall yield themselves up to the law and shall not be sheltered, that for the prevention of cattle stealing no beef shall be sold in any fair or market without the hide, that all horses, sheep and cattle shall be sold only in open fair or market, that notorious offenders shall be sent to Virginia and other foreign parts, that the use of weapons and horses be forbidden except to noblemen and gentlemen, that the overlords shall require sufficient bonds of their tenants, and that offenders shall be remanded to the place where their offense was committed. Only the paragraph regarding America is quoted.]

Item, for the more speedy suppressing, and freeing the said Countreis and places of notorious and wicked offenders that will not be reformed, but by severity of punishment; Wee have taken order for the making out a Commission to speciall Commissioners, to survey, search and finde out, and enforme Us of the most notorious and lewd persons, and of their faults, within the said Counties of Northumberland, Cumberland, and Westmerland, Riddesdale, and Bewcastle within the same: And We hereby signifie our pleasure to be upon Certificate of the said Commissioners, to send the most notorious ill livers, and misbehaved persons of them that shall so be certified, into Virginia, or to some other remote parts to serve in the Warres, or in Colonies, that they may no more infect the places where they abide within this our Realme.

*   *   *   *   *

Given at Our Pallace of Westminister, the three and twentieth day of December, in the fifteenth yeere of Our Raigne of Great Britaine, France and Ireland.

Anno 1617.

GOD SAVE THE KING.

    Imprinted at London by Bonham Norton and John Bill, Deputies and Assignes of Robert Barker, Printer to the Kings most Excellent Majestie. Anno M.DC.XVII.

    4 pp. folio. Copies in Antiq., I. T., P. C., P. R. O., and Q. C. Entered on Patent Rolls; entered in Privy Council Register (Scotland), xi, 288.

1618, JUNE 9.

[CENSURING SIR WALTER RALEIGH FOR SACKING ST. THOMAS.]

BY THE KING.

A Proclamation declaring His Majesties pleasure concerning Sir Walter Rawleigh, and those who adventured with him.

Whereas We gave Licence to Sir Walter Rawleigh,[6] Knight, and others of Our Subjects with him, to undertake a Voyage to the Countrey of Guyana, where they pretended great hopes and probabilities to make discovery of certain Gold Mines, for the lawfull enriching of themselves, and these Our Kingdoms: Wherein We did by expresse limitation and Caution restraine, and forbid them and every of them, from attempting any Acte of hostility, wrong, or violence whatsoever, upon any of the Territories, States, or Subjects of any forraine Princes, with whom Wee are in amitie: And more peculiarly of those of Our deare Brother the King of Spaine, in respect of his Dominions and Interests in that Continent. All which notwithstanding, We are since informed by a common fame, that they, or some of them have, by an hostile invasion of the Towne of S. Thome (being under the obedience of Our said deare Brother the King of Spaine) and by killing of divers of the inhabitants thereof, his Subjects, and after by sacking and burning of the said towne, (as much as in them for their owne parts lay) malitiously broken and infringed the Peace and Amitie, which hath beene so happily established, and so long inviolably continued betweene Us and the Subjects of both our Crownes.

Wee have therefore held it fit, as appertaining neerely to Our Royall Justice and Honor, eftsoones to make a publique declaration of Our owne utter mislike and detestation of the said insolences, and excesses, if any such have beene by any of Our Subjects committed: And for the better detection and clearing of the very trueth of the said common fame; Wee doe heereby straitly charge and require

---

[6] Raleigh's voyage for the discovery of gold mines in Guiana (the modern Venezuela) was projected in 1616. He was released from the Tower in March of that year and sailed from Plymouth with a fleet of fourteen ships in June, 1617. The expedition seemed doomed to failure from the start, and after St. Thomas was attacked and burned in December, 1617, Raleigh was compelled to return to England without having attained his object. He landed at Plymouth in June, 1618, and after the due form of trial was executed, although upon a sentence of 1603, on October 29, 1618 (*Dictionary of National Biography*, vol. 47, pp. 197-200, where authorities are cited). Raleigh's commission for undertaking the voyage, dated August 26, 1616, is printed in Rymer's *Fœdera*, xvi, 789.

all Our Subjects whatsoever, that have any particular understanding and notice thereof, upon their duety and alleagiance which they owe Us, immediately after publication of this Our pleasure, to repaire unto some of Our Privy Counsell, and to discover and make knowne unto them their whole knowledge and understanding concerning the same, under paine of Our High displeasure and indignation; that Wee may thereupon proceede in Our Princely Justice to the exemplary punishment and coertion of all such, as shal be convicted and found guilty of so scandalous and enormous outrages.

Given at Our Mannor of Greenwich, the ninth day of June, in the sixteenth yeere of Our Raigne of England, France and Ireland, and of Scotland the one and Fiftieth.

GOD SAVE THE KING.

Imprinted at London by Bonham Norton, and John Bill, deputie Printers for the Kings most Excellent Majestie. Anno M.DC.XVIII.

1 p. folio. Copies in Antiq., B. M., I. T., P. C., P. R. O., and Q. C. Entered on Patent Rolls. Printed in Rymer's "Fœdera," xvii, 92, where it is dated June 11, 1618.

1619, MAY 18.

[IMPORTATION OF WHALE-FINS FROM GREENLAND.]

BY THE KING.

A Proclamation inhibiting the Importation of Whale Finnes into his Majesties Dominions by any, but the Muscovy Company.

Whereas Wee by Our Proclamation given at Wansted, the eleventh day of September in the twelfth yeere of Our reigne of Great Brittaine, France, and Ireland,[7] for the reasons therein expressed, and for the incouragement of Our welbeloved Subjects, the company of Merchants trading for Muscovia, Greeneland[8] and the parts adjoyning, commonly called the Muscovia Company, did straitly and expresly forbid and prohibit all Aliens and Strangers whatsoever, and also all Our owne Subjects (others then the sayd Muscovia Merchants, and that in their joynt stock) to bring into any Our Kingdomes, and Dominions any Whale Finnes upon paine of confiscation of the same, and of Our high indignation and displeasure, and of such further punishment as should be meet to be inflicted upon the Offenders for their contempt in that behalfe.

Now forasmuch as We are given to understand, That Our sayd Proclamation took not that good effect, nor found that due obedience and conformity which We expected: We have therefore in further manifestation of our former intentions and gracious favor towards the sayd Company, thought good eftsoones to publish Our Royall pleasure heerein, and to revive and quicken Our sayd former Proclamation, which We cannot but take in ill part, hath beene so much neglected: And therefore We doe by these presents straitly charge, prohibit, and forbid, aswell all Alliens and Strangers whatsoever, as also Our naturall born Subjects and Denizens, That they nor any of them (other then the sayd Muscovia Merchants, and that in their joynt stocke onely) shall from hencefoorth directly or indirectly import, or bring into Our Kingdomes and Dominions, or any of them, any Whale Finnes, upon paine of forfeiture, and confiscation of the same, whether they be found on board of any Ship, Hoy, Boate, or Bottome, or layd on land in any warehouse, storehouse, shop, cellar, or any other place whatsoever, and upon paine of Our high Indigna-

---

[7] Refers to the proclamation of September 11, 1614. In 1618 the East India Adventurers had joined stock with the Muscovy Company to form one joint company for the whale fishery, but after two years of unsuccessful adventuring the agreement was dissolved (Anderson, *Origin of Commerce*, ii, 360, 367).

[8] Spitzbergen, rather than Greenland proper.

tion and displeasure, and such other punishment, as by Our Court of Starre chamber shalbe thought meet to be inflicted upon them, or any of them, as contemners of Our Royall will and commandement in this behalfe.

And Wee doe likewise straitly charge, prohibite and forbid, aswell all Aliens and Strangers, as Our naturall borne Subjects and Denizens (other then the sayd Muscovia Merchants) that they nor any of them doe presume to buye, utter, sell, barter or contract for, any Whale finnes, knowing the same to be imported into any of our Realmes or Dominions contrary to Our wil and pleasure heerein declared, upon paine of Our high indignation and displeasure, and such further punishment as by Our said Court of Starre chamber shall bee thought meet to be inflicted upon such offenders, as contemners also of Our Royall commandement. And to the end this Our pleasure may take the better effect, We doe heereby charge, and command all Customers, Comptrollers, Searchers, Waiters, Farmors, and Collectors of Our Customes, and other our Officers and Ministers, carefully to attend every one in his severall place, the execution heereof, and in no wise to permit or suffer any Whale finnes directly or indirectly, openly or privately to be brought, or imported into any Our Kingdomes or Dominions, contrary to Our Royal pleasure heerein expressed, or being so imported, that they doe not permit, or suffer the same to bee colourably customed for other goods and Merchandize, but that foorthwith they or some of them doe seize and take to Our use all such Whalefinnes as shall be so imported, and immediately upon such seizure made, to give notice thereof in writing to Our Register for forfeitures in Our Custome house in the Port of London, upon paine to undergoe such punishment, as shalbe thought meet by the Lords of Our Privie Councell.

Neverthelesse Our intent and meaning is, That the sayd Muscovie Company, and none other, shall or may buy, and sell, barter, or contract for, any such Whalefinnes, as being imported contrary to this Our Proclamation shalbe confiscate and seized, and the same, being sold by the sayd Company, may be afterward bought, contracted for, and used by any other Our Subjects at their wil and pleasure. Any thing heerein contained to the contrary notwithstanding.

Given at Our Mannour of Greenwich, the eighteenth day of May, in the seventeenth yeere of our Raigne of England, France, and Ireland, and of Scotland the two and fiftieth.

Imprinted at London by Bonham Norton and John Bill, Printers to the Kings most excellent Majestie. Anno. M.DC.XIX.

2 pp. folio. There are two issues slightly varying in set-up. Copies in Antiq., B. M., Dalk., I. T., P. C., P. R. O., and Q. C.

1619, OCTOBER 6.

[MANUFACTURE OF TOBACCO-PIPES.]

An abstract of some branches of his Majesties late Charter, Granted to the Tobacco-Pipe makers of Westminster; declaring his Majesties pleasure touching that Manufacture, and also all persons whom it may concerne.

James by the grace of God, King of England, Scotland, France and Ireland, &c. Whereas Wee have been informed by the complaint of divers of Our poore Subjects, the ancient Makers of Tobacco-Pipes within this Our Realme, That for want of power and priviledge to retaine their Apprentises and Servants during their Apprentiship (who commonly depart from them before they have served their tearmes, or attained to the knowledge of their Art) they are much prejudiced both in their Trades and meanes of living, by their excessive making and uttering of ill Ware, And Our Subjects who have use of that Manufacture, are thereby greatly abused and deceived: And not only so, but to their Masters farther impoverishment, these loose and idle persons doe instruct and teach others of as bad qualitie as themselves, to make and sell like ill and deceitful ware. Besides, for that the said Art of making Tobacco Pipes is easily learned, sundry of our Subjects trained up in other Trades more useful for the Realme, doe forsake the same and take up this of making Tobacco-Pipes: And others who have other good Trades to live upon, intrude themselves into this also, and use both, to the hinderance and overthrow of those who anciently practised the same. And whereas for the better reforming of all those disorders, to cut off the superfluous straglers and late intruders, to reduce them to a competent number, and to settle good government amongst them (this Trade being a new Trade, never yet ordered by any Law or Policie, and which concerneth not any Commoditie of necessitie for our Common-weale, but a superfluous pleasure, necessarie to be regulated by Our Royall power and authoritie) We have therefore thought fit by Letters Patents under Our Great Seale, to Incorporate a certaine number of choice and selected persons, who have either served as Apprentices, or have otherwise practised that Art by the space of seven yeers, to whom and whose Servants, Apprentices, and such others as shall be by them admitted into that Societie for their skill and honest conversation, Wee intend to appropriat the said Art, and to restraine all others from taking that benefit which in no right belongeth unto them.

And to the end that all our loving Subjects may take knowledge of Our pleasure expressed in our Charter, that it may be duly observed without pretext of ignorance, Wee doe heereby declare Our expresse will and pleasure to be, and doe straightly charge and command, That no person or persons whatsoever, other then such as are members of the said Societie of Tobacco-pipe makers of Westminster, or which have by the space of seven yeares at the least beene bound to (or exercised) that Art, or such others as shall be chosen into the Societie by the said Societie, shall not presume (from the date of these presents) directly nor indirectly to make any manner of Tobacco-pipes within this Our Realme of England or Dominion of Wales, nor shall bring in or import any manner of Tobacco-pipes from beyond the Seas, or from Our Realme of Scotland; Nor shall utter, sell, or put to sale any Tobacco-pipes so made or brought into this Our Realme of England and Dominion of Wales, contrary to Our pleasure heerein declared Upon paine not only of forfeiture of all such Manufacture, but of incurring such penalties, imprisonments and punishments, as by the Lawes and Statutes of this Our Realme, or by Our prerogative Royall may be inflicted upon the offenders in this kind for their contempt or neglect of Our Royall Will and Commandment. And further, for the better discovering and suppressing of all secret and under-hand making or uttering of the said Manufacture by such as are not members of this Societie or otherwise enabled as aforesaid, Wee doe require, charge, and straightly command all Our loving Subjects (especially such Retaylers as shall buy Tobacco-pipes to sell againe) that they, nor any of them directly, nor indirectly, shall buy, acquire, get or obtaine any Tobacco-pipes whatsoever of or from the hands of any person or persons, not being knowne members of the said Societie, And to that end it is provided, that all Tobacco-pipes made by the said Company, shall be brought to the Common Hall of the said Societie, there to be proved whether the same be good and marchantable ware, before they shall be uttered or put to sale; (where they may be bought of all Our loving Subjects) Upon paine of undergoing of Our displeasure, and such paines and penalties as shall or may ensue thereupon for such contempt against Our will and Our prerogative Royall. And for the full effectuating of Our pleasure heerein, These are to command and straightly charge, That all the said Tobacco-pipe Makers aforesaid, shall forthwith take knowledge of our Charter by these presents, and by resorting to the said Societie in London, where they shall receive such Orders and Ordinances as shall be constituted and made by the Master, Wardens, and Assistances of the said Societie for the benefit of the said Societie. And lastly, We will and do hereby require all Mayors, Sherifes, Justices of Peace, Bailifes, Constables, and all other Officers and Ministers whatsoever, That they and every of them in their severall Offices and Places be from time to time ayding and assisting to the said Master, Wardens, and Societie in the due execution and accomplishment of this Our Royall Will and Commandment, as they tender Our pleasure, and will avoid the contrary.

Witnesse Our selfe at Westminster the sixth day of October, in the seventeenth yeere of Our Raigne of England, France, and Ireland, and of Scotland, the three and Fiftieth.

1 p. folio. Copy in Antiq.

1619, NOVEMBER 10.

[INSPECTING OF TOBACCO.]

BY THE KING.

A Proclamation concerning the viewing and distinguishing of
Tobacco in England and Ireland, the Dominion of Wales,
and Towne of Barwicke.

Whereas divers good and necessarie provisions have beene heretofore made, as well by Act of Parliament, as otherwise, for the well garbling of Spices and Drugges, to the intent the Subjects of this Our Realme should not bee occasioned to use any unwholesome Spices or Drugges, to the impayring of their health, or to buy the bad instead of the good, to the impairing of their substance. And for as much as the Drugge called Tobacco, being of late yeeres growne frequent in this Our Realme and other Our Dominions, is daily sold ungarbled, whereby more inconvenience groweth and ariseth to Our loving Subjects, then by any other Drugge whatsoever. And for that also by the manie and sundrie abuses practised and committed by Merchants, Masters of Ships and others, in concealing and uttering the said Tobacco without paying any Impost or Custome for the same, great losse and dammage accrueth to Us, notwithstanding any Lawes, Statutes or other course heretofore taken for preventing thereof: For remedie of all which Inconveniences, Wee, by our Letters Patents under our great Seale of England, bearing Date, at Westmynster the five and twentieth day of May now last past, did prohibite and forbid, That no person or persons should at any time after the day of the Date of our said Letters patents within Our Realme of England, the Dominion of Wales, and Port and Towne of Barwicke, or any of them; or within Our Realme of Ireland, or any part of them or any of them, by himselfe or themselves, or his or their servants or factours, or any others, directly or indirectly sell or put to sale; or attempt, presume or goe about any manner of way to sell or put to sale, either in grosse or by retaile, any Tobacco, of what sort, kind or growth soever, before the Custome and Impost thereof due, were paid; and the same Tobacco were viewed, distinguished and sealed by the Officer or Officers of Us, Our Heires and Successours, in that behalfe to be constituted and appointed; For whose labour, travell, charges and expences in that behalfe to be sustained and taken in the execution of the said Office: Wee did by the said Letters Patents, constitute and appoint, That they should and might from time to time, demand, take and receive·to their owne use, of every person and persons whose Tobacco they should so garble, viewe and seale, the summe of foure pence of currant English money, for every pound weight thereof so viewed and sealed.

And Wee did also by Our said Letters Patents (for the considerations therein mentioned) give and grant the said Office, with the powers, fees and authorities before mentioned to Our welbeloved Subjects, Francis Nichols, Jasper Leake and Philip Eden, Gentlemen, to be executed by them or their Deputies or Assignes for thirtie and one yeeres next ensuing the Date of the said Letters Patents.

And Wee did further by Our said Letters, for Us, Our Heires and Successours, give and grant unto the said Francis Nichols, Jasper Leake and Philip Eden, and their Assignes, and to all and every person and persons, which by them or any of them, by writing under their or any of their hands and Seales, should bee in that behalfe deputed and assigned, full power and authoritie during the terme aforesaide, as well to bee present and to have place in all manner of Custome-houses, Ports, Havens, Creekes and places of lading or unlading of any manner of Goods, Wares or Merchandizes, into or out of the said Realmes and Dominions: As also to be present with all and every the Customers, Collecters, Searchers, Surveyers, Waiters, and other Officers and Ministers having charge for or concerning the lading or unlading of any Goods, Wares or Merchandizes, for their better executing of all and everything and things thereby appointed, and for their better receiving and enjoying of the benefit of Our said Grant at all times and places, where the said Officers and Ministers or any of them, should by reason of their said severall Offices have cause or occasion to be: And also in all and every place or places, as well in Ships arrived with Tobacco, and riding in any Port, Roade or River, as on the Land, to make and appoint such and so many Watchmen, Waiters and Officers, and to provide and use such reasonable waies, orders and meanes, as they the said Francis Nichols, Jasper Leake and Philip Eden, and their Assignes and Deputies should and might be just and truely informed of all parcels and quantities of Tobacco, as should at any time or times during the said Grant, be brought into any Port or place, or be planted or growing in any place or places of the said Realmes and Dominions or any of them.

And also that it should and might be lawfull, to and for the said Francis Nichols, Jasper Leake, and Philip Eden, and their Assignes, and their and every of their Deputies and Substitutes, at all and every time and times during the terme aforesaid, in lawfull and convenient maner, with a Constable or other Officer of the place, as well to goe on board, view, and survay all Shippes, Vessels, or Bottomes, riding or lying within any of the Ports, Havens, Creekes and places of lading or unlading, within Our saide Realme of England, Dominion of Wales, Port or Towne of Barwicke, or Realme of Ireland, or any the members or places thereunto belonging, as to goe into any House, Celler, Vault, Warehouse, Shop, or other place within the said Realmes and Dominion, and Port, or Towne of Barwicke, or any part of them, or any of them to search and view if there be any Tobacco uttered, sold, or put to sale, or offered to be sold, or put to sale before the same be viewed, distinguished, and sealed contrary to the true meaning of the said Letters patents.

And We did also by the said Letters for Us, Our Heires and Successors, require, charge and Command all and singular Maiors, Shiriffes, Justices of Peace, Bailiffes, Constables, Headboroughes, Customers, Comptrollers, Searchers, Surveyors, Waiters, and all other Officers, Ministers, and Subjects whatsoever, of Us, Our Heires and Successors, as well of the said Realme of England, Dominion of Wales, and Port and Towne of Barwicke, as of the said Realme of Ireland, That they and every of them, should from time to time during the continuance of that Our graunt, be aiding and assisting to the said Francis Nichols, Jasper Leake, and Philip Eden, and their Assignes, and to every of them, their and every of their Deputie and Deputies, Substitute and Substitutes, in the due Execution of all and every the powers and authorities expressed in the said Letters Patents, upon paine of the displeasure of Us, Our Heires and Successors, and as they would answere the contrary at their perils; as by the said Letters Patents more at large appeareth.

Wee now, to the intent Our will and pleasure in the premisses may be the better knowne to all Our loving Subjects whom it may concerne, Doe hereby notifie, publish and declare the same Our pleasure, willing and commanding that all and every the premisses, be from time to time in every respect duely performed, executed and observed according to the true intent and meaning of the same Our Letters Patents. And that no person or persons doe attempt or presume to violate or infringe Our Command hereby; or by Our said Letters Patents declared or expressed, upon the paines and penalties therein contained. And We doe also hereby Charge and Command, as well all and singular Merchants, and other person and persons whatsoever, which shall import any Tobacco of what sort soever, That they cause the same to be duely entred in the Custome house belonging to the Port or place where it shall bee landed, in the name or names onely of the true proprietor or owner, proprietors or owners thereof, and not in the name or names of any other person or persons which is not the true owner thereof; As also all Our Customers and other Officers whatsoever, That they take speciall care and regard to the due performance of the same, as they tender Our pleasure, and will avoide the contrary.

Given at Theobalds the tenth day of November, in the seventeenth yeere of Our Reigne of Great Brittaine, France, and Ireland.

God save the King.

Imprinted at London by Bonham Norton, and John Bill, Printers to the Kings most Excellent Majestie. Anno MDC.XIX.

2 pp. folio. There are two issues varying only in set-up. Copies in Antiq., Camb., I. T., P. C., P. R. O., and Q. C.

1619, DECEMBER 30.

[FORBIDDING PLANTING OF TOBACCO IN ENGLAND.]

BY THE KING.

A Proclamation to restraine the planting of Tobacco
in England and Wales.

It is not unknowen what dislike Wee have ever had of the use of Tobacco, as tending to a generall and new corruption, both of mens bodies and maners: Neverthelesse it is of the two, more tolerable, that the same should be imported amongst many other vanities and superfluities which come from beyond the Seas, then permitted to be planted here within this Realme, thereby to abuse and misimploy the soile of this fruitfull Kingdome: For which purpose by Our direction, Letters of late have beene addressed from our Councell of State, prohibiting the plantation thereof within a certaine distance of Our City of London: But entring into further consideration of the manifold inconveniences of suffering this nourishment of vice, (and nothing else) as a noysome and running Weede, to multiply and overspread within this Our Kingdome, Wee are resolved upon many and weightie reasons of State, to make the said Prohibition generall.

For first, Wee are informed, That whereas the use of forreine Tobacco was chiefly vented, and received in Cities and great Townes, where ryot and excesse useth to take place, it is now by the Inland plantation become promiscuous, and begun to be taken in every meane Village, even amongst the basest people.

Secondly, Wee are given to understand from divers persons of skill and experience, That the English Tobacco, howsoever some doe presume or imagine by industrie and experience to rectifie it, and make it good (wherein it is easie for opinion to doe mischiefe) yet it is certeinly in it selfe more crude, poysonous and dangerous for the bodies and healths of Our Subjects, then that that comes from hotter Climates; So that the medicinall use of Tobacco (which it is that that is onely good in it, and to be approved) is in this kind also corrupted and infected.

Thirdly, Whereas Our Colonies and Plantations in Virginia and the Sommer Islands, (being proper and naturall Climates for that plant, and the true temper thereof) receive much comfort by the Importation thereof into this Kingdome, (which it is to be respected at least in the Interim, untill Our said Colonies may grow to yeeld better and more solide commodities) Now the said Trading from thence is and will be by the Plantation within this Realme, choaked and overthrowen.

Fourthly, Wee doe find also, that the reason that mooved Us to interdict the planting thereof neere the Citie of London, (which was in regard of the conversions of garden grounds, and rich soyled grounds from divers Roots and Herbes, fit for victuall and sustenance, unto this harmefull vanitie) extendeth likewise unto all Cities, Townes and Villages, and rather more, by how much the povertie is greater there, then here above.

And lastly, for that it doeth manifestly tend to the diminution of Our Customes, which is a thing, that although in case of good Manufactures, and necessary commodities Wee doe little esteeme; Yet where it shall be taken from Us, and no good but rather hurt thereby redound to Our people, Wee have reason to preserve.

Wee therefore intending in time to provide a remedie for this spreading evill, which hath in a very few yeeres dispersed it selfe into most parts of Our Kingdomes, doe hereby straightly charge and command all and every person and persons of what degree or condition soever, That they or any of them, by themselves, their servants, workemen or labourers, doe not from and after the second day of Februarie next, presume to sow, set, or plant, or cause to be sowen, set or planted, within this Our Realme of England, or Dominion of Wales, any sort or kinde of Tobacco whatsoever, And that they or any of them, shall not, or doe not hereafter maintaine, or continue any olde stockes, or plants of Tobacco, formerly sowen or planted, but shall foorthwith utterly destroy and roote up the same, converting and imploying the ground and soyle thereof to some other lawfull uses and purposes, as to them shall seeme best, upon paine of contempt of Our Royall commandement, to be proceeded with according to Our Lawes, and Prerogative Royall with all severitie.

And therefore, for the more due execution of the premisses, Wee doe further will, require and command all Mayors, Sheriffes, Justices of Peace, Bayliffes, Constables, and other Officers and ministers, to whom it shall or may appertaine, That they and every of them, shall from time to time diligently and carefully intend the due and exact observation of this Our Royall pleasure, And that they permit not, nor suffer any thing to be done, contrary to the true intent and meaning of this Our Proclamation, but withstand the same to their uttermost power, as they tender Our service: And further that they take order that such offenders, labourers, or workemen, as shal persist in the sowing or planting of Tobacco, in this Our Realme or Dominion of Wales, or in the maintaining or continuing any old stocks, or former plantations thereof hereafter, may be called before them, and be bound in Recognizances of good summes to Our use, to appeare in Our Court of Starrechamber, there to be prosecuted by Our Attourney generall, as contemners of Our expresse Commandement, Proclamation, and Prerogative Royall; wherein (especially in a cause of this nature) Wee will expect, and require of all Our Subjects, their due conformitie and obedience.

Given at Our Palace of Westminster the thirtieth day of December, in the seventeenth yeere of Our Reigne of Great Britaine, France and Ireland.

God save the King.

Imprinted at London by Robert Barker, and John Bill, Printers to the Kings most Excellent Majestie. Anno MDC.XIX.

2 pp. folio. Copies in Antiq., I. T., P. C., P. R. O., and Q. C.

1620, MAY 15.

[FORBIDDING ROGER NORTH'S EXPEDITION TO BRAZIL.]

BY THE KING.

A Proclamation declaring his Majesties pleasure concerning
Captaine Roger North, and those who are gone foorth
as adventurers with him.

Whereas Roger North[9] Esquier, with divers others of Our Subjects, as Adventurers for the intended Plantation and setling of Trade and Commerce in those parts of the Continent of America neare and about the River of Amazones (which were presupposed not to be under the obedience and governement of any other Christian Prince or State) hath secretly conveyed himselfe away and hath disloyally precipitated and imbarqued himselfe, and his fellowes, and sodainly set to Sea with a pretended purpose to prosecute that designe, contrary to Our Royal pleasure and Commandement expresly signified unto him by one of Our principall Secretaries, Our Admirall of England having also refused him leave to go: We then having out of weightie considerations, and reason of State, and upon the deliberate advise of Our Privy Councell resolved to suspend and restraine the said Plantation and voyage for a time, and having thereupon streightly charged and commanded him the said North upon his duty and aleageance, that hee and his Associates should for a while surcease their Provisions, and should stay them-

---

[9] Capt. Roger North, who had been a member of Raleigh's unfortunate expedition to Guiana, petitioned the King in 1619 for letters patent authorizing him to establish the King's right to the coast and country adjoining the Amazon River and to found a Plantation there. On April 18, 1619, the Privy Council authorized the Solicitor General to prepare a bill for granting him privileges for a Plantation which should "extend from the River of Wyapoco [Oyapok] to five degrees of southerly latitude, from any part or branch of the River of Amazons otherwise called Oreliana and for longitude into the Land to be limited from sea to sea." This was then esteemed to be part of Guiana, but is now territory of Brazil. Provided with a passport, but without express leave from the King, North sailed from Plymouth in May, 1620. The King, inspired by the remonstrances of Spanish agents, then issued the proclamation of recall. Although his cruise prospered, his ship being "well fraught" with 7000 pounds of tobacco, he returned to England as soon as he heard of the warrant against him. He was imprisoned in the Tower in January, 1621, and his cargo was confiscated. He soon succeeded in obtaining his release and later made good his claim to the restitution of the tobacco (see *Acts of Privy Council, Colonial*, i, 23-48; *Calendar of State Papers, Colonial, 1574-1660*; *Dict. of National Biography*, xli, 174.)

selves and their Shipping, which they had already prepared, untill Our further pleasure should be made knowen unto them.

Wee have therefore held it fit hereby to make a publique Declaration of Our utter mislike and disavowement of this their rash, undutiful and insolent attempt; and do hereby revoke, annihilate and disanull all Power, Authoritie, jurisdiction, or Commission whatsoever, which he the said North, or any of his Complices may pretend in any sort to derive and hold from or under Us; and do hereby charge aswell him the said North, as all his Companions and followers, immediately upon the first notice that shall be given him or them of this Our pleasure, that they shall make their speedie returne directly home, with all their shipping and munitions into this Our Kingdome of England, assoone as the windes and weather shall permit them; and being heere arrived shall foorthwith present themselves in person unto some of Our Privie Councel, under paine of being heereby declared guiltie of high contempt and rebellion, in case they shall disobey this Our expresse commandement.

And Wee doe further heereby straitly require and charge aswell the Governours, as all other the Partenors and Adventurers, any wayes concerned, or interested as members of the Companie and Incorporation intended for that Plantation, as all other Merchants, Captaines, Masters, and Officers, of Ships, Saylors, Marrinors, and all other our loving subjects whatsoever, that they shall in no sort ayd or abette, nor comfort him the said North, nor any of his Complices with any supply of shipping, men, money, munition, victuals, merchandise, or other commodities or necessaries whatsoever: but that aswell all and every Our Admirals, Vice-Admirals, and other Our Officers and Commanders of Our Ships, or Pinnaces, as all other Captaines and Masters of any of Our subjects ships and vessels whatsoever, that shall happen to meete with him the saide North, or any of his Company at sea, or in any Harbour, Port, or Creeke wheresoever, shall in Our Name attach, seize, and summon him, or them, and their shipping, to returne immediately home, and shall foorthwith bring them backe to some of Our Ports of this Our Kingdome, and there commit them and their Ships to the charge of such Our Officers, as it shall respectively appertaine unto, untill Wee (having received information of their such returne, which Wee will expect from Our said Officers, who shall so stand incharged with them) shall give further order concerning them, aswell their persons as their shipping and munitions. Wherein Wee doe expresly charge and command aswell him the said North, and all his Company, Abettors, and Adherents, and all the rest of that Company and Incorporation intended, as all and every other Our Officers by Land or Sea, and all other Captaines, Masters, and Marriners in any of Our subjects ships, and all other Our loving subjects whatsoever, faithfully, diligently, and carefully to observe, doe, and performe in their severall qualities and places, that which Wee have heereby required of them, according to every of their duties, charges, and imployments, upon paine of Our high displeasure and indignation, and as they will answere the contrarie at their uttermost perill.

Given at Our Manour of Greenwich this fifteenth day of May, in the eighteenth yeere of Our Reigne of Great Britaine, France and Ireland.

God save the King.

Imprinted at London by Robert Barker, and John Bill, Printers to the Kings most Excellent Majestie. Anno Dom. M.DC.XX.

2 pp. folio. Copies in Antiq., I. T., P. C., P. R. O., and Q. C. Entered on Patent Rolls. Printed in Rymer's "Fœdera," xvii, 215.

1620, MAY 27.

[MANUFACTURE OF TOBACCO-PIPES.]

BY THE KING.

A Proclamation commanding Conformity to his Majesties pleasure, expressed in his late Charter to the Tobacco-pipe-makers.

Whereas divers of the poorer sort of Our Subjects have heretofore lived by the trade of making Tobacco pipes, but for want of power to retaine and keepe their Apprentices and servants in due obedience, and to restraine others from intruding upon their Arte, the auncient Makers have not so well prospered as was desired: For prevention of which inconveniences, and for reducing the workemen in that trade to such a competent number, as they might bee governed after the example of other Societies, who florish by ranging themselves under good Orders; We did by Our late Charter Incorporate a selected number of the most ancient, and such others as they for skill and honestie should admit into their Socitie: Thereby prohibiting all others who were not members thereof, to make any sort of Tobacco-pipes within Our Realme of England or Dominion of Wales; And thereby also commanding, that no person or persons directly, or indirectly should buy Tobacco-pipes to sell againe, of, or from the hands of any others then the knowne Members of the said Societie. Yet neverthelesse being lately informed by Certificate from sundry Our Justices of Peace of Our Counties of Middlesex and Surrey (who in due obedience of Our Royall pleasure, declared in Our said Charter, did in person assist the execution of the same) That divers lewde and obstinate offenders, had fortified themselves in their houses with weapons, And in contempt of Our Regall Authority resisted them, comming with the severall Warrants of the Lord Chiefe Justice of Our Bench, and other the Justices of Peace within Our Citie of London, and the said counties of Middlesex and Surrey; And also that there were divers il disposed persons (who delighting to oppose al good orders) contemptuously maintained these underhand offendors, some by harboring the unlawfull Makers of Tobacco-pipes secretly in their houses, there to make them contrary to Our Charter, to the end to partake of the stolne profit thereof; Others, by buying secretly this under-hand made ware, in contempt of Our Authority, and with an evill intent of overthrowing this Societie which we have sought to establish.

Now therefore, that by the presumptuous example of these disobedient persons, others may not be incouraged hereafter by impunity to presume to resist and contemne Our Royall Commandement in matters of greater moment, or to withstand the authority of Magistrates and government, These are to charge and straitly command, that no persons whatsoever within this Our Realme of England and Dominion of Wales shall hereafter presume to make any manner of Tobacco-pipes, but such as are or shall bee members of the said Societie: nor shall presume to harbour in their houses any Tobacco-pipe-makers to use their trade there, who are not of the said Societie; nor that any person or persons (especially who buy Tobacco-pipes to sell againe) shall at any time, or in any place buy or obtaine by any meanes, directly or indirectly any Tobacco-pipes whatsoever, from any under-handmakers or others, but only from such as are knowne members of the said Societie, and that at their common Hall, or other knowne Warehouses appointed, or hereafter to bee appointed, where they may bee bought by all Our loving Subjects, upon paine of Our high displeasure, and such punishments as are due for such contempts, whereof We shall require a strict account by proceeding against the offendours in Our Court of Starre-Chamber.

Further commanding, that if at any time heereafter any person shall bee so audacious as to fortifie themselves in their houses, or in the houses of any other, or to withstand Our will and pleasure heerein, or to resist Our authoritie given and imparted to Our Lord chiefe Justice and others, in the search or apprehension of them, or any of them; Then Wee doe heereby will and require, that sufficient power be had and taken by such who shal have such Warrants, to apprehend such obstinate and contemptuous persons, and to carry them before Our said chiefe Justice, or other Justice of the Peace, that punishment may be inflicted on them in the severest manner Our Lawes will permit by imprisoning their bodie, till they have put in sufficient suretie for their good behaviour afterwards. Heereby further, straitly charging Our Atturney generall for the time being, that he cause all and every such wilfull and disobedient persons, for such their high contempt in this behalfe, to be prosecuted in Our Court of Starre-Chamber (where Our will is they shall bee sharpely punished) according to the measure of such their audacious and bold resistance of Our Royall commandement. And to the intent that these fraudes and abuses may the better be found out and punished, Our pleasure is, that it shall and may bee lawfull for any two, or more of the said Societie, together with a lawfull officer to enter into any suspected place or places, at lawful and convenient times, there to search for, and finde out any under-hand made, or sold Tobacco-pipes; And all such so found to seize, take, and carry away, and them safelye to keepe to bee disposed of, according to the tenor of Our sayd Charter.

And lastly, for the full execution of this Our Royall Commandement, Wee will and require the Lord Maior of our Citie of London, for the time being, and all other Maiors, Shiriffes, Justices of Peace, Bailiffes, Constables, and all other Officers and Ministers whatsoever; That they and every of them in their severall Offices and places, bee from time to time ayding and assisting to the Master, Wardens, and Societie of Tobacco-pipe makers in the due execution and accomplishment of this Our Royall will and Commandement, as they tender Our pleasure, and will answere the contrary at their perill.

Given at Our Court at Theobalds the seven and twentieth day of May, in the eighteenth yeere of Our Reigne of Great Britaine, France and Ireland.

God save the King.

Imprinted at London by Robert Barker, and John Bill, Printers to the Kings most Excellent Majestie. Anno Dom. M.DC.XX.

2 pp. folio. Copies in Antiq., I. T., P. C., P. R. O., and Q. C. Entered on Patent Rolls.

1620, JUNE 29.

[RESTRAINING DISORDERLY TRADING IN TOBACCO.]

BY THE KING.

A Proclamation for restraint of the disordered trading for Tobacco.

Whereas Wee, out of the dislike Wee had of the use of Tobacco, tending to a generall and new corruption both of mens bodies and maners, and yet neverthelesse holding it of the two more tolerable, that the same should be imported amongst many other vanities and superfluities, which came from beyond the Seas, then permitted to be planted here within this Realme, thereby to abuse and misimploy the soile of this fruitfull Kingdome, did by Our Proclamation dated the thirtieth day of December now last past straitly charge and commaund all and every person and persons, of what degree or condition soever, That they or any of them by themselves, their servants, workemen or labourers should not from and after the second day of February then next following, presume to sow, set or plant, or cause to be sowen, set or planted within this Our Realme of England, and the Dominion of Wales, any sort or Kinde of Tobacco whatsoever, and that they, or any of them, should not maintaine or continue any olde stockes or plants of Tobacco formerly sowen or planted, but should forthwith utterly destroy and root up the same. And whereas We have taken into Our Royall consideration as well the great waste and consumption of the wealth of Our Kingdomes, as the endangering and impairing the health of Our Subjects, by the inordinate libertie and abuse of Tobacco, being a weede of no necessary use, and but of late yeeres brought into Our Dominions, and being credibly informed, that divers Tobacconists, and other meane persons taking upon them to trade and adventure into the parts beyond the Seas for Tobacco, to the intent to forestall and engrosse the said commoditie, upon unmerchantlike conditions, doe transport much Gold bullion and Coyne out of Our Kingdomes, and doe barter and vent the Staple commodities of Our Realme at under-values, to the intent to buy Tobacco, to the discredit of Our native merchandizes, and extreame enhansing of the rates and prices of Tobacco, and the great disturbance and decay of the Trade of the orderly and good Merchant: We taking the premisses into Our Princely consideration, and being desirous to put a remedie to the said inconveniences, which Wee have long endeavoured, though with lesse effect then Wee expected, have resolved to make some further redresse, by restraining the disordered traffique in that commoditie, and reducing it into the hands of able persons that may manage the same without inconvenience, whereby the generall abuse may be taken away, and the necessary use (if any be) may be preserved. We doe therefore not only by these presents, straitly charge and commaund, That Our said Proclamation restraining the planting of Tobacco, be in every respect observed and performed according to the tenour thereof, upon the penalties therein contained; but also that no person or persons whatsoever, Englishmen, Denizens or Strangers, (other then such as shall be authorized and appointed thereunto by Letters Patents under Our great Seale of England) doe import or cause to be imported into this Our Realme of England or Dominion of Wales, or any part of them or either of them, any Tobacco, of what nature, kind, or sort soever, after the tenth day of July next ensuing the date hereof, from any the parts beyond the Seas, upon paine of forfeiture to Us of all such Tobacco so to be imported contrary to the true meaning of these Presents, and upon such further paines and penalties as by the Lawes and Statutes of this Realme, or by the severitie or censure of Our Court of Starrechamber may be inflicted upon the offendors, for contempt of this Our Royall command. And likewise that no Master, Merchant, or Purser of any Ship or other Vessell, doe at any time or times after the said tenth day of July, presume or attempt to take into their ships to be imported into this Realme and Dominion, or either of them, any sort, maner, or quantity of Tobacco whatsoever, but onely to the use of such person and persons as shalbe so as aforesaid authorized and appointed under Our great Seale of England to import the same, and which shalbe by them, their deputies, servants or factors delivered to the said Masters, Merchants or Pursers of Ships to be imported, upon the paines and penalties aforesaid.

And to the intent that no such offendor may colour or hide his offence and contempt, by shadowing the Tobacco to be brought in, contrary to Our pleasure before expressed, under pretence of former store, We doe hereby signifie and declare Our will and pleasure, and doe straitly charge and command, That all and every person and persons which now have, or hereafter shall have within or neere the Cities of London or Westminster, in their hands, custody or possession, any Tobacco heretofore imported, or hereafter and before the said tenth day of July now next ensuing to be imported into this Realm, amounting to the quantitie of ten pounds weight or above, shall before the said tenth day of July now next comming, bring the same unto the house commonly called, The Hawke and Feasant, situate in Cornehill in the said citie of London, and shall cause the same to be there sealed and marked by such person and persons, and with such marke or Seale as by Us shalbe for that purpose assigned and appointed, without giving any Fee or allowance for the said Seale or marke.

And to the intent that the Tobacco to be hereafter imported by Warrant or Authoritie under Our great Seale, may be knowen and distinguished from such as shall be secretly and without Warrant brought in by stealth, We doe likewise charge and command, that all such Tobacco as from and after the said tenth day of July shall be imported by force of any such warrant or Authoritie and none other, except the old store aforesaid to be sealed as aforesaid, shall be sealed and marked with such Seale and marke as aforesaid. And we doe hereby prohibite all person and persons from and after the said tenth day of July, to buy, utter, sell or vent within the said Kingdome and Dominion, or either of them, any Roll or other grosse quantitie of Tobacco whatsoever, before the same be so as aforesaid marked or sealed, upon paine of forfeiture unto Us of all such Tobacco so bought, uttered, solde or vented contrary to the intent of these Presents, and upon such further penalties as by Our Lawes, or by the censure of Our Court of Starrechamber may be inflicted upon the offenders, as contemners of Our Royall command.

And for the better execution of this Our Pleasure, Wee doe hereby command all and singular Customers, Comptrollers, Searchers, Waiters, and other officers attending in all and every the Ports, Creeks, or places of lading or unlading, for the taking, collecting, or receiving of any Our Customers, Subsidies or other duties, to take notice of this Our pleasure: and We do hereby command, and give power and authority unto them, and every or any of them, from time to time, as well to search any Ship or other Vessell or Bottome, riding or lying within any Port, Haven or Creeke within their severall charge and place of attendance, for all Tobacco imported contrary to the intent of this Our Proclamation, and the same being found, to seize and take to Our use; as also to take notice of the names, and apprehend the bringers in, and buyers of the same, to the end they may receive condigne punishment for their offences, upon paine that every of the said Officers which shalbe found negligent, remisse or corrupt therein, shall lose his place and entertainment, and undergoe such paines and penalties as by Our Lawes, or the censure of Our said Court of Starrechamber may be inflicted upon them for the same.

And likewise We doe hereby will, ordaine, and appoint, That it shal and may be lawfull to and for such person and persons, as shalbe so as aforesaid authorized and appointed by Letters Patents under Our great Seale, to import Tobacco by himselfe or themselves, or his or their Deputie or Deputies, with a lawfull Officer to enter into any suspected places at lawfull and convenient times, and there search, discover and finde out any Tobacco imported, uttered, solde or vented, not marked or sealed as aforesaid, contrary to the true meaning hereof, and all such Tobacco so found, to seize, take away and dispose of, and the owners thereof, or in whose custody the same shalbe found, to informe and complaine of, to the end they may receive punishment according to Our pleasure before herein declared.

And further, We doe by these Presents will and require all and singular Mayors, Sheriffes, Justices of Peace, Bayliffes, Constables, Headboroughes, Customers, Comptrollers, Searchers, Waiters, and all other Our Officers and Ministers whatsoever, That they and every of them in their severall places and offices be diligent and attendant in the execution of this Our Proclamation, and also aiding and assisting unto such person and persons, and his and their Deputies and Assignes as we shall so as aforesaid authorize and appoint to import Tobacco, aswell in any search for discovery of any acte or actes to bee performed contrary to the intent of these Presents, as otherwise in the doing or executing of any matter or thing for the accomplishment of this Our Royall Command. And lastly Our will and pleasure is, and Wee doe hereby charge and command Our Atturney generall for the time being, to informe against such persons in Our Court of Starrechamber from time to time, whose contempt and disobedience against this Our Royall command shall merit the censure of that Court.

Given at Our Manour of Greenwich the nine and twentieth day of June, in the eighteenth yeere of Our Reigne of England, France and Ireland, and of Scotland the three and fiftieth.

GOD SAVE THE KING.

Imprinted at London by Robert Barker, and John Bill, Printers to the Kings most Excellent Majestie. Anno Dom. M.DC.XX.

2 pp. folio. Copies in Antiq., I. T., P. C., P. R. O., and Q. C. Entered on Patent Rolls. Printed in Rymer's "Fœdera," xvii, 233.

1621, MARCH 8.

[SUPPRESSING LOTTERIES IN VIRGINIA.]

BY THE KING.

Whereas, at the humble suit and request of sundry Our loving and well disposed Subjects, intending to deduce a Colony, and to make a Plantation in Virginia, Wee, for the inlarging of Our Government, increase of Navigation and Trade, and especially for the reducing of the savage and barbarous people of those parts to the Christian faith, did incorporate[10] divers Noblemen, Gentlemen and others, adventurers in the sayd Plantation, and granted unto them sundry Priviledges and Liberties; amongst which, for their better helpe and assistance to raise some competent summes of money to prosecute the same Plantation to a happy end, Wee did grant them licence to set foorth, erect, and publish Lotteries, to continue for one yeere after the opening of the same, and further, during Our pleasure; which liberty hath been by the same Company put in use divers yeeres past. Now forasmuch as We are given to understand, that although Wee in granting the sayd Licence, had Our eye fixed upon a religious and Princely end and designe, yet the sayd Lotteries, having now for a long time been put in use, doe dayly decline to more and more inconvenience, to the hinderance of multitudes of Our Subjects.[11]

Wee whose care continually waiteth upon the generall welfare of Our people, have thought it expedient, for the generall good of Our Subjects, to suspend the further execution of the saide Lotteries, untill upon further deliberation and advisement, We shall be more fully informed of the inconveniences and evils thereby arising, and may ordaine due remedy for the same, without any conceit of withdrawing Our favour in any degree from the said Company or plantation, and good worke by them intended.

[10] The third charter to the Virginia Company, granted March 12, 1612, contained four clauses, sections xvi-xix, regarding the conduct of lotteries (Brown's *Genesis of the United States*, ii, 552).

[11] The Privy Council, upon complaint of the House of Commons, took action regarding the suspension of lotteries in Virginia on March 4, 1621 (*Acts of Privy Council, Colonial*, i, 39). For the general subject of lotteries in Virginia, see Bruce, *Economic History of Virginia*, ii, 275; Kingsbury, *Records of Virginia Company*, i, 93; Brown, *Genesis of the United States*, index; and Brown, *First Republic in America*, index. In the last reference, p. 394, this proclamation is incorrectly dated March 18. The proclamation is reproduced in fac-simile in *Three Proclamations concerning the Lottery for Virginia*, published by the John Carter Brown Library, Providence, R. I., 1907, in which volume are also reproduced a broadside of 1613 issued by the Council for Virginia regarding the drawing of the lottery and "A Declaration for the certaine time of drawing the great standing Lottery," printed February 22, 1615 [-16].

And therefore We doe heereby expresly charge and command the sayd Company and their successors, and all their Officers, Ministers, and Servants, and all others, That from hencefoorth they desist and forbeare, to use or execute any manner of grant or Licence from Us, for the keeping and continuing of any Lotterie, or to keepe or continue any Lotterie, within this Our Realme of England or the Dominions thereof, untill such time as Wee shall declare Our further pleasure therein. And Wee likewise require all Justices, Officers, and Ministers whatsoever, from hencefoorth, diligently and carefully to see this Our pleasure executed, and to punish the infringers thereof, as contemners of Our Royall command.

Given at Our Palace of Westminster the eighth day of March, in the eighteenth yeere of Our Reigne of Great Britaine, France and Ireland.

GOD SAVE THE KING.

Imprinted at London by Robert Barker, and John Bill, Printers to the Kings most Excellent Majestie. M.DC.XX.

1 p. folio. Copies in Antiq., I. T., P. C., P. R. O., and Q. C.; also John Carter Brown Library.

1622, NOVEMBER 6.

[PROHIBITING DISORDERLY TRADING
TO NEW ENGLAND.]

BY THE KING.

A Proclamation prohibiting interloping and disorderly trading
to New England in America.

As it hath ever beene held a principall Office of Christian Kings, to seeke by all pious meanes the advancement of Christian Religion; so the consideration thereof, hath beene a speciall motive unto Us, from time to time, as often as cause hath required, to further, by Our Royall authority, the good disposition of any of Our well affected Subjects, that have a will to attempt the discovering and planting in any parts of the World, as yet savage and unpossessed by the Subjects of any Christian Prince or State. And now for that, by Gods sacred favour, there is likely to ensue great advancement of his glory, Our Crown, and State, by reason of Our grant heeretofore made to the Counsell for the managing of the affaires of New England in America, being in breadth from forty degrees of Northerly latitude from the Equinoctiall line to forty eight degrees of the sayd Northerly latitude, and in length by all the breadth aforesayd, thorowout the maine land from Sea to Sea[12]; We cannot but continue Our speciall respect and favour unto them in their endevours, and exercise Our Royall authority against the hinderers thereof. Wherefore, having received certaine information of many and intolerable abuses offered by sundry interlopers, irregular and disobedient persons, that seeking principally their present and private profits, have not only impeached some of the Planters there, of their lawfull possessions, but also taken from them their Timber without giving any satisfaction, as in justice they ought to have done: and not therewith contented, have rined whole woods to the utter ruine of the same for ever after; as also, by casting of their ballast in the harbors of some of their Ilands, have almost made them unserviceable: And yet not so contented, by their promiscuous trading, as well Mariners as Masters with the Savages, have overthrowne the trade and commerce that before was had, to the great profit of the Planters, and which were indeed their principall hopes for the advancement of that plantation, next unto the commodities that coast affords of Fishing: Neither heerwith satisfied, but as if they resolved to omit nothing that might be impious and intolerable, they did not forbeare to barter away to the Savages, Swords, Pikes, Muskets, Fowling peeces, Match, Powder, Shot, and other warlike weapons, and teach them the use thereof;

---

[12] The patent of November 3, 1620.

not only to their owne present punishment (divers of them being shortly after slain by the same Savages, whom they had so taught, and with the same weapons which they had furnished them withall) but also to the hazard of the lives of Our good subjects already planted there, and (asmuch as in them lay) to the making of the whole attempt it selfe (how pious and hopefull soever) frustrate, or so much the more difficult.[13] We, for reformation and prevention of these or the like evils heerafter, and for the more cleare declaration of Our Kingly resolution and just intents, both to maintayne Our Royall grant already made, and to uphold and encourage by all wayes and meanes the worthy dispositions of the undertakers of those designes, have thought fit, and doe heerby straitly charge and command, That none of Our Subjects whatsoever, (not Adventurers, Inhabitors or Planters in New England) presume from hencefoorth to frequent those Coasts, to trade or traffique with those people, or to intermedle in the woodes or freehold of any the Planters or Inhabitants (otherwise then by the licence of the sayd Counsell, or according to the orders established by Our Privy Counsell for the releese or ease of the transportation of the Colony in Virginia) upon paine of Our high indignation, and the confiscation, penalties and forfeitures in Our sayd Royall grant expressed: Leaving it neverthelesse, in the meane time, to the discretion of the sayd Counsel for New England, to proceed against the foresayd offenders according to the same, especially, seeing We finde the armes of the sayd Counsell to bee open to receive into that plantation any of Our loving Subjects, who are willing to joyne with them in the charge, and participate in the profits thereof.

Given at Our Court at Theobalds, the sixt day of November, in the yeere of Our Reigne of England, France, and Ireland, the twentieth, and of Scotland the sixe and fiftieth.[14]

God save the King.

Imprinted at London by Bonham Norton and John Bill, Printers to the Kings most Excellent Majestie. M.DC.XXII.

1 p. folio. Copies in Antiq., B. M., Dalk., I. T., P. C., P. R. O., and Q. C.; also John Carter Brown Library. Entered on Patent Rolls. Printed in Rymer's "Fœdera," xvii, 416.

---

[13] These "irregular and disobedient persons" were undoubtedly the members of Thomas Weston's colony at Weymouth. The Council for New England, in May, 1622, took notice of the complaints against Weston and moved that a proclamation be secured warning those who went to New England in contempt of authority (Records in Amer. Antiquarian Society *Proceedings* for April, 1867, p. 59). The proclamation was ordered by the Privy Council on October 23, 1622 (*Acts of the Privy Council, Colonial*, i, 55).

[14] A note on the original proclamation in the privy seal bundles, no. 1955, in the Public Record Office, reads, "I have prepared this proclamation readie for your Majesty's signature upon an order made at the Councell Board. Thomas Coventry."

1624, SEPTEMBER 29.

[ENCOURAGING GROWTH OF TOBACCO IN PLANTATIONS.]

BY THE KING.

A Proclamation concerning Tobacco.

Whereas Our Commons, assembled in Our last Sessions of Parliament, became humble Petitioners unto Us, That, for many waightie reasons, much concerning the welfare of Our Kingdome, and the Trade thereof, We would by Our Royall power, utterly prohibite the use of all foreigne Tobacco, which is not of the growth of Our owne Dominions[15]: And whereas We have upon all occasions made knowen Our dislike, We have ever had of the use of Tobacco in generall, as tending to the corruption both of the health and manners of Our people, and to that purpose have at severall times heretofore prohibited the planting of Tobacco, both in England and Wales, as utterly unfit, in respect of the Climate, to cherish the same for any medicinall use, (which is the onely good to bee approoved in it;) And at other times have also prohibited the disorderly Trading for Tobacco, into the parts beyond the Seas, as by Our severall Proclamations, published to that purpose, it may appeare. Neverthelesse, because Wee have beene earnestly and often importuned by many of Our loving Subjects, Planters and Adventurers in Virginia, and the Sommer Islands, and lately by Our Commissioners for Virginia, that We would be pleased to take into Our Royall care that part of Our Dominions, by Our Royall authoritie, and by the industrie of Our loyall Subjects, added to the rest of Our Empire, for the propagation of Christian Religion, and the ease and benefite of this populous Realme, and to consider, that those Colonies and Plantations, are yet but in their infancie, and cannot be brought to maturitie and perfection, unlesse We will bee pleased for a time to tolerate unto them the planting and venting of the Tobacco, which is, and shall be of the growth of those Colonies and Plantations; We, taking into Our Princely consideration these, and many other important reasons of State, have beene graciously pleased to condescend to the desires and humble petitions of Our loving Subjects in this behalfe.

And therefore We doe by these presents straitly charge and command, That no person whatsoever, of what degree or qualitie soever, doe at any time hereafter, import, or cause to be imported from any part beyond the Seas, or out of Our

[15] The Commons vote, dated May 24, 1624, is in the *Journal of the House of Commons,* i, 794. The several documents leading up to the issuing of this Proclamation are listed in Kingsbury's *Records of the Virginia Company,* i, 192-200.

Kingdome of Scotland, into this Our Realme of England, or Dominion of Wales, or into Our Realme of Ireland, any Tobacco, which is not of the proper growth of the Plantations of Virginia, and the Sommer Islands, or one of them, upon paine of forfeiture unto Us of all such Tobacco so to be imported, contrary to the true meaning of these presents, in whose hands soever the same shall be found, and upon such further paines and penalties, as by the Lawes and Statutes of these Our Realmes, or by the severity or censure of Our Court of Starre-chamber, in either of those Kingdomes respectively, may be inflicted upon the Offendors, for contempt of this Our Royall command, and to be reputed and taken as enemies to Our proceedings, and to those Plantations which so much concerne Our Honour, and the honour and profit of these Our Kingdomes. And We further will and command, upon the penalties aforesaid, that from hencefoorth, no person or persons whatsoever, presume to sow, set, or plant, or cause, or permit, or suffer to be sowed, set, or planted, in any of his or their grounds, any Tobacco whatsoever, within these Our Realmes of England, or Ireland, or Dominion of Wales, or any Isles or places belonging thereto, or permit or suffer any old stocke, plant, or root of Tobacco formerly set, sowed, or planted there to continue, not plucked up and utterly destroyed, contrary to the tenour and true meaning of a former Proclamation, made and published by Us to that purpose, bearing date the thirtieth day of December, in the seventeenth yeere of Our Reigne of England.

And Wee further straitly charge and command, upon the paines and penalties aforesaid, That no person whatsoever, presume to buy, or sell any Tobacco, which from hencefoorth shall be imported, or brought from any the parts beyond the Seas, or from Our Realme of Scotland, which is not, or shall not be of the proper growth of the Colonies aforesaid, of Virginia, and the Sommer Islands, or one of them. And because Wee understand, that some, who intend their owne private, more then the publique, conceiving it to be probable, that We would grant the petition of Our Commons in Parliament, to prevent the effect thereof, have lately imported secretly, and by stealth, great quantities of forreigne Tobacco, for which they have payd no Subsidie, or other duety unto Us; We further will and command, under the paines and penalties aforesaid, that no person whatsoever, from, and after the five and twentieth day of March, now next ensuing, presume to sell, or offer, or put to sale within these Our Realmes or Dominion, any Tobacco, which hath beene formerly imported into this Realme, which is not of the proper growth of the Colonies, or Plantations aforesaid, or one of them, nor that any person whatsoever, willingly and knowingly, take, or use any Tobacco, from, and after the first day of May, now next ensuing, which is not, or shall not be of the proper growth of the sayd Colonies, or Plantations, or one of them. Yet, because the said forreigne Tobacco may not lie on the hands of the owners thereof, Wee are graciously pleased, that at any time, within fortie dayes after the sayd five and twentieth day of March, such forreigne Tobacco may be freely exported by any person whatsoever, without paying any Subsidie or other duetie for the same. And because no man shall pretend ignorance, and thereby endevour to excuse his offence in any of the premisses; Wee doe further charge and command, and doe hereby signifie and declare Our will and pleasure to be, that all, and every person and persons, Merchant or other, who useth to sell, or hath any purpose to sell Tobacco, who have in his, or their hands, custodie or possession, or in the hands, custodie or possession of any other by their delivery, or to their use, any Tobacco heretofore imported into this Our Realme, or planted, set, or sowen within this Realme, shall before the twentieth day of October, now next comming, bring the same into Our Custome-house, within Our Citie of London, if such Tobacco be within five miles of Our said Citie, or if such Tobacco be in any other Citie, Towne, or Place, within this Our Realme of England, or Dominion of Wales, or Realme of Ireland, shall bring the same to the Towne-house, or other fit place, which shall be to that purpose appointed by Us, in that City or Corporate Towne, neerest unto which the said Tobacco shall be, and shall before the first day of December, now next comming, there require and cause the same to be Marked and Sealed by such person or persons, and with such Seale and Marke, as We shall thereunto assigne or appoint for that purpose, without giving any fee or allowance for the said Seale or Marke, and whatsoever Tobacco shall not be Sealed or marked, as aforesaid, within the severall times aforesaid, shall be confiscate et forfeited unto Us for such their default and contempt. And for the avoyding of all deceit and abuse in disguising of forraigne Tobacco, or mingling the same with the Tobacco of Virginia, or the Sommer Islands, thereby to defraud the true intent of these presents, We further straitly charge and command, under the paines and penalties aforesaid, That no person, who is, or shall be a seller of Tobacco, shall have, or keepe ready cut, above the quantity of one pound of Tobacco at once, nor shall mingle any forraigne Tobacco, with any Tobacco of the growth of the Sommer Islands or Virginia.

And Wee straitly charge and command, that all the planters of Tobacco in the Colonies aforesaid, or any part thereof, shall make the same good, and merchantable, and shall not presume to send over into this our Realme of England, any Tobacco, which shall not be good and merchantable, and well made up in rolle without stalkes, or other bad or corrupt stuffe, upon paine of confiscation thereof, or so much thereof, as upon due triall made, shall be found to be otherwise, to the intent that such of Our Subjectes, as shall desire to use the same, may not be abused, or deceived therewith, to the impairing of their health. And to the intent that the Tobacco of the Colonies, and Plantations aforesaid, thus tolerated by Us, may be knowen and distinguished, from such as shall bee secretly, and without warrant brought in by stealth; Wee doe likewise straitly charge and command, upon the paines and penalties aforesaid, That all such Tobacco, as shall bee brought from the Colonies aforesaid, shall be all brought, and landed at the Key of Our Custome house, in Our citie of London, and not elsewhere, in any of Our Realmes or Dominions, and shal be there registred, et shall not be removed from Our said Custome house, untill it shall bee there first tryed, sealed, and marked, by such person, or persons, et with such seale or marke, as We shall thereunto assigne and appoint; such seale or marke to bee set thereto, without Fee, or other reward whatsoever. And Wee doe further straitly charge and command, upon the paines and penalties aforesaid, That all owners of ships, bee carefull to imploy such masters in their ships, or other vessels, from whom they will take good caution, not to offend in the importation of any Tobacco, contrary to this Our Royall pleasure. And We do further signifie and declare by these presents, that We will require an exact accompt of the master of every ship, or other vessell, that he shall make such diligent, and carefull search, over the mariners and passengers in his ship, or other vessell, that none of them shall conveigh over into these Our Realmes of England, or Ireland, or dominion of Walles, or into any Port, Haven, Creeke, or other parts thereof, any Tobacco, to be imported, contrary to the true intent and meaning of these presents: And that Our Customers, or their deputies, in every Port of these Our Realmes of England, and Ireland, shall, upon oath, examine every Master of a ship, or other vessell, or other Officers and Mariners in the said ship, or vessell, whether they have made search in the said ship or vessell, for Tobacco, and whether any Tobacco bee in the said ship, or vessell, to their knowledge, and whether any Tobacco were laden in the said ship or vessell, and bee taken out thereof, and what is become of the same: And if any Master of a ship, or other vessell, shall wilfully, or negligently permit, or suffer any Tobacco to be imported, or shall otherwise offend, contrary to these presents, every such Master (because it is in his power to prevent the same) shall also be answerable unto Us for his contempt herein, and shall be subject, et lyable to all the paines and penalties aforesaid, as well as if he himselfe had actually and purposely committed the said offence. And whereas We are informed, that some traders in Tobacco, doe use to import Tobacco in forreigne Bottomes; Wee strictly charge and command, that no person whatsoever, either Stranger, Denizen, or naturall borne Subject, presume to import any Tobacco whatsoever, in any forreigne bottome, at any time hereafter, upon paine of confiscation, not onely of the said Tobacco, but also of the ship, or vessell, wherein the same is so imported, and upon the other paines and penalties aforesaid.

And for the better execution of Our pleasure herein, We doe hereby command all and singuler Customers, Comptrollers, Searchers, Wayters, and other Officers, attending in all, and every the Ports, Creekes, or places of lading or unlading, for the taking, collecting, or receiving of any of our Customes, Subsidies, or Duties, to take notice of this Our pleasure: And We do hereby command, and give power and authoritie unto them, and every of them, from time to time, as well to search any shippe, or other vessell, or bottome, ryding, or lying within any Port, Haven, or Creeke, within their severall charge of attendance, for all Tobacco imported, contrary to the intent of this Our Royall Proclamation; and the same being found, to seize and take to Our use, and also to take notice of the names, and apprehend the bringers in and buyers of the same, to the end they may receive condigne punishment for their offences, upon payne, that every of the said Officers, which shall bee found negligent, remisse or corrupt therein, shall lose his place and entertainement, and undergoe such paines and penalties, as by Our Lawes, or by the censure of Our said Court of Starre-chamber, may be inflicted upon them for the same.

And We doe likewise, will, ordaine, and appoint, that it shall and may bee lawfull, for such person or persons, as shall be thereunto authorized and appointed, by him, or themselves, or his, or their Deputy or Deputies, with a lawfull Officer to search any shippe, or other vessell, and to enter into any shoppe, house, seller, warehouse, or other suspected places, at lawfull and convenient times, and there to search, discover, and find out any Tobacco, imported, uttered, sold, or vented, or to be uttered, sold, or vented, not marked or sealed, as aforesaid, contrary to the true meaning hereof, and all such Tobacco so found, to seize, take away, and dispose of, and the owners thereof, or in whose custodie the same shall be found, to informe and complaine of, to the end they may receive punishment, according to Our pleasure before herein declared.

And further, We doe by these presents, will and require all and singuler Mayors, Sheriffes, Justices of Peace, Bayliffes, Constables, Headboroughs, Customers, Comptrollers, Searchers, Wayters, and all other Our Officers and ministers whatsoever, That they, and every of them, in their severall places and Offices, be diligent and attendant in the execution of this Our Proclamation, and also ayding and assisting unto such person and persons, and his and their Deputies and Assignes, as We shall so, as aforesaid, authorise et appoint,[16] as well in any search for discovery of any act, or acts to be performed contrary to the intent of these presents, as otherwise, in the doing or executing of any matter or thing, for the accomplishment of this Our Royall command. And further Our will and pleasure is, and Wee doe hereby charge and command Our Atturney generall, for the time being, to informe against such persons in Our Court of Starre-chamber, from time to time, whose contempt and disobedience against this Our Royall command, shall merit the censure of that Court, and to prosecute every such information speedily and effectually, untill the same shall bee brought to sentence. And Our pleasure and command is, that all the Tobacco which upon any seizure shall become forfeited, shall bee brought to Our Custome house, next adjoyning to the Port, or place where the same shall be seized, where the seizor thereof shall deliver the same to Our use, and the same shall be forthwith burnt, consumed, and destroyed; but the offendour, before he be discharged, shall pay to the partie, who seized the said Tobacco, the one halfe of the true value thereof: And that such person or persons, whom Wee shall appoint specially by Our Privie Seale, to take care and charge of the execution of Our pleasure in the premisses, shall have the one halfe of all the Fines, to bee imposed upon every offendour against this Our Proclamation, for their encouragement to bee diligent and faithfull, in, and about the performance of that service, We shall so commit unto them.

Given at Our Honour of Hampton Court, the nine and twentieth day of September, in the two and twentieth yeere of Our Reigne of England, France, and Ireland, and of Scotland the eight and fiftieth.

God save the King.

Imprinted at London by Bonham Norton and John Bill, Printers to the Kings most Excellent Majestie. 1624.

4 pp. folio. There are two issues varying only in set-up. Copies in Antiq., B. M., Canterbury, Dalk., I. T., P. C., and P. R. O.; also in John Carter Brown Library. Entered on Patent Rolls. Printed in Rymer's "Fœdera," xvii, 621.

---

[16] The commission, dated November 9, 1624, appointing Edward Dichfield and five others officers to take charge of the execution of the provisions of this Proclamation, is printed in Rymer's *Fœdera*, xvii, 633.

1625, MARCH 2.

[ENCOURAGING GROWTH OF TOBACCO IN PLANTATIONS.]

BY THE KING.

A Proclamation for the utter prohibiting the importation and use of all Tobacco, which is not of the proper growth of the Colonies of Virginia and the Summer Islands, or one of them.

Whereas, at the humble suite of Our Commons in Parliament, by Our Royall Proclamation, bearing date the nine and twentieth day of September now last past, for the reasons therein contained, We have prohibited the importation and use of all Tobacco, which is not of the proper growth of Our Colonies of Virginia and the Summer Islands, or one of them; And whereas, upon the humble Petition of many Our loving Subjects, being Planters or Adventurers in those Colonies, and for the support and incouragement of those Plantations (whose prosperous estate We much affect, and shall by all good meanes be alwayes ready to cherish and protect) We have beene contented to tolerate the use of Tobacco, of the growth of those Plantations for a time, untill by more solid Commodities they be able to subsist otherwise, which (as We are informed) they cannot as yet by any meanes doe; And therefore by Our said Proclamation, Wee did thinke fit to give particular directions in many things tending to those ends, and did straitly command the due execution and observation thereof, under the penalties therein contained: Now because Wee have beene informed, as well by the humble Certificate of Our Commissioners for Virginia, as by the humble Petition of divers of Our loving Subjects, the Planters and Adventurers of, and in those Colonies, That, notwithstanding Our Royall pleasure was so expressly signified, and the reasons of State are so plainely laid downe, as might have perswaded every well affected Subject to the due observance thereof; yet divers, out of an inordinate desire of private gaine, have wilfully disobeyed Our commandement herein, and thereby have indeavoured, as much as in them lieth, to destroy so noble a worke as the support of those Plantations, which so much concernes Our Honour, and the honour and profit of Our people.

Wee therefore, being very sensible of this neglect and contempt, have thought good to renew Our said Proclamation; And doe hereby signifie and declare unto all Our loving Subjects, and unto all others, Our expresse will and pleasure to be, That Our said former Proclamation, and every clause, prohibition, article and thing therein contained, shall from hencefoorth be duly observed and obeyed, with such alterations and additions, as are in these presents contained and expressed, upon paine of Our high displeasure, and such penalties and punishments, as in Our said former Proclamation are, or in these presents shall be limited or appointed for the offenders thereof.

And whereas some have since Our said last Proclamation, unmerchantlike, secretly and cunningly stollen in great parcels of Tobacco, contrary to Our said Proclamation; Wee would have those persons, and all others by their example know, That they must expect the severitie of that censure, which Our Court of Starre-Chamber shall thinke fit to inflict upon them, and that Wee are resolved not to relent or remit their deserved punishment, but to cause them and all others, that shall dare to offend herein, to bee prosecuted and punished in such measure, as such their high contempt doth deserve.

And because We conceived it would be utterly in vaine to prohibite the importation of such forreine Tobacco, as aforesaid, unlesse the care and charge of the execution thereof were committed by Us, to some fit and able persons, who besides the respect to Our service, might for their owne particular interests take the same to heart; Therefore We have by Our Letters Patents under Our great Seale of England, authorized certaine persons, Citizens of London, well affected to those plantations, and to Our service, by themselves, and their Deputies, to search and inquire into the offences, and offenders against Our said Proclamation: And Wee have also contracted with them to bee Our Agents for Us, and to Our use to receive the Tobacco of those Colonies, at, and for such prices as Wee have agreed to give for the same; and besides those prices, to bee given to the Planters and owners of the said Tobacco, Our said Agents have further contracted with Us, to give and pay unto Us, and to Our use, such summes of money more, as may give Us reasonable satisfaction for that losse, which otherwise Wee should sustaine in Our Customes and other Dueties, and may inable Us to beare that charge, which Wee have undertaken yeerely to disburse for the generall defence and support of those Plantations. And We doe further by this Our Proclamation publish and declare, that We will constantly and inviolably observe and performe Our said contract, and on Our parts, will allow and disburse out of Our revenew, those summes of money for the safety of those Plantations, and for the ease of the Planters and Inhabitants there, which by the said contract hath beene on Our parts undertaken; whereof We would have, aswell Our said Agents, as the Planters and Adventurers in those Colonies, and all other whom it may concerne, to rest confidently assured.

And because Wee are given to understand, that divers using to trade in Tobacco, and having a purpose to import, or buy, or sell the same, contrary to the intent of this Our Proclamation, doe usually land the same at private Wharffes, Staires, or other places, and send, or conveigh the same unto the Houses, Cellers, Warehouses, or other places, of, or belonging to others, who are lesse suspected then themselves, thereby to conceale the same from Us, and Our Agents; Wee further will and command, That from hencefoorth no person whatsoever, presume, or suffer the said prohibited Tobacco to bee landed at any Wharffe, Staire, or other place, nor receive, or conceale any such prohibited Tobacco, or suffer the same to be bestowed in any of their Houses, Cellers, Warehouses, or other places, upon paine of Our high displeasure, and upon such paines and penalties, as by this, or Our former Proclamation, are to be inflicted upon the principall offenders, And to the intent that all the prohibited Tobacco brought in, shall be justly and truely exported againe, et no part thereof sold, or vented within these Our Kingdomes; Our will and command is, That all the prohibited Tobacco which shall be seized within Our Kingdome of England, shall be brought and delivered into the Warehouse, or Storehouse which shall be to that purpose provided by the said Agents, in Our city of London; and all the prohibited Tobacco, which shall be seized within Our Kingdome of Ireland, shall bee brought and delivered into the Warehouses, or Storehouses which shall to that purpose bee appointed by Our Agents in Our city of Dublin, or elsewhere within Our said Kingdome of Ireland.

And for the incouragement of those, who shall take paines in the discovery and seizing thereof, Our will and pleasure is That the one halfe of the reasonable value thereof, shall bee paid unto the seizers thereof in money by Our Agents, et the Tobacco it selfe shall be exported againe by Our said Agents, or by their appointments: And for the better execution of Our service herein, We doe hereby give full power and authority, as well to Our Agent and Agents, as to their Deputy and Deputies, at all time and times, to enter into, and to search for any prohibited Tobacco, contrary to this Our Proclamation, in any Ship, Boate, or vessell, or in any House, Ship, Celler, Soller, Warehouse, or in any Trunke, Chest, Case, Barrell, or Pack, Cabbin, or any other suspected place whatsoever, and finding any such prohibited Tobacco, the same to seize and cary away, to be conveyed to such place or Warehouse, as Our said Agent shall appoint for that purpose, as aforesaid.

And Our expresse will and command is, That neither Our said Agents, nor any others, doe sell, or utter any part of the said prohibited Tobacco, within any Our owne Dominions, there to bee spent and used, whereby the vent of the Tobacco of our Colonies aforesaid may any way bee hindred, upon paine of Our heavy displeasure, and such other paines and penalties, as other offenders against this Our Proclamation are liable unto.

And whereas by Our former Proclamation, We did command, that from, et after the five et twentieth day of March, then, and now next ensuing, no person should sell, utter, or offer to put to sale, or use any Tobacco, which is not of the proper growth of the Colonies aforesaid, and before the ende of forty dayes then next ensuing, should transport out of Our said Kingdome, all other Tobacco, then that of the growth of those Colonies; Wee doe now by this Our Proclamation, ratifie and confirme the same, and command, the same to be duely put in execution: And to the ende there may be no evasion used to avoyd the same, Wee doe hereby give full power and commandement to Our said Agents, by themselves and their Deputies, at any time, or times after the said five and twentieth day of March now next ensuing, to search for the said prohibited Tobacco, and to take a true and exact note and accompt of the quantity thereof, to the intent that the Owners thereof, before the ende of forty dayes next ensuing after the said five and twentieth day of March, either by themselves, or some other, may export the same by the privity of the said Agents, according to the true intent of this, and of Our said former Proclamation, and at the end of the said forty dayes, may give a just account unto

Our said Agents, what is become thereof; et whatsoever Tobacco, which is not of the proper growth of the Plantations aforesaid, shall after the said forty dayes be found in the hands of any person whatsoever, shall bee seized by Our said Agents, or their Deputies to Our use, and the said person or persons having or using the same, shall incurre Our high displeasure, and bee subject to such further paines and penalties, as by Our said Proclamation are to be inflicted upon any other offenders.

And Our further will and command is, that all the Tobacco of the growth of Our Colonies aforesaid, shall be brought to the Custome-house-key of Our port of London, and there be delivered to Our Agents, or their Assignees to Our use, according to Our contract aforesaid, or be kept in Our said Custome-house to bee transported out of Our Dominions; and whatsoever Tobacco of the growth of those Plantations, or either of them, shall not be brought to that Key, and be delivered as aforesaid, or for which there shall not bee good security given to Our Agents, within foureteene dayes after the landing thereof, to export the same as aforesaid, the same shall bee forfeited and seized to Our use by Our Agents or their Deputies, as other prohibited Tobacco, and this to bee duely observed under the paines and penalties aforesaid.

And whereas Wee are given to understand, that divers using to trade in Tobacco, have and still doe secretly and underhand steale into Our Kingdomes the said prohibited Tobacco, and doe so privily hide and conceale the same, that they cannot be easily discovered, nor found out; and doe either by themselves, or others by them to that purpose imployed, carry the same by small quantities to the houses or shops of Our subjects, inhabiting within Our said Kingdomes, and doe sell or profer the same to bee sold, or else doe secretly and covertly offer to contract for the sale of such prohibited Tobacco; Our will and pleasure is, and Wee doe hereby straitly charge and command all and every Our loving subjects, to whom any the said prohibited Tobacco shall be offered to be sold or contracted for, as aforesaid, that immediately upon the sight of any such prohibited Tobacco, or upon offer to contract for any such Tobacco, they make stay thereof, and of such person or persons, as shall either profer the same to sell, or shall offer to contract for any the said prohibited Tobacco, and that they and every of them, who shall have the said prohibited Tobacco so proffered unto them to be sold, as aforesaid, shall give notice thereof, and charge the next Constable, Head-borough or other Officer, with such person or persons, who shall offer to put the same to sale, upon paine of Our high displeasure, and of such other paines and penalties, as other offenders against this Our Royall Proclamation are liable unto. And Wee doe hereby further charge and command all and singuler Constables, Head-boroughs et other Our Officers aforesaid, that they and every of them, upon notice unto them given of any such prohibited Tobacco, as aforesaid, or of any such person and persons so offending, as aforesaid, that they seize the said Tobacco, and detaine all such person and persons so offending as they shal have knowledge of, untill they have given notice thereof unto Our said Agents or their Deputie or Deputies, and untill by their meanes the person offending may be brought before such Officer as hath power by this Our Proclamation to take sufficient bond for the appearance of such person, in some of Our Courts of justice, to answer for their faults as the same shall deserve.

And for the better finding out and discovery of the offences and offenders against Our former and this Our Proclamation, We are well pleased, and doe hereby require and command, that Our Treasurer, Commissioners for Our Treasury, Chancellour and Barons of Our Exchequer now, and for the time being, within Our said Kingdomes of England and Ireland, respectively shall and may award such and so many Commissions, as they shall thinke meet, to be directed to discreet and fit persons in all or any Our Ports, or elsewhere, to enquire of and examine upon oath, or otherwise, all such persons as are, or shall be suspected to have heretofore offended, or which hereafter shall offend against this, or Our former Proclamation in this behalfe, or any other person or persons whatsoever, for the finding out and discovery of the said offences and offenders, as is before mentioned; to the end that, as well the importers of such Tobacco as the buyers, sellers, spenders, receivers and concealers thereof, may receive such condigne punishment by fine or otherwise, for their offences, as by Our Court of Star-chamber, or Court of Exchequer shall be thought fit: And in case such Tobacco shall not, or cannot be taken, or found to bee seized, that then every such offender shall forfeit and pay to the hands of Our Agent or Agents, in this behalfe for Our use, the full value of such Tobacco, as the said offenders heretofore have, or hereafter shall have imported, bought, sold, vented or received, as aforesaid, beside such further punishment, as shall be fit to be inflicted upon them for their contempt.

And Our further will and pleasure is, and We doe hereby declare, That whatsoever Our said Agent or Agents, their Assignee or Assignees, under the hands and seales of the greater number of them, have already done, or shall doe hereafter against any offender or offenders, in requiring and taking the forfeiture of any Tobacco, or the value thereof so imported or uttered as aforesaid, or in the mitigating or taking any lesse summe then the value of the same of any such offender in the premisses, or otherwise according to the good discretion of Our said Agent or Agents, Wee doe and will from time to time approve and allow of by these presents: And this signification of Our pleasure shall be as well unto Our said Agent or Agents for the time being, as unto all and every such Commissioner and Commissioners which have beene, or shall be imployed, in, or about this Our service, a sufficient warrant and discharge in that behalfe, without any account to be by them, or any of them respectively yeelded to Us, Our Heires or Successors, and without incurring any penalty in the doing or executing of this Our Service and Royall Command.

And forasmuch as heretofore divers great quantities of Tobacco have beene imported into this Realme, under the name or names of sundry poore Mariners, and other, which are not able to pay the value thereof, nor give satisfaction for the same, Our will and pleasure is, the better to avoyd such frauds and deceipts in time to come, That in whatsoever Ship, or other Vessell, any such Tobacco in greater or lesser quantities, shall be found or discovered to have beene, or to be so imported, and to be shifted away that seizure thereof cannot, or shal not be made, That then such Mariners, or others, who shall so import or couler the said

Tobaccoes, shall not onely be punished, as aforesaid, but that every Master of such Ship or Vessell, wherein such Tobacco shall be so imported or shifted away, as aforesaid, shall forfeit to Us the value of the said Tobacco, and that such Ship or Ships shall be arrested, and stayed by the Officers of every Port, or any of Our Agents, their Deputies or Assignees respectively, untill the said forfeiture be duly answered and paid to the hands of Our said Agent or Agents to Our use, or such others as they shall appoint in that behalfe.

And for the better execution of the premisses, Wee doe straitly charge and command all Justices of Peace, Mayors, Sheriffes, Bailiffes, Constables, Headboroughs, Tythingmen, Our Warden and Constable of Our Cinque Ports, and all other Our Officers and Ministers, as well of Our Admiralties, as otherwise, and all other Our loving Subjects, to whom it shall or may appertaine, that they and every of them at all times et times hereafter, and from time to time, upon sight of Our Letters Patents, granted to Our said Agents, or of a Deputation under the hands et seales of Our Agents, or any three of them, be ayding and assisting to Our said Agent and Agents, and their Deputie and Deputies, and to such Our Commissioners, as shall be from time to time appointed for or about this Our service, And also to be from time to time ayding and assisting to all Our Searchers, Waiters, and to all such other person and persons as shall be authorized by Our said Agent or Agents, or by Our Customers or Farmers of Our Customes, for the searching, seizing, taking, and carying away of all such Tobacco imported, or hereafter to be imported or uttered, or intended to be put to sale contrary to this Our Royall prohibition and command. And if any person or persons shall bee found, privily or secretly to oppose or animate any others, to contradict or withstand them in the due execution of this Our service and Royall command, or to neglect the due execution thereof, That then We do by these presents, straitly charge and command, all and every Our sayd Officers respectively, that every such person and persons shall be apprehended and brought before Our Treasurer, Chancellour of Our Exchequer, or before any the Lords or others of Our Privy Councell, or before Our chiefe Baron, or some other of the Barons of Our Exchequer for the time being, to receive such order for condigne punishment to be inflicted upon them according to their demerits, as shall be fit.

Given at Our Court at Theobalds, the second day of March, in the two and twentieth yeere of Our Reigne of Great Britaine, France, and Ireland.

GOD SAVE THE KING.

Imprinted at London by Bonham Norton and John Bill, Printers to the Kings most Excellent Majestie.

M.DC.XXIIII.

4 pp. folio. Copies in Antiq., B. M., Dalk., P. R. O., and Q. C. Entered on Patent Rolls. Printed in Rymer's "Fœdera," xvii, 668.

1625, APRIL 9.

[IMPORTATION OF TOBACCO.]

BY THE KING.

A Proclamation touching Tobacco.

Whereas Our most deare Father, of blessed memorie, deceased, for many weighty and important Reasons of State, and at the humble suit of His Commons in Parliament, did lately publish two severall Proclamations, the one dated the nine and twentieth day of September, now last past, and the other the second of March following, for the utter prohibiting of the importation, and use of all Tobacco, which is not of the proper growth of the Colonies of Virginia and the Sommer Islands, or one of them, with such Cautions, and under such Paines and Penalties, as are in those Proclamations at large expressed:

Wee, tendring the prosperity of those Colonies and Plantations, and holding it to bee a matter of great consequence unto Us, and to the honour of Our Crowne, not to desert, or neglect those Colonies, whereof the foundations, with hopefull successe, have been so happily layd by Our Father, beeing given to understand, that divers persons intending onely their private gaine, and neglecting all considerations of the publique, in this short time, whilest Wee have been necessarily taken up in ordering of the great affaires of Our Kingdomes and State, have taken the boldnesse, secretly, and by stealth, to import and utter great quantities of Tobacco, which is not of the growth of the Plantations aforesaid, to the utter destruction of those Plantations, as much as in them lieth; Wee have thought fit, for the preventing of those inconveniences, which may otherwise ensue, to the irrecoverable dammage of those Plantations, and of Our service, to publish and declare Our Royall pleasure for the present, touching the premisses, untill upon more mature deliberation Wee shall see cause to alter, or adde unto the same, in any part.

And Wee doe therefore straitly charge and command, that no person whatsoever, of what degree or qualitie soever, doe at any time hereafter, either directly or indirectly, import, buy, sell, or utter, plant, cherish, or use, or cause to bee imported, sold, or uttered, cherished, planted, or used, in Our Realmes of England, or Ireland, or Dominion of Wales, or in any Isles or places thereunto belonging any Tobacco, of any sort whatsoever, which is not of the proper growth of the said Colonies, or one of them; And that no person whatsoever, by any shift or device whatsoever, doe receive, or conceale, or colour the Tobacco of any other, so imported, planted, bought, sold, uttered, or used within Our sayd Realmes, or Dominions, or the Isles or places aforesaid, or any part thereof, upon paine of forfeiture unto Us, of all such Tobacco so to be imported, bought, sold, planted, uttered, or used, contrary to the true meaning of these presents, in whose hands soever the same shall be found, and upon such further paines and penalties, as by the Lawes and Statutes of these Our Realms, or by the Censure of Our Courts of Star-Chamber, in either of Our said Kingdomes respectively, can or may be inflicted upon the offenders, for contempt of this Our Royall Command; and to be reputed and taken as enemies to Our proceedings, and to those Plantations, which so much concerne Our honour, and the honour and profit of Our State.

And Our further will and command is, that all the forreigne Tobacco, of what sort soever, which is not of the proper growth of those Plantations, or one of them, shall before the fourth day of May, now next ensuing, bee transported out of Our Realmes and Dominions, as by the sayd former Proclamations it was directed and commanded, upon paine of forfeiture thereof, and upon the other paines and penalties aforesayd to be inflicted upon the offenders.

And Our pleasure is, That all such forreigne Tobacco may bee freely exported by any person whatsoever, without paying to Us, or to Our use, any Subsidie, or other duetie for the same.

Given at Our Court at White-Hall, this ninth day of April, in the first yeere of Our Reigne of Great Britaine, France, and Ireland.

GOD SAVE THE KING.

Printed at London by Bonham Norton and John Bill, Printers to the Kings most Excellent Majestie. M.DC.XXV.

2 pp. folio. Copies in Antiq., B. M., Crawf., I. T., P. C., and P. R. O. Entered on Patent Rolls. Printed in Rymer's "Fœdera," xviii, 19.

1625, MAY 13.

[SETTLING THE AFFAIRS OF VIRGINIA.]

BY THE KING.

A Proclamation for setling the Plantation of Virginia.

Whereas the Colonie of Virginia, Planted by the hands of Our most deare Father of blessed memory, for the propagation of Christian Religion, the increase of Trade, and the enlarging of his Royall Empire, hath not hitherto prospered so happily, as was hoped and desired, A great occasion whereof his late Majesty conceived to be, for that the government of that Colony was committed to the Company of Virginia, encorporated of a multitude of persons of severall dispositions, amongst whom the affaires of greatest moment were, and must be ruled by the greater number of Votes and Voyces; And therefore his late Majestie, out of His great Wisedome, and depth of Judgement, did desire to resume that popular government, and accordingly the Letters Patents of that Incorporation, were by his Highnesse direction in a Legall course questioned, and thereupon judicially repealed, and adjudged to bee voyde[17]; wherein his Majesties ayme was onely, to reduce that government into such a right course, as might best agree with that forme which was held in the rest of his Royall Monarchy, and was not intended by him, to take away, or impeach the particular Interest of any private Plantor, or Adventurer, nor to alter the same, otherwise then should be of necessity for the good of the publique: And wheras We continue the like care of those Colonies and Plantations, as Our late deare Father did, and upon deliberate advice and consideration, are of the same Judgement that Our said Father was of, for the government of that Colony of Virginia; Now lest the apprehension of former personall differences, which have heretofore happened (the reviving and continuing whereof Wee utterly disallow, and strictly forbid) might distract the mindes of the Plantors and Adventurers, or the opinion, that We would neglect those Plantations, might discourage men to goe or send thither, and so hinder the perfecting of that worke, wherein We hold the honor of Our deare Father deceased, and Our owne honour to be deeply engaged; We have thought fit to declare, and by Our Royal Proclamation to publish Our owne Judgement, and resolution in these things, which by Gods assistance Wee purpose constantly to pursue. And therefore Wee doe by these presents publish and declare to all Our loving Subjects, and to the whole world, that Wee hold those Territories of Virginia and the Sommer-Ilands,

---

[17] For the proceedings whereby the patent was overthrown by the *quo warranto*, June 26, 1624, see Brown, *First Republic in America*, p. 601.

as also that of New England, where Our Colonies are already planted, and within the limits and bounds whereof, Our late deare Father, by His Letters Patents, under His great Seale of England, remaining of Record, hath given leave and liberty to His Subjects to plant and inhabite, to be a part of Our Royall Empire, descended upon Us and undoubtedly belonging and appertaining unto Us; And that We hold Ourselfe, as well bound by Our Regal office, to protect, maintaine, and support the same, and are so resolved to doe, as any other part of Our Dominions:

And that Our full resolution is, to the end that there may be one uniforme course of Government, in, and through Our whole Monarchie, That the Government of the Colonie of Virginia shall immediately depend upon Our Selfe, and not be committed to any Company or Corporation, to whom it may be proper to trust matters of Trade and Commerce, but cannot bee fit or safe to communicate the ordering of State-affaires, be they of never so meane consequence: And that therefore Wee have determined, That Our Commissioners for those Affaires, shall proceed according to the tenor of Our Commission directed unto them, untill Wee shall declare Our further pleasure therein. Neverthelesse We doe herby declare, That Wee are resolved, with as much convenient expedition, as Our Affaires of greater importance will give leave, to establish a Councell, consisting of a few persons of understanding and qualitie, to whom We will give trust for the immediate care of the Affaires of that Colony, and who shall be answerable to Us for their proceedings, and in matters of greater moment, shall be subordinate and attendant unto Our Privie Councell heere; And that We will also establish another Councell to be resident in Virginia, who shall be subordinate to Our Councell here for that Colonie; and that at Our owne charge we will maintaine those publique Officers and Ministers, and that strength of Men, Munition, and Fortification, as shall be fit and necessary for the defence of that Plantation, and will by any course that shall be desired of Us, settle and assure the particular rights and interests of every Planter and Adventurer, in any of those Territories, which shall desire the same, to give them full satisfaction for their quiet and assured enjoying thereof.

And lastly, whereas it is agreed on all sides, that the Tobacco of those plantations of Virginia and the Sommer Islands (which is the onely present meanes for their subsisting) cannot be managed for the good of the Plantations, unlesse it be brought into one hand, whereby the forreigne Tobacco may be carefully kept out, and the Tobacco of those Plantations may yeeld a certaine and ready price to the owners thereof; Wee doe hereby declare, That to avoid all differences and contrariety of opinions, which will hardly be reconciled amongst the Planters and Adventurers themselves, We are resolved to take the same into Our owne hands, and by Our servants or Agents for Us, to give such prices to the Planters and Adventurers for the same, as may give them reasonable satisfaction and encouragement; but of the maner thereof, Wee will determine hereafter at better leisure: And when We shall have concluded the same, We shall expect, that all Our loving Subjects will readily conforme themselves thereunto.

And in the meanetime, because the importation and use of forreigne Tobacco, which is not of the growth of those Plantations, or one of them, will visibly and assuredly undermine and destroy those Plantations, by taking away the meanes of their subsistence, We doe hereby strictly charge and command, That Our late Proclamation, bearing date the ninth day of April last, intituled, (A Proclamation touching Tobacco) shall in all points and parts thereof, be duely and strictly observed, upon paine of Our high displeasure, and such further penalties and punishments, as by the sayd Proclamation are to be inflicted upon the offenders. And We doe hereby advise all Our loving Subjects, and all others whom it may concerne, not to adventure the breach of our Royall Commandement in any of the premisses, We being fully resolved, upon no importunitie or intercession whatsoever, to release or remit the deserved punishment of such, as shall dare to offend against the same, seeing We holde not Our Selfe onely, but Our people interested therein.

Given at Our Court at White-Hall, the thirteenth day of May, in the first yeere of Our Reigne of Great Britaine, France, and Ireland.

GOD SAVE THE KING.

Imprinted at London by Bonham Norton, and John Bill, Printers to the Kings most Excellent Majestie. Anno Dom. M.DC.XXV.

2 pp. folio. There are two issues, varying only in the cut of the royal arms. Copies in Antiq., B. M., Crawf., I. T., P. C, and P. R. O. Entered on Patent Rolls. Printed in Rymer's "Fœdera," xviii, 72.

1627, FEBRUARY 17.

[IMPORTATION OF TOBACCO.]

BY THE KING.

A Proclamation touching Tobacco.

Whereas Our most deare Father, of blessed memory, deceased, for many weighty and important reasons of State, and at the humble suit of his Commons in Parliament, did heretofore publish two severall Proclamations, the one bearing date the nine and twentieth day of September, in the two et twentieth yeere of His Highnesse Reigne of England, France, and Ireland, and of Scotland the eight and fiftieth, and the other the second day of March then next following, by both of them utterly prohibiting the importation et use of all Tobacco, which is not of the proper growth of the Colonies of Virginia, and the Summer-Ilands, or one of them, with such Cautions and under such Paines and Penalties, as are in those Proclamations at large expressed.

And whereas Our sayd Father by another Proclamation bearing date the thirtieth day of December, in the seventeenth yeere of His Highnesse Reigne of England, did straitly charge all and every person or persons, of what degree or condition soever, that they should not from the second day of February then next following, presume to Sowe, Set, or Plant, or cause to be sowen, set, or planted within this Realme of England or Dominion of Wales any sort or kinde of Tobacco whatsoever, and that they, or any of them should not maintaine and continue any old Stockes or Plants of Tobacco formerly sowen or planted, but should foorthwith destroy and roote up the same.

And whereas We, finding the said Proclamations to be grounded upon many weighty reasons and considerations, did since Our Accesse to Our Crowne, by Our Proclamation lately published, renew and confirme the said former prohibitions: Neverthelesse, because the immoderate desire of taking of Tobacco hath so farre prevailed in these Our Kingdomes, as that it cannot on a sodaine bee utterly suppressed, and the difference, or, at least, the opinion of difference betweene Spanish or forreine Tobacco, and Tobacco of the Plantations of Virginia, and of Our owne Dominions, is such, that Our Subjects can hardly be induced totally to forsake the Spanish Tobacco; whereby it commeth to passe, That where Wee were willing to have suffered losse in Our Customes, so as the said forreigne Tobacco might have been kept out, the same is secretly, and by stealth brought in in great quantities, and many great quantities of Tobacco are set and so wenwithin this Our Realme of

England and Dominion of Wales, and so the mischiefe, intended to be redressed, is not avoided, and yet Our Revenue in Our Customes is much diminished.

Wee therefore, taking into Our Princely consideration, as wel the present estate of these times, and how many important necessities doe at this instant presse Us, that by all good meanes Wee should husband Our Revenue to the best, and also considering the many inconveniencies which doe and will arise, both to Our selves and to Our Subjects, by the secret importation of Spanish Tobacco, and planting of English Tobacco, whereby divers of Our Subjects have taken liberty to themselves, for the desire of private gaine, without respect to the publique, to make such frequent sale of the same, as that thereby not onely Our Plantations abroad are much hindered, but Our Customes also are much impayred, Wee have thought fit, by the advice of Our Commissioners for Our Revenue, as Our first part of proceeding concerning Tobacco, to restraine wholly the planting of Tobacco within these Our Realmes, or any the Iles thereto belonging, and to forbid the importation of forreine Tobacco. And yet to give way to the infirmitie of Our Subjects for the present, by the allowing the importation of some smal quantity of Spanish or forreine Tobacco, not being of the growth of the English Plantations, not exceeding the quantitie of fiftie thousand weight in any one yeere to bee brought in by Our owne Commissioners onely, and to Our owne particular use onely, and not otherwise.[18]

And to the end that the extraordinary liberty now taken, may be restrained, the said Colonies or plantations not hindered, nor Our Selfe deceived in Our Customes, Wee have likewise by the advice aforesaid, thought it requisite, to imploy some persons of trust and qualitie to be Our Commissioners in this Service, to, and for Our owne proper use, and upon accompt to be given to Us for the same.

Wee doe therefore hereby publish and declare Our Royall will and pleasure, that, notwithstanding the severall Proclamations before mentioned, We are well contented to give way to the importation and sale of so much Spanish and forreine Tobacco, as shall not exceede the quantitie of fifty thousand weight in any one yeere, as aforesaid, and that the same shall bee Our owne Merchandise and Commodity, and be managed and disposed of by Our owne Commissioners, or such as they shall appoint for Our use, and not otherwise.

And, because that no man shall presume, by colour of this Our Licence or toleration, to import any other, or greater quantity of Spanish or forreine Tobacco, nor utter or put the same to sale, to the prejudice of Our Service hereby especially intended, and to the overthrow of Our Colonies and Plantations abroad, Wee doe hereby straitly charge and command, that no man other then Our owne Commissioners, for Our owne proper use, presume to import any forreine Tobacco into Our Realmes of England or Ireland, or any parts thereof. And for their better assistance therein, and the prevention of all abuses, Wee have thought fit, and so ordaine, and doe by these presents publish Our Royall pleasure, That all Tobacco that shall from hencefoorth be imported into this Our Realme of England, whether it be Spanish, or of the growth of Virginia, the Sommer-Ilands, or the West-Indies,

---

[18] In a commission issued to Sir John Wolstenholme and ten others to execute the regulations regarding the importation of tobacco, dated January 31, 1627, this provision as to Spanish tobacco had been inserted. (Printed in Rymer's *Fœdera*, xviii, 831.)

or other adjacent Ilands, beeing English Plantations, shall be brought into Our Port of London onely: Also that there shall bee three severall Seales kept by Our Commissioners in some convenient place, where they shall appoint, under three lockes, whereof three of Our Commissioners shall keepe three severall Keyes, wherewith both all such forreine Tobacco, as shall bee so imported, as aforesaid, as also such other Tobacco of the growth of Virginia, and the Sommer-Ilands, and other the sayd Plantations as shall bee imported, shall be sealed, That is to say, for that of Virginia, and the Sommer-Ilands, a Seale engraven with Our Armes, and for that of the other English Plantations, a Seale engraven with a Lion and a Crowne, and for the other forreine Tobacco, a Seale engraven with a broad Arrow and a Portcullice, without paying anything for the sealing of the Tobacco of Virginia, and Sommer-Ilands, and other the sayd Plantations, but onely what the parties themselves shal thinke fit to allow for the sealers paines, waxe, and threed.

And We doe hereby will et Command, that no person or persons whatsoever, whether Denizen, or Stranger, or borne within any of Our Realmes or Dominions, doe presume, attempt, or go about to counterfeit the said Seales, or any of them, and that no person or persons whatsoever, other then Our Commissioners, their deputy or deputies, do presume, attempt, or go about to import any Spanish or forraine Tobacco whatsoever, or to buy, utter, or sell any Tobacco, of what sort soever, but such as the Roule thereof shall bee sealed with one of the Seales aforesaid, or to import any other, or greater quantity of Spanish Tobacco, then the said fifty thousand weight onely in any one yeere, or to sowe, set, or plant, or cause to be sowen, set, or planted in any of his, or their grounds, any Tobacco whatsoever, within Our Realmes of England, or Ireland, or Dominion of Wales, or any Isles or places belonging thereto, or permit, or suffer any old stockes formerly set to continue, upon paine of forfeiture unto us, of all such Tobacco as shall be imported, set, sowen, planted, suffered, uttered, or put to sale, contrary to the true meaning of these presents, and to have the same English Tobacco utterly destroyed, in whose hands soever the same shall be found, and upon such further paines, and penalties, as by the Lawes and Statutes of this Our Realme of England, or by the severity, or censure of Our Court of Star-chamber, or by Our Prerogative Royall may be inflicted upon the offenders for their contempt of this Our Royall Command, the one moity of all which fines to be imposed upon any the said offenders, We are graciously pleased shall be bestowed upon the persons that shall informe against them for the same; and that such person or persons as shall discover any planting of Tobacco within Our Realme of England, or other Our Realmes or Dominions, shall have his charges expended in following of Suite against the offendors, allowed out of Our part of the fines to be imposed, besides his moity aforesaid.

And further, that every person or persons, that shall discover the falsifying, or counterfeiting of any the Seales aforesaid, shall have an hundred Crownes for such his discovery out of Our part of the fine to be imposed for the same, besides the one moity for himselfe, as aforesaid.

And for the better execution of Our will and pleasure, We doe hereby Command, all and singular Customers, Comptrollers, Searchers, Waiters, and other Officers, attending in all, and every, or any of Our Ports, Creekes, or places of lading, or unlading, for the taking, collecting, or receiving of any Our Customes, Subsidies, or other duties, to take notice of this Our pleasure.

And We doe hereby command, and give power and authority unto Our said Commissioners, and those whom they shall thinke fit to imploy in Our said service, and every, or any of them from time to time, and at all times when they shall thinke fittest, with a Constable, or other officer, for their assistance to search any ship, or other vessell or bottome, riding or lying within any Port, Haven, or Creeke within their severall charge and place of attendance, for all Tobacco, imported contrary to the intent of this Our Proclamation, and the same being found, to seize and take to Our use, as also to take notice of the names, and apprehend the bringers in, and buyers of the same, to the end they may receive condeigne punishment for their offence.

And further, to take speciall care, that no more of the said Spanish, or other forraine Tobacco, shall be imported, then the said fifty thousand weight onely, in any one yeere, and that the same be brought into Our Port of London onely, as aforesaid, upon paine that every of the said officers that shall be found negligent, corrupt, or remisse herein, shall lose his place, and entertainement, and undergoe such paines and penalties, as by the Laws, or the censure of Our said Court of Star chamber may be inflicted upon them for the same.

And likewise We doe hereby ordaine, will and appoint, that it shall and may be lawfull, to and for Our said Commissioners, authorised, as aforesaid, to import the said fifty thousand weight of Spanish or other forraine Tobacco, by him, or themselves, or his, or their deputy or deputies with a Constable, or other officer, for their assistance, to enter into any suspected place or places, at such time or times, as they shall thinke to be most convenient, and there to search, discover, and finde out any Tobacco, imported, uttered, planted, set, sowed, sold or vented, not marked, or sealed, as aforesaid, contrary to the true meaning hereof, and such Tobacco so found to seize, take away, et dispose of et the owners thereof, or in whose custome the same shal be found, to informe, and complaine of, to the end they may receive punishment, according to Our pleasure herein before declared.

And further, We doe by these presents, will and require, all and singular Mayors, Sheriffes, Justices of peace, Bailiffes, Cõstables, Headboroughs, Customers, Controllers, Searchers, Waiters, and all other Our Officers, and Ministers whatsoever, that they, and every of them, in their severall places and offices, be diligent and attendant in the execution of this Our Proclamation, and also ayding and assisting, to Our said Commissioners thereunto by Us appointed, or to be appointed, and to their Deputies, as well in any search for discovery of any act, or acts to bee performed, contrary to the intent of these presents, as otherwise in the doing, or executing of any matter or thing for the accomplishment of this Our Royall Command.

And lastly, Our will and pleasure is, and We doe hereby, charge and command Our Atturney generall, for the time being, to informe against such persons in Our Court of Star-chamber, or Exchequer-chamber, as the case shall require from time to time, whose contempt and disobedience against this Our Royall Command, shall merit the censure of these Courts.

Given at Our Court at Whitehall, the seventeenth day of Februarie, in the second yeere of Our Reigne of Great Britaine, France, and Ireland.

GOD SAVE THE KING.

Imprinted at London by Bonham Norton and John Bill, Printers to the Kings most Excellent Majestie. M.DC.XXVI.

3 pp. folio. Copies in Antiq., B. M., Crawf., I. T., P. C., and P. R. O. Entered on Patent Rolls. Printed in Rymer's "Fœdera," xviii, 848.

1627, MARCH 30.

[SEALING OF TOBACCO.]

BY THE KING.

A Proclamation touching the Sealing of Tobacco.

Whereas We (by the advice of Our Commissioners for Our Revenue) have resolved to import a quantity of Spanish Tobacco (not exceeding fifty thousand weight in any one yeere) and utterly to prohibite the importation of any other forreine Tobacco, which is not of the growth of Our owne Plantations, and to prohibite also the planting of all Tobacco within these Our Realmes of England and Ireland, and Islands thereto belonging or adjacent, As by Our Proclamation, dated the seventeenth day of February last (for the reasons therein expressed) it doth at large appeare: Now, because Wee are informed, that it will much conduce to Our Service, and the setling of that businesse, for the preventing of the stealing in of all forreine Tobacco, and discovery of the offendours, and for the clearing of all others, who are not offendors, from future trouble, that all the Tobacco of the growth of Our plantations already imported, shal be sealed by Our Commissioners to that purpose appointed, aswell as that which shal be hereafter imported, in such sort as by our sayd Proclamation is already directed, That so the Tobacco of Our Plantations may bee distinguished from the forreine Tobacco, and the Tobacco planted within these Our Realmes, which are prohibited: Our will and command therfore is, and We doe hereby declare et publish Our Royall pleasure to be, That Our said Commissioners appointed by Us for this Service, shal with al cõvenient speed, Seale all the Tobacco of the growth of Our said Plantations already imported in such sort, as they are directed to Seale that which shall be hereafter imported.

And if any person whatsoever, having any such Tobacco, of the growth of Our said Plantations, or any of them, which shall refuse to have the same Sealed, or which shall not offer the same to be Sealed, as aforesayd, and the same shall hereafter, at any time after one moneth, from the date hereof, be discovered, that the same shall bee taken and reputed for forreine Tobacco, or for Tobacco of the growth of these Our Realmes, which hath been prohibited, and which they durst not avow the keeping of, and as such Prohibited Tobacco shal be taken, and seized as other prohibited Tobacco, according to the Tenor and true meaning of Our said former Proclamation, whereof Wee will, that every person, whom it may concerne, do take notice at their perill.

Given at Our Court at White-Hall, the thirtieth day of March, in the third yeere of Our Reigne of Great Britaine, France and Ireland.

GOD SAVE THE KING.

Imprinted at London by Bonham Norton and John Bill, Printers to the Kings most Excellent Majestie. M.DC.XXVII.

1 p. folio. Copies in Antiq., B. M., Crawf., P. C., and P. R. O. Entered on Patent Rolls. Printed in Rymer's "Fœdera," xviii, 886.

1627, AUGUST 9.

[IMPORTATION OF TOBACCO.]

BY THE KING.

A Proclamation for the ordering of Tobacco.

The Kings most Excellent Majestie, and His Royall Father of blessed memory, having at severall times and upon severall occasions, published their Proclamations concerning Tobacco, as well that which hath beene indeavoured to bee planted within this Realme, as that which is of the growth of Virginia and the Sommer Islands, and other English Colonies and Plantations, and also concerning Spanish and other forraigne Tobacco; And finding that the inordinate desire of taking Tobacco, and the immoderate thirst of gaine, by the planting and selling of Tobacco, cannot otherwise be allayed or moderated; Hath at the last, by the advice of His Privie Counsell, determined upon this finall resolution touching all sorts of Tobacco, in manner following.

First, His Majestie doth heereby declare His Royall Pleasure to be, and doth heereby Will and Command, that no person whatsoever doe at any time hereafter, plant, cherish, or preserve any Tobacco, within these His Realmes of England or Ireland, or Dominion of Wales, or any the Isles, parts, or places, of, or belonging to them or any of them, and if any bee now planted or growing there, that the same bee presently plucked up and utterly destroyed, by the Owners, Planters, Tenders, or Dressers thereof, and lest they or any of them, should adventure to neglect the performance hereof, His Majestie doeth further straitly charge and command all Constables, Tything-men, Headboroughs, and other Officers within their severall limits and Jurisdictions, carefully and effectually to see the same executed and performed accordingly. And His Majestie doth further Will and Command all Justices of Peace, Mayors, Sheriffes, and other principall Officers in their severall places, within the compasse of their severall Jurisdictions and authorities, upon complaint to them made, to cause the same to be duly performed and executed without partialitie, as they and every of them will answere their contempts in that behalfe at their uttermost perils.

And that the Tobacco of His Majesties own Plantations and Colonies may not bee planted and imported hither without limitation or measure, or under colour thereof, the Tobacco of the growth of Spaine and other forraigne parts, may not be brought into these His Realmes, or sold or uttered heere, to the overthrow of His Colonies abroad, and to the wasting of the wealth and treasure of His Kingdomes at home. His Majesty doeth further Will and straitly Command, that no person whatsoever doe at any time heereafter import any Tobacco of the growth of Spaine, and other forraigne parts out of His owne Dominions, nor sell, utter, or offer to sell, or utter, or otherwise dispose or keepe any such Tobacco, to the intent to sell or utter the same without His Majesties speciall Commission in that behalfe, upon paine of confiscation and forfeiture thereof, in whose hands soever the same shall be found, and upon such further paines and penalties, as by the Lawes of these His Realmes, or by His Prerogative Royall which in this case He will not admit to be disputed, may be inflicted upon the offendors.

And because such forraigne Tobacco, may not be received and uttered, under the pretence of the Tobacco of the growth of Virginia, the Summer-Ilands, and other Colonies and Plantations, under and within His Majesties owne Dominions, nor the Planters, Owners, or Adventurers, of, and in these Plantations, give themselves over to the planting of Tobacco onely, to make a present returne of profit, and neglect to applie themselves to solide Commodities fit for the establishing of Colonies, which will utterly destroy these and all other Plantations; His Majestie doth further will and command, that from henceforth no Tobacco of the growth of Virginia, the Summer-Ilands, or any other Plantations, or Colonies, of, or within His owne Dominions, bee imported into these his Realmes or Dominions, or any the Ports, Havens, Creekes, or places thereof, without His Majesties especiall licence in that behalfe, under the great Seale of England, and that upon the importation thereof, the same bee delivered into the hands of such Commissioners, for his Majesties owne immediate use, as His Majestie under His great Seale of England shal appoint, at, and for such Prices and Rates to be paid for the same, as shall be reasonable agreed upon, betweene the Owners or Factors of the same, and the Kings Commissioners on His Majesties behalfe, or if they shall not agree thereon, then to be transported againe, and sold elsewhere, upon paine of confiscation and forfeiture thereof, and upon further paines and penalties, as by the Law, or His Majesties Prerogative Royall may be inflicted upon them.

And further His Majestie doth straitly charge and command, that no person whatsoever presume to buy any sort of Tobacco, within these Realmes or Dominions, or any Haven, Port, Creeke, or place thereof, of any other person, then of His Majesties Commissioners onely to bee authorised under the great Seale of England, as aforesaid, and after the same shall bee sealed with a Seale to that purpose appointed, and that they, upon the buying thereof, doe expresse the true time when the same was bought, the quantitie and qualitie thereof, in and by a note in writing indented betweene the Buyer and Seller, testifying the same upon the paines and penalties aforesayd.

And if during these times of Hostility, any Tobacco shall bee imported by any of His Majesties owne Shippes, or by the Ships of any of his Subjects, by way of Prize, or Letters of Marque, his further will and pleasure is, that all such Tobacco shall be delivered unto his Majesties Commissioners, at, and for reasonable prices, to bee accomptable therefore to his Majesties use.

And his Majesty doeth hereby straitly charge and command, all Customers, Controllers, Searchers, Wayters, and all other Officers, Ministers, of, or belonging to His Customes, And also all Justices of Peace, Mayors, Sheriffes, Constables, and other Our Officers, Ministers and loving Subjects, in their severall places and degrees, to take knowledge of this his Royall pleasure and Commandement, and to bee ayding, helping and assisting to His Majesties Commissioners, and their Deputies, Factors and servants, in all things touching and concerning this His Service, whereof his Majestie is resolved to require a due and strict accompt.

Given at His Majesties Court at Windsore, the ninth day of August in the third yeere of His Reigne of England, Scotland, France, and Ireland.

GOD SAVE THE KING.

Imprinted at London by Bonham Norton and John Bill, Printers to the Kings most Excellent Majestie. M.DC.XXVII.

2 pp. folio. Copies in Antiq., B. M., Crawf., I. T., P. C., and P. R. O. Entered on Patent Rolls. Printed in Rymer's "Fœdera," xviii, 920.

1630, NOVEMBER 24.

[FORBIDDING DISORDERLY TRADING
WITH THE SAVAGES.]

BY THE KING.

A Proclamation forbidding the disorderly Trading with the Salvages in New England in America, especially the furnishing of the Natives in those and other parts of America by the English with Weapons, and Habiliments of Warre.

Whereas a Proclamation was heretofore published by Our deare Father King James of blessed memorie, in the twentieth yeere of His Reigne,[19] for the better supportation and Reiglement of the Plantations within Our Territory of New England in America, whereby, amongst divers other things, the insufferable abuses committed by divers Interloping and irregular Merchants, and disobedient Fishermen and Mariners, were prohibited, who seeking only their present and private profit, did Trade with the Salvages of that Countrey, and to the great prejudice and danger of Our loving Subjects the Planters there, did Barter away to the Salvages, Swords, Pikes, Muskets, Fowling-Pieces, Match, Powder, Shotte, and other Warlike Armes, Weapons, and Munition, and teach them the use thereof, not onely to their owne present ruine (divers of them having been slaughtered by the barbarous people with their owne Weapons formerly sold by them) but also to the great hazard of the lives of the English already, planted there, and to the apparant destruction of that hopefull Plantation.

Wee, being informed that these abuses are still continued to the indangering of that Plantation,[20] and that the like abuses are also practised in other Forreigne Plantations: Out of Our Princely care for the prosperity of these Colonies, which being well governed may be of great use to this Nation, for the reformation and prevention of these and the like enormities for the future.

And to the end that the Royal Grant of Our late Father to the President and Counsell of New England aforesayd, may bee maintained and upholden, and that the Planters there, and adventurers thither, may bee encouraged by all good wayes and meanes to proceede in their worthy designes, have thought it fit, and doe

---

[19] Refers to proclamation of November 6, 1622.

[20] The Privy Council, September 29, 1630, had acted upon a petition from Massachusetts and had requested the attorney-general to draw up a proclamation (see *Acts of Privy Council*, i, 154, and *Cal. State Papers, Colonial, 1574-1660*, p. 120).

hereby straitly charge and command, That none of Our Subjects whatsoever (who are not Adventurers, Inhabiters, or Planters, authorised by Our President and Counsell for New England, according to the sayd Letters Patents) doe presume from hencefoorth to frequent those Coasts to Trade or Traffique at all with the Native people of those Countreys, or to intermeddle with the Woods, or Grounds of any of the Planters, or English Inhabitants there, otherwise then by the Licence of the sayd President and Counsell, or for the necessary use of their Fishing on those Coasts, in which case of Fishing, or under colour thereof, they are not to use any Trade or Traffique there, nor to challenge any Right to the Soyle there, or the Woods growing or beeing thereon, and especially Wee doe charge and command, that neither any Interlopers, Fisher-men, or Mariners, or any other of Our Subjects whatsoever, being of the said Company of New England or otherwise, doe at any time hereafter dare to Sell, Barter, or any wayes to deliver or convey unto any of the Salvages or Natives of America, where any of Our English Colonies are or shall bee planted, any Weapons or Habiliments of Warre of any kinde whatsoever, or to teach them or any of them the use of Gunnes, or how to make, or amend them, or any thing, belonging to them, upon paine of Our high indignation, and the Confiscation, Penalties and Forfeitures expressed in the said Royall Graunt of Our sayd Father, wherein Wee shall proceede against those who have offended, or shall offend in any of the premisses, in such manner and measure as the qualitie of their Offences shall deserve. And yet further Wee leave it to the discussion of the said President and Counsell for New England, and to other the Governours and Counsell in any other Forreigne English Colonie in their severall places respectively, to proceede against the Offenders in any the kindes aforesaid, according to the powers already granted unto them, and according to Our Lawes in that behalfe.

Given at Our Court at Whitehall, the foure and twentieth day of November, in the sixt yeere of Our Reigne of Great Britaine, France and Ireland.

GOD SAVE THE KING.

Imprinted at London by Robert Barker, Printer to the Kings most Excellent Majestie: and by the Assignes of John Bill. 1630.

2 pp. folio. Copies in Antiq., Crawf., P. C., and P. R. O. Entered on Patent Rolls. Printed in Rymer's "Foedera," xix, 210. A photographic fac-simile of this proclamation was printed by the Museum Book Store of London, about 1898.

1631, JANUARY 6.

[RESTRICTING IMPORTATION OF TOBACCO.]

BY THE KING.

A Proclamation concerning Tobacco.

Whereas in the Reigne of Our most deare and Royall Father, King James of blessed memory, et since Our accesse to the Crowne, severall Proclamations have been made and published concerning Tobacco, Yet notwithstanding all the care and providence which hath hitherto been used, We finde the unlimited desire of gaine, and the inordinate appetite of taking Tobacco, hath so farre prevailed, that Tobacco hath been continued to bee planted in great quantities, in severall parts of this Our Realme, and a vast proportion of unserviceable Tobacco made and brought from Our Colonies of Virginia, Summer Ilands, and other Our Forreigne Plantations, besides an incredible quantity of Brasill and Spanish Tobacco imported hither, and secretly conveyed on Land. And it is now come to passe, That those Our Forreigne Plantations, that might become usefull to this Kingdome, lingering onely upon Tobacco, are in apparant danger to be utterly ruined, unlesse Wee speedily provide for their subsistence; The bodies and manners of Our people are also in danger to bee corrupted, and the wealth of this Kingdome exhausted by so uselesse a Weede as Tobacco is; which beeing represented unto Us by the humble Petition of Our loving Subjects the Planters and Adventurers in Virginia, and also by the like humble Petition of the Retailers and Sellers of Tobacco in and about Our Cities of London and Westminster, Wee have thought it worthy of Our Princely care, as a matter not only fit for Our profit, et the profit of Our people, but much concerning Us in Our honour and government so to regulate the same, and compell due obedience thereto, that Our forreigne Plantations and Colonies may bee supported and encouraged, and they made usefull to this Kingdome, by applying themselves to more solide commodities, that the healths of Our Subjects may be preserved, the wealth of this Kingdome enlarged, and the manners of Our people so ordered and governed, that the world may not justly taxe Us, that these are at once endangered only by the licentious use of Tobacco. And therfore having seriously advised hereof, Wee, by the advice of Our Privie Councell, have now resolved upon, and published these Our Commands following concerning Tobacco, which Our Royall will and pleasure is, shall be in all things observed upon paine of Our highest displeasure, and of such paines, penalties and punishments, as by Our Court of Exchequer, and Court of Starre-Chamber, and by any other Courts and ministers of Justice, or by Our Prerogative Royall can be inflicted upon the offenders.

And first, Our will and Command is, that no person whatsoever doe at any time hereafter plant, preserve, or maintaine any Tobacco, which is, hath been, or shall be planted in Our Kingdomes of England or Ireland, or Dominion of Wales, or in the Islands of Jersey or Guernesey, but that the same bee utterly displanted and destroyed, and that none presume or adventure to Buy, Sell, or utter any such Tobacco, the same being utterly unwholesome to bee taken.

And further, that no Tobacco whatsoever be from hencefoorth imported into these Our realms, or any Haven, Port, Creeke or place therof, which is, or shal be of the growth of any the parts or places beyond the Seas, belonging to, or under the obedience of any foreine King, Prince, or State whatsoever; But such, and so much thereof onely, as Wee shall specially allow to be imported, untill it shal be fully setled betweene those Forreine Princes and Us, according to those Treaties which are betweene Us, that Our Subjects may not unthriftily vent the solide Commidities of Our owne Kingdomes, and returne the proceed thereof in Smoake.

And further We will and command, that no Tobacco of the growth of any of Our English Plantations in Virginia the Sommer Islands, Caribee Islands, or other Islands or places in America, or the Coasts thereof, be at any time hereafter imported or brought into Our Kingdomes of England or Ireland, or Dominion of Wales, at any other Port then at, or in Our Port of London onely, and the same duely entred in Our Custome-houses there, nor that any greater quantitie thereof bee imported there, then Wee by the advice of Our Privie Councell shall hold fit, and under Our Privie Seale, shall declare to bee competent for the expence of these Our Kingdomes, Wee not thinking it fit to admit of an immeasurable expence of so vaine and needlesse a Commoditie, which ought to bee used as a Drugge onely, and not so vainely and wantonly as an evill habite of late times hath brought it unto.

And these sorts of Tobacco which shall be thus brought from Our owne Colonies, Wee will take present order shall bee well ordered and made up, and so certified to bee, under the hand of the Governour of that place, and when the same shall be brought hither, shall bee againe Searched, Tryed and Sealed, that Our Subjects be not abused by corrupt Tobacco.

And Our expresse Command is, that whatsoever Tobacco shall bee taken, which shall be imported contrary to this Our Proclamation, the same shall be forfeited and confiscate, and by the Officers of that Port or place where it shall bee taken, shall be immediately burnt.

And for the ordering and governing of the expence and use of Tobacco when it shall be imported, Wee, by the advice of Our Privie Councell, shall speedily direct such a course as Wee shall hold fit, which Wee expect shall be also in all things observed.

And Wee straitly charge and Command all Our Customers, Comptrollers, Searchers, and all other the Officers and Ministers of Our Ports, that they and every of them in their severall places, doe carefully and faithfully observe Our Royal Command, in, and concerning the premisses; and if any of them shall be found remisse or negligent therein, or to connive at any such offender, that hee or they shall for such their fault, without any remission be remooved from the place or places of his or their attendance on Our service.

And to the end Our pleasure and Command hereby published, may be the better executed, Wee doe hereby will, require and Command, all Maiors, Sheriffes, Justices of peace, Bayliffes, Headboroughs, and other Our Officers and loving Subjects whatsoever, to be aiding and assisting, and so much as in them lyeth, to take care that the premisses herein mentioned, be duly put in execution, as they tender their duetie and allegeance to Us, and will answere the contrary at their uttermost perils.[21]

Given at Our Court at Whitehall the sixt day of January, in the sixt yeere of Our Reigne.

GOD SAVE THE KING.

Imprinted at London by Robert Barker, Printer to the Kings most Excellent Majestie: and by the Assignes of John Bill. 1630.

2 pp. folio. Copies in Antiq., B. M., Canterbury, Crawf., and P. C.; also in Va. State Library. Entered on Patent Rolls. Printed in Rymer's "Fœdera," xix, 235.

---

[21] A communication from the Privy Council to the Governor of Virginia, inclosing the proclamation and directing the observance of its regulations, is preserved among the records in the Public Record Office. An order from the Council to the farmers and officers of customs, issued at the same time, directs that Spanish tobacco will pay a duty of 2s. per pound, St. Christopher's, Barbadoes, and the adjacent islands 12d. per pound, and Virginia and the Somers Islands 9d. per pound. (*Cal. State Papers, Colonial, 1574-1660*, p. 125). For the various restrictions upon the growth of tobacco in the plantations, see Bruce, *Economic History of Virginia*, i, 304-309.

1633, OCTOBER 13.

[RESTRICTING SALE OF TOBACCO.]

BY THE KING.

A Proclamation for preventing of the abuses growing by
the unordered Retailing of Tobacco.

Whereas the Plant or Drugge called Tobacco scarce knowne to this Nation in former times, was in this Age first usually brought into this Realme in small quantity, as Medicine, and so used, and by divers taken as Medicine, but in processe of time, to satisfie the inordinate appetite of a great number of men and women it hath been brought in in great quantity, and taken for wantonnesse and excesse, provoking them to drinking and other inconveniences, to the great impairing of their healths, and depraving of their manners, so that the care which His Majesty hath of his people hath enforced Him to thinke of some meanes for the preventing of the evill consequence of this immoderate use thereof. And albeit His Majesties dearest father of blessed memorie had given directions therein, as well by Proclamation as otherwise, yet those waies tooke not so good effect as was desired, for that therein was no restraint of the number of those that should sell Tobacco by retaile, nor care taken of the quality of those that should make such sale, but Victuallers, Taverners, Alehouse-keepers, Tapsters, Chamberlaines, Hostlers and others, of the meanest condition have promiscuously used to regrate the same as allurements to other naughtinesse, keeping therein no Assize, to the prejudice of the rest of His Majesties loving Subjects. For repressing therefore of all such excesses and for preventing of future inconvenience, Our Soveraigne Lord the King, by the advice of the Lords and others of His Privie Councell hath resolved to reduce the venting, selling and uttering of Tobacco into some good order, and that none but men of sufficiency, and such as shall bring certificate of their meetnesse, shall hereafter sell or utter any Tobacco by retaile. And to that purpose His Majestie hath lately caused Letters from His Lords, and others of His Privie Councell to bee directed unto the Justices of Peace of the severall Counties of this Kingdome, and Dominion of Wales, and also unto the Maiors, Bailiffes and other chiefe Officers of divers Cities and Townes Corporate; Commanding them to certifie in what Townes and places it may bee fit to suffer selling and retailing of Tobacco, and how many in each place were fit to bee licensed to use that Trade. In answere of which Letters, Certificates have beene made from divers of the Justices of Peace, and from the Maiors, Bailiffes, and other Magistrates of divers Cities and Townes Corporate, who therein have acknowledged the abuses that daily arise by the ungoverned selling and retailing of Tobacco, expressing their desire of reformation.

Whereupon His Majestie by like advice of his Counsell hath caused other Letters to be directed to the Justices and Conservators of the Peace in severall Counties; thereby declaring in what Townes and places Tobacco shall be permitted to be sold or uttered by Retayle, and hath Commanded the said Justices and Conservators of the Peace, to cause the names of those Townes and places specified in those Letters, to be written and affixed in publique places where the Assises and Sessions of the peace shall be kept, in those Counties, to the end that all His people may take notice that other places are not admitted or allowed for selling or uttering of Tobacco by Retaile. And by Letters directed to the said Maiors, Bayliffes, and other head Officers of Cities and Townes, His Majestie hath given notice unto them of the names of those that are permitted there to sell or deliver Tobacco in that manner, and hath Commanded them to give publique notice in the said Cities and Townes, of the names of those persons that are so admitted to sell or deliver it.

Now our said Sovereigne Lord the King doth straightly prohibite all His people, that after the feast of Candlemas next[22] comming after the date of these presents, none of them out of the said Cities or Townes so appointed as aforesaid, or within the said Cities, or Townes, no others but those named as aforesaid, and such as from time to time shall bee permitted in like manner, doe sell or deliver any Tobacco by Retayle, and that none of them that are permitted or allowed in this behalfe, keepe any Taverne, Alehouse, or Victualling, or otherwise sell any distilled or hot Waters, Wine, Ale, Beere, or Cyder in their houses, so long as they shall bee permitted to sell Tobacco by Retayle: And for that the necessities of these times require it, His Majestie doth charge and command all His Subjects to obey these His Ordinances, under the paines to bee inflicted upon contemners of the same, and of His Royall will and pleasure, being for the good of His people: All which His pleasure is shall bee observed untill Hee shall by His Proclamation, or Letters of His Privie Counsell make other publique signification of His pleasure herein. And Hee doth charge and command all Justices of Peace, and all Maiors, Bayliffes, and head Officers of all His Cities and Townes within His said Kingdome of England, and Dominion of Wales, and all those who are permitted to sell Tobacco by Retaile, that they make diligent enquirie of all those that shall presume to doe against this Command, and from time to time to make certificate of their names, and places of their residence, with the particular of their contempts, to the Lords of His Majesties Privie Councell.

Given at the Court at Whitehall the thirteenth day of October,[23] in the ninth yeere of the Reigne of our Sovereigne Lord Charles by the grace of God King of England, Scotland, France, and Ireland, Defender of the Faith, etc.

GOD SAVE THE KING.

Imprinted at London by Robert Barker, Printer to the Kings most Excellent

[22] February 2, 1634.

[23] This proclamation is entered in the Privy Council Register under date of August 14 (*Acts of Privy Council*, i, 191), probably the date of the original draft by the attorney general. Rushworth, in his *Historical Collections*, ii, 191, lists it under the date of August 13. Rymer's *Fœdera* assigns to it the date of October 13, as given in the printed proclamation.

Majestie: and by the Assignes of John Bill. M.DC.XXXIII.

2 pp. folio. There are two issues, varying only in the cut of the royal arms. Copies in Antiq., Bodl., B. M., Camb., Crawf., Dalk., P. C., P. R. O., and Q. C. Printed in Rymer's "Fœdera," xix, 474.

1634, MARCH 13.

[REQUIRING LICENSES FROM TOBACCONISTS.]

BY THE KING.

A Proclamation restraining the abusive venting of Tobacco.

Whereas the Kings most excellent Majestie being informed of the abuses dayly arising of the ungoverned Selling and Retailing of Tobacco, by his Proclamation lately published, did prohibit all his people, that after the feast of Candlemas, which is now last past, none of them out of certaine Cities and Townes therein specified to have beene appointed, and within those Cities and Townes no other but certaine persons named, as in the said Proclamation is expressed, and such as from time to time as should be permitted, should sell or deliver any Tobacco by Retaile, herein requiring due obedience untill his Majestie should make other declaration, as by the same Proclamation appeareth.

Sithence which, a great number of his Majesties loving subjects have repaired to some Lords, and others of his Majesties Privie Councell, being his Majesties Commissioners appointed to treat with them, and have humbly desired Letters Patents of Licence to sell Tobacco by Retaile, whereunto his Majesties said Commissioners have consented: but because it is both convenient and necessary that the number of those that be Licensed to sell Tobacco by Retaile, and also their names be knowne, that in time convenient notice may be taken from them how much Tobacco in each yeere they Retaile and Vent: that upon knowledge thereof, his Majesty for preventing of the issuing out of the Realme too great a proportion of the Stocke of this Kingdome, may give order for the quantity of Tobacco that shall be yeerely brought in: And being resolved that any who from henceforth shall presume to utter or sell Tobacco, not being Licensed, shall severely be proceeded against: For these and for other causes, the King our Soveraigne Lord straightly defendeth and commandeth, that neither such as by pretext of being formerly nominated as meet men to Retaile Tobacco, nor any other from henceforth presume to sell or utter Tobacco by Retaile, untill they shall have obtained his Majesties Licence in that behalfe, any permission or tolleration that may be pretended by the said Proclamation, or any other signification notwithstanding, upon such paines of censure in the Court of Star-Chamber and elsewhere, as may be inflicted upon contemners of his Majesties commands publiquely proclaimed. Wherein his Majestie is pleased, that a part of the Fines set upon the Contemners of this Command, be conferred upon those that give notice of the Offenders, so as they may be brought to judgement.

Given at Our Court at Newmarket, the thirteenth day of March, in the ninth yeere of Our Reigne.

God save the King.

Imprinted at London by Robert Barker, Printer to the Kings most Excellent Majestie: And by the Assignes of John Bill. 1633.

1 p. folio. There are two issues, varying only in the cut of the royal arms. Copies in Antiq., B. M., Crawf., Hodg., P. C., and Q. C. Entered on Patent Rolls. Printed in Rymer's "Fœdera," xix, 522.

1634, MAY 19.

[CONCERNING TOBACCO.]

BY THE KING.

A Proclamation concerning Tobacco.

Whereas in the Reigne of Our late deare Father, and since Our accesse to the Crowne, upon mature deliberation there have been sundry Proclamations published for restraining the landing of Tobacco to certain Ports and Harbours within this Kingdome, and against planting of the same within this Realme; And for that they have not been put in due execution, divers fraudes and abuses have beene of late invented and put in execution by mixing of Tobacco, not onely with other Tobacco of worse condition, but also with other Materials, falsifying and corrupting the same, to the great hurt and damage of Our people, both in their estates and persons, which growing evill may in some measure bee prevented, if the Tobacco brought into this Our Realme shall be layd or landed onely in one Port and place.

For remedie therefore in that behalfe, and to the end Wee may bee the more truely answered of the Custome, Impost, and other dueties due unto Us for Tobacco brought into this Realme by way of Merchandize, whereof Wee have been sundry times defrauded by landing the same at the pleasures of the Owners: Wee doe hereby publish and declare Our Royall will and pleasure, That no Tobacco bee hereafter landed, or imported to bee landed at any other Porte, then in Our Port of London, and at no other place of the sayd Port then at the Key and Wharfe commonly called the Custome-house Key, scituate in Our Citie of London, and other Port or place for landing of Tobacco Wee doe not admit or allow, but them inhibite.

And Wee doe hereby straitly charge and command all and singular Customers, Comptrollers, Searchers, Waiters and other Officers, attending in all Our Ports, Creekes, or places of lading or unlading, (except Our said Port of London) not to take entries of any Tobacco, nor suffer the same to be taken, landed, or layd on shoare in any other Harbour, Port, Creeke or place within this Kingdome, upon paine that every of the said Officers that shall bee found negligent, corrupt or remisse herein, shall undergoe such paines and penalties, as by the Lawes or Censure of our Court of Starre-chamber may bee inflicted upon them for the same.

And it is Our further will and pleasure, that if any Ship or Barque wherein Tobacco shall be loaden shall arrive at any other Port or place then at Our sayd Port of London, Wee doe hereby give full power and Authoritie to all and every the Customers, Comptrollers, Surveyours, Searchers and Waiters, and every of them there attending, and doe command them to take and arrest the same Tobacco, and forthwith to make Certificate to the Customers of the Port of London, of the Owners name of such Ship or other Vessell, and his place of dwelling, the number and names of the Officers, and Mariners in the same, the place from whence the same Tobacco came, with the quantitie of Tobacco that shall bee contained therein.

And also, that Our said Officers, or some of them, shall with all convenient speed cause and procure the Tobacco so by them arrested, to bee carefully transmitted to the said Port of London, to the Customer there, that the same may bee there viewed, and the dueties thereof belonging unto Us, may be duely payed and satisfied, and such further order taken with the same, and with the Owners thereof, as shall be fit.

And whereas notwithstanding former Proclamations published to the contrary, yet Wee are informed, that Tobacco is still planted and sowen in divers parts of Our Realmes of England and Ireland, in contempt of Us and Our Royall Commands declared to the contrary; We do therefore hereby againe absolutely prohibit the Planting thereof in Our said Kingdomes, as also the bringing into the same of any Seed for the increase thereof, from the parts beyond the Seas; The Tobacco growing in the Northerne and moist Climats being not onely unwholesome for mans body, but the same maketh fertill grounds become for a long space lesse fruitfull, that might otherwise produce Corne, Herbes and Rootes for the sustenance of Our Subjects.

And for the more certaine depressing of the same, We doe hereby straitly command Our Justices of Assize within their severall Circuits, Our Justices of Peace within Our severall Counties of this Kingdome, Maiors, Sheriffes, Bayliffes, and other Our Officers within each Cittie and Towne Corporate, that they at their severall Sittings, Quarter Sessions, and meetings, give the same in charge as an Offence, whereof Wee expect due reformation, requiring a Returne thereof amongst other the grievances of the Countrey in their Presentments, And the names and dwelling places of any Offenders herein, and the qualities of their Offences, to present to the Lords of Our Privie Councel, the then next Tearme after every such Sitting or meeting, to the end the Offenders may bee proceeded against by sentence in Our Court of Starre-chamber, or otherwise, as in justice shall be thought fit.

And lastly, We doe by these Presents will and require all and singular Maiors, Sheriffes, Justices of Peace, Bayliffes, Constables, Headboroughes, Customers, Comptrollers, Searchers, Waiters, and all other Our Officers and Ministers whatsoever, that they and every of them in their severall places and Offices, be diligent and attendant in the execution of this Our Proclamation, as they will answere the contrary at their uttermost perils.

Given at Our Court at Greenewich, this nineteenth day of May, in the tenth yeere of Our Reigne of England, Scotland, France and Ireland.

GOD SAVE THE KING.

Imprinted at London by Robert Barker, Printer to the Kings most Excellent Majestie: And by the Assignes of John Bill. 1634.

2 pp. folio. Copies in Antiq., B. M., Crawf., P. C., P. R. O., and Q. C. Entered on Patent Rolls. Printed in Rymer's "Fœdera," xix, 553.

2 pp. folio. Copies in Antiq., B. M., Crawf., P. C., P. R. O., and Q. C. Entered on Patent Rolls. Printed in Rymer's "Fœdera," xix, 553.

1636, MAY 16.

[LIMITING WHALE-TRADE TO MUSCOVY COMPANY.]

BY THE KING.

A Proclamation inhibiting the Importation of Whale Finnes, or Whale Oile, into His Majesties Dominions by any, but the Muscovia Company.

Whereas Our late deare and Royall Father, of ever blessed memory, King James, by His Proclamation, bearing date the eighteenth day of May, in the seventeenth yeere of His Reigne, for the reasons therein expressed, and for the encouragement of His welbeloved Subjects, the Company of Merchants trading for Muscovia, Greenland,[24] and the parts adjoyning, commonly called the Muscovia Company, did inhibit the Importation of Whale Finnes, into any of His Kingdomes or Dominions, by any persons other then by that Company, and that in their Joynt-stock only, under the penalties therein mentioned; We now being minded to give the like encouragement and assistance to the said Company, and for the better support of the Fishing-Trade to Greeneland, and the parts adjacent, which by the increase of Navigation conduceth much to the common good of Our Kingdome and People, have thought fit to publish Our Royall pleasure therein; And therefore We do by these presents straightly Charge, prohibite, and forbid, as well all Aliens and Strangers whatsoever, as Our naturall borne Subjects and Denizens, That they, nor any of them, (other then the said Muscovia Merchants only, and that in their Joynt-stock for the Whale-Fishing;) shall from henceforth directly or indirectly Import or bring any Whale Oyle, or Whale Finnes, (whether the said Finnes be whole, or cut, in what manner soever) into any Our Kingdomes or Dominions, upon Paine of the forfeiture and confiscation of the same; whether they bee found on Board of any Ship, Hoye, Boat, or Bottom, or laid on land in any Ware-house, Store-house, Shop, Cellar, or any other place whatsoever; and upon Paine of Our high Indignation and displeasure, and such other punishments, as by Our Court of Starre-Chamber shall bee thought meet to be inflicted upon them, or any of them, as Contemners of Our Royall Will and Commandment in this behalfe.

And Wee do likewise straightly Charge, prohibite, and forbid, as well all Aliens and Strangers, as Our naturall borne Subjects and Denizens, (other then the said Muscovia Merchants in their Joint-stock as aforesaid) that they, nor any of them do presume to Buy, Utter, Sell, Barter, or Contract, for any Whale Oyle, or Whale

[24] Spitzbergen, rather than Greenland proper.

Finnes, knowing the same to bee Imported into any Our Realmes or Dominions, contrary to Our Will and Pleasure herein declared; whether the said Finnes bee whole, or cut as aforesaid, upon Paine of Our high Indignation and displeasure, and such further punishments, as by Our said Court of Starre-Chamber shall bee thought meet to bee inflicted upon such Offendours, as Contemners also of Our Royall Commandments.

And to the end, that Our Pleasure hereby declared may take the better effect; Wee do hereby Charge and Command, all Customers, Collectours, Farmours, Comptrollers, Searchers, Waiters, and all other Our Officers and Ministers whatsoever, in all or any Our Ports, Havens, or Creekes; that they and every of them in their severall places, do carefully attend and see to the due execution hereof; and in no wise to permit or suffer any Whale Oile, or Whale Finnes whole, or cut, directly, or indirectly, openly, or covertly, to be brought or imported into any Our Kingdomes or Dominions contrary to Our Royall pleasure herein expressed; or being so imported, that they do not permit, or suffer the same to be colourably Customed for other Goods and Merchandise; but that they forthwith do seise, and take to Our use all such Whale Finnes, and Whale Oyle as shall bee so Imported, contrary to Our pleasure herein declared, upon Paine to undergo such punishments as shall be thought meet by the Lords of Our Privie Councell.

Neverthelesse, Our intent and meaning is, That the said Muscovia Company in their Joynt-stock only, and none other, shall or may Buy and Sell, Barter, or Contract, for any such Whale Finnes, or Whale Oyle, as being imported contrary to this Our Proclamation, shall be confiscate and seised, and the same being sold by the said Company, may be afterwards bought, contracted for, and used by any other Our Subjects, at their will and pleasure; Any thing herein contained to the contrary notwithstanding.

Given at Our Palace of Westminster, the sixteenth day of May, in the twelfth yeere of Our Reigne.

GOD SAVE THE KING.

Imprinted at London by Robert Barker, Printer to the Kings most Excellent Majestie: And by the Assignes of John Bill. 1636.

2 pp. folio. Copies in B. M., Crawf., Guild., and P. C. Entered on Patent Rolls. Printed in Rymer's "Fœdera," xx, 16.

1637, APRIL 30.

[REGULATING EMIGRATION TO AMERICA.]

BY THE KING.

A Proclamation against the disorderly Transporting His Majesties Subjects to the Plantations within the parts of America.

The Kings most Excellent Majestie being informed that great numbers of His Subjects have bin, and are every yeare transported into those parts of America, which have been granted by Patent to severall persons, and there settle themselves, some of them with their families and whole estates: amongst which numbers there are also many idle and refractory humors, whose onely or principall end is to live as much as they can without the reach of authority: His Majestie having taken the premisses into consideration, is minded to restraine for the time to come such promiscuous and disorderly departing out of the Realme; And doth therefore straitly charge and command all and every the Officers and Ministers of his severall Ports in England, Wales, and Barwick, That they doe not hereafter permit or suffer any persons, being Subsidie men, or of the value of Subsidie men,[25] to embarque themselves in any of the said Ports, or the members thereof, for any of the said Plantations, without Licence from His Majesties Commissioners for Plantations first had and obtained in that behalfe; Nor that they admit to be embarqued any persons under the degree or value of Subsidymen, without an Attestation or Certificate from two Justices of the Peace living next the place where the party last of all, or lately then before dwelt, that he hath taken the Oaths of Supremacie, and Allegiance, and like Testimony from the Minister of the Parish of his conversation and conformity to the Orders and discipline of the Church of England.[26] And further His Majesties expresse will and pleasure is, That the Offi-

[25] Men who could pay the "subsidy," or tax assessed in favor of the Crown.

[26] Adam Anderson, the early historian of British commerce, in referring to this proclamation, says: "This was levelled against the Puritans, then going in great numbers to New England, to avoid persecution at home; and a better example need not be desired of the wisdom and character of this King, and his favourites and ministers" (*Origin of Commerce*, ii, 492). The proceedings against the Massachusetts charter had just been brought to a close in April, 1637, with a judgment decreeing that it should be vacated. On April 30 came this proclamation. On May 3 the Privy Council ordered that the attorney-general should "call in" for the patent for New England and present it to the Committee for Foreign Plantations (*Acts of Privy Council*, i, 217). A commission was issued which arrived at Boston, June 3, establishing a general government for New England (Winthrop, *History of New England*, i, 269). Among the papers in the Public Record Office is the draft of a "Manifesto" of the King, dated July 23, 1637, establishing a general government in New England and declaring his

cers and Ministers of his said severall Ports, and the Members thereof, do returne to His Majesties said Commissioners for Plantations every halfe yeare a particular and perfect List of the names and qualities of all such persons as shall from time to time be embarqued in any of the said Ports for any of the said Plantations. And of these His Majesties Royall Commands, all the Officers and Ministers of His said Ports, and the Members thereof are to take care, as they will answer the neglect thereof at their perils.

Given at Our Court at Whitehall the last day of Aprill, in the thirteenth yeare of Our Reigne.

GOD SAVE THE KING.

Imprinted at London by Robert Barker, Printer to the Kings most Excellent Majestie: And by the Assignes of John Bill. 1637.

1 p. folio. Copies in B. M., Camb., Canterbury, Crawf., and P. C.; also in Boston Public Library. Entered on Patent Rolls. Printed in Rymer's "Fœdera," xx, 143.

intention of appointing Sir Ferdinand Gorges as governor (*Cal. State Papers, Colonial, 1574-1660*, p. 256). These various restrictive measures all grew out of the Anglican unwillingness to countenance this Puritan asylum in the New World.

1638, MARCH 14.

[IMPORTATION OF TOBACCO.]

BY THE KING.

A Proclamation concerning Tobacco.

Whereas We have had especiall care to provide, That Our loving Subjects the Planters of and in Virginia, the Summer Islands, Caribee Islands, et other Our Forrein Plantations might be encouraged to apply themselves to staple Commodities, fit for the establishing of Colonies, that so the said Plantations might the better flourish and become usefull to Our Kingdomes, and the Planters might be enabled to fortifie and secure themselves as well against the invasion of Forrein Enemies, as the assaults and incursions of the Natives; yet notwithstanding this Our care, the said Planters finding a present though small return of profit for Tobacco, have hitherto wholly betaken themselves to the planting thereof, little minding more solid commodities, their own safetie, or any better or other way or means of supportation and subsistence.

And whereas Our Merchants working upon the necessities of the Planters, have from time to time bought their Tobacco at low and small prices, thereby occasioning the said Planters to grow negligent and carelesse of the well ordering their Tobacco, by means whereof much unserviceable Tobacco hath from Our said Colonies been imported hither, and hath been sophisticated, mixed and stamped with rotten fruits, stalks of Tobacco, and other corrupt ingredients, and afterwards sold and uttered to Our people.

And whereas the vain and wanton taking of Tobacco being at length grown to an excesse, and this excesse having begotten an inordinate desire thereof in those that use it, and much of the Tobacco of Our said Colonies imported hither, being unserviceable as aforesaid, divers of Our Merchants for their own private gain have returned the proceed of the solid Commodities of Our Kingdoms by them vented in Forreign parts in Spanish Tobacco, et many of Our Subjects here have planted great quantities of Tobacco in severall parts of this Our Realme, which Tobacco here planted through the coldnesse of the Climate, and unaptnesse of the Soil, not coming to a perfect maturitie, is altogether unwholesome to be taken. By all which means the forreigne Plantations of Our Subjects remain unfortified, and are in apparant danger to be ruined, the Planters are grieved and discouraged, the Colonies of other Nations do flourish, the wealth of Our Kingdoms is exhausted, the immoderate use of a vain and needlesse weed is continued, the health of Our

Subjects is much impaired, and their manners in danger to be depraved.

And although Wee out of Our Princely care of Our said Plantations abroad, and the good of Our Subjects at home, have formerly as well by Proclamation as otherwise, given direction in the premisses, and have provided against all the afore-mentioned evils, yet this Our care hath not hitherto produced that good effect which We intended and desired, for that fit, diligent and able Agents have not hitherto been imployed in these Our services, to see Our purposes deduced into Act: For these causes, and for divers other weighty considerations tending to the honour of Our said Plantations, et to the good as wel of Our said Planters, as of Our people here, Wee by the advice of the Lords and others of Our Privy Councell, have resolved to regulate Our said Plantations, and the planting, making up, and ordering of Tobacco there, and to limit and appoint what quantities of Tobacco shall henceforth be imported into Our Kingdoms, as well for the expence of Our Realmes, as for Our own services, and also to buy and take into Our own hands and mannaging all Tobacco from henceforth so to be imported, at such reasonable prices to be given for the same, as shall be expedient for the relief and better encouragement of the said Planters, and likewise to regulate the trade and sales of Tobacco here at home, and to commit the care and trusts of the premisses unto such fit Agents as Wee shall nominate in that behalf; All which Wee intend to put in speedy execution.[27]

And to the end Our Royall intentions touching the premisses may the better take effect, Wee do hereby will and command, That no person whatsoever, do at any time hereafter plant or cause to be planted any Tobacco within Our Kingdoms of England and Ireland, or either of them, or within Our Dominion of Wales, or Town of Barwick, or within Our Islands of Jersey and Gernesey, or either of them, or within Our Isle of Man: And that all Tobacco already planted, and now growing there, be presently displanted and utterly distroyed.

And to the end the doing hereof be not in any wise omitted or neglected, Wee do charge and command all Constables, Tithingmen, Headboroughs, and other Officers within their severall limits and jurisdictions carefully to see the same executed accordingly. And further Wee do will and command all Justices of Peace, Maiors, Sheriffes, and other principall Officers in their severall places, within the compasse of their severall jurisdictions and authorities, upon complaint to them made, to cause the same to be duly performed, without partialitie, and they and every of them will answer their Contempts at their perils.

And Wee do further will and command, that no person or persons whatsoever, within our said Realms and Dominions, do from henceforth presume to buy, sell, or utter any Tobacco of the growth of our said Kingdomes of England and Ireland, Dominion of Wales, Town of Barwick, and Islands of Jersey, Gernsey and Man, or any of them, or to let their grounds to Farm to any person or persons, to plant the same with Tobacco, or to stamp, beat, or mixe any Tobacco whatsoever with rotten fruits, the stalks of Tobacco, or any other bad or corrupt Ingredient, the

---

[27] The Privy Council on the day of the issuance of this proclamation, March 14, took action providing for a conference regarding tobacco between those interested in its growth and sale (*Acts of Privy Council*, i, 226).

same being utterly unwholesome to be taken as aforesaid. And Wee do likewise will and command, That no Tobacco of the growth of any parts or places beyond the Seas, belonging to, or under the obedience of any Forreigne King, Prince or State whatsoever, or of the growth of Our said Colonies and Forreign Plantations, be from henceforth imported into Our Kingdomes of England, and Ireland, and Dominion of Wales, or any of them, or into any other Our Dominions, or into any Port, Haven, Creek, or place to them or any of them belonging, more or other, then only such and so much of the Tobacco of the growth of the Plantations of the King of Spaine, as We by Our Letters under Our Privie Seal, or otherwise shall be pleased to allow; and such and so much of the Tobacco of the growth of Our own Colonies, as We shall in like manner declare to be competent for the expence of Our Kingdomes, and fit for Our own services, and for the better relief and encouragement of the said Planters.

And We do further will and command, That no Tobacco of the growth of Our said Plantations, or any of them be from thence transported in any English or other Ship or Bottome unto any Forreigne parts under the obedience of any Forreigne King, Prince, or State whatsoever; but that the same Tobacco be first imported unto Our Port of London, and entred in Our Custome-house there: And that no Tobacco of what sort soever be from henceforth imported, landed, or unladed to, in, or at any other Port, Haven, Creek, or place within Our said Kingdomes of England and Ireland, and Our Dominion of Wales, or any of them, or within any other Our Dominions, then to, in, or at Our Port of London onely. And that all Merchants, Masters and Owners of any Ship or Ships, and other persons whatsoever within or under Our obedience, do take notice of Our Royall command and pleasure herein, and do carefully and duely observe the same accordingly.

And We do hereby further will and command, That all Tobacco so imported and entred as aforesaid (other then such as shall be imported and entred by Our said Agents) shall from henceforth be sold and delivered unto the hands of Our said Agents to Our own immediate use, at, and for such valuable rates and prices to be given for the same, as shall be reasonably agreed upon between the Planters, Owners and Factours thereof, and Our said Agents on Our behalfe.

And Our pleasure further is, and We do hereby charge and command, That none of Our loving Subjects comercing, or any way trading in or about Tobacco, no other person or persons whatsoever, do from henceforth presume to buy any Tobacco in grosse of what sort soever, in any Port, Haven, Creek, or place within Our said Realms and Dominions, at the first hand, or of any person or persons whatsoever, other then of Our said Agents onely; And that all Tobacco bought of Our said Agents, shall be sealed with a seal to be appointed for that purpose, and that the quantity and quality thereof with the time when the same was bought be expressed, in and by a Note in writing indented between the Buyer and Seller, if to Our said Agents it shall seem fitting for this Our service.

And Wee do further charge and command, That no Tobacco whatsoever be from henceforth shipped or laded to be transported from any Port, Haven, Creek, or other place of Our Realm of England, Dominion of Wales, Port or Town of Barwick, or from any other Port within Our Dominions, without the Licence and consent of Our said Agents, and the same to be done in such manner, and upon such security to be given to the use of Us, Our Heirs and Successours, as to Our said Agents in their discretions shall seem expedient for Our service in that behalf.

And further Wee do hereby strictly command, That Our Royall pleasure hereby declared be in all things duely and truely observed upon pain of confiscation and forfeiture of all Tobacco of what sort soever imported or exported, laded or unladed, bought or sold contrary to the effect and true meaning of this Our Proclamation, and under such further pains and penalties, as by the Lawes of Our Realms, or Our Prerogative Royall may be inflicted upon the Offenders. Which Tobacco so forfeited and confiscated, shall be immediately brought to Our Custome-house in London, or to such other place as shall hereafter bee appointed in that behalfe, there to bee valued or apprized; and after such valuation or apprizement made, the Officer or other person by whose diligence such forfeiture was discovered, shall have the one moity of the same forfeiture or value for his service and future encouragement, and the other part therof shall go to Our own use.

And Wee do hereby straitly charge and command all Customers, Controllers, Searchers, Waiters, and all other Officers and Ministers of and belonging to Our Customes; And also all Justices of Peace; Maiors, Sheriffs, Constables, and other Our Officers, Ministers, and loving Subjects in their severall places and degrees, to take notice of this Our Royal pleasure and commandment, and to be aiding, helping and assisting to Our said Agents and their Deputies, Factours and servants in all things touching and concerning this Our service, whereof Wee are resolved to require a due and strict account.

Given at Our Court at Whitehall, this fourteenth day of March, in the thirteenth yeer of Our Reign.

God save the King.

Imprinted at London by Robert Barker, Printer to the Kings most Excellent Majestie: And by the Assignes of John Bill. 1637.

4 pp. folio. Copies in B. M., Crawf., Dalk., and P. C. Entered on Patent Rolls.

1638, MAY 1.

[REQUIRING LICENSES FOR NEW ENGLAND.]

BY THE KING.

A Proclamation to restrain the transporting of Passengers
and Provisions to New England, without Licence.

The Kings most Excellent Majestie, for divers weighty and important causes well known to His Majesty, doth hereby straitly charge and command all Merchants, Masters and Owners of Ships whatsoever, That from henceforth they or any of them do not presume to set forth any Ship or Ships with Passengers or Provisions for New England, untill they shall have first obtained speciall Licence from His Majestie, or such of the Lords, and others of His Privy Councell, as by His Majesties speciall Commission now are or shall be appointed for the Businesse of Forrain Plantations, upon pain of His Majesties high displeasure, and such penalties and punishments as shall be thought meet to be inflicted on offenders herein for their contempt of His Majesties Royall Commands.[28] And His Majesty doth hereby further require and command all the Customers and other Officers and Ministers of or belonging to all or any His Ports within the Realm of England, and Dominion of Wales, That they and every of them in their severall Offices and places do take speciall care of the due execution of His Majesties Royall will and pleasure herein declared, as they will answer for the contrary at their uttermost perils.

Given at the Court at Whitehall, the first day of May, in the fourteenth yeer of His Majesties Reign.

God save the King.

Imprinted at London by Robert Barker, Printer to the Kings most Excellent Majestie: And by the Assignes of John Bill. 1638.

1 p. folio. Copies in Crawf. and P. C.; also in N. Y. Public Library. Entered on Patent Rolls. Printed in Rymer's "Fœdera," xx, 223.

[28] Since the issuance of the proclamation of April 30, 1637, the tide of emigration to New England had not perceptibly slackened. After the receipt of a letter informing Archbishop Laud that a convoy of ships was preparing to sail for New England (*Cal. State Papers, Colonial, 1574-1660*, p. 266), the Privy Council ordered, March 30, 1638, that eight ships in the Thames should be detained and their passengers and provisions landed. Two days later a more comprehensive order was passed, applying to all ships bound for New England. On April 6 the Council relented and allowed the ships to depart, but ordered that a proclamation should be issued requiring a special license before such voyages were made (*Acts of Privy Council*, i, 227-229).

1639, MARCH 25.

[CONCERNING TOBACCO.]

BY THE KING.

A Proclamation concerning Tobacco.

Having been heretofore informed, that thorow the immoderate taking of Tobacco, provoking the takers thereof to excessive Drinking and other inconveniences, the health of many of Our Subjects had been much impaired, which had the rather been occasioned for that no restraint had been made of the number, nor regard had of the quality of those that sold Tobacco by Retail but persons of the meanest condition had promiscuously used to Retail the same, keeping no order or assize therein: Whereupon We out of Our Princely care, to represse all such excesses, and to prevent such future inconveniences as might occur thereby, did by the advice of the Lords and others of Our Privy Councell, resolve to regulate the ungoverned Selling and Retailing of Tobacco, and to reduce the same into some good order; and that none but men of sufficiency, and such as should bring certificate of their meetnesse, should from thenceforth be permitted to sell or utter Tobacco by Retail, and those onely in certain fit places, and to a certain number in every such place, which places and number We did by the like advice of the Lords, and others of Our Privie Councell, appoint accordingly: And afterwards by Our Proclamation, dated the thirteenth day of March, in the ninth yeer of Our Reign, for the reasons therein expressed We did straitly charge and command, that none should from thenceforth presume to sell or utter Tobacco by Retail, untill they should have obtained Our Licence in that behalf.

In conformity whereunto, divers of Our loving Subjects have since taken severall and respective Licences under Our great Seal of England, to sell and utter forrain Tobacco by Retail, in such respective Cities, Towns, and places, as in the same Licences are expressed, rendring to Us, Our Heirs and Successors, such Rents as in and by Our said Licences are respectively reserved in that behalf: By which means not onely the afore mentioned excesses have in some good measure been repressed, and many inconveniences prevented, but also some small addition and improvement hath been made to Our Revenue.

But notwithstanding the Premisses, divers ill affected persons, endeavouring for some small advantage to themselves, to bring the Retailing of Tobacco to that confused and ungoverned liberty it had before, have in contempt of Our said Proclamation presumed without Our Licence to vent and utter Tobacco by Retail, as well in London, and the parts adjacent, as in divers other Cities, Towns, and places of this Our Realm, thereby discouraging, and in some sort disabling Our said Subjects, who have taken Our Licences, as aforesaid, to pay their Rents thereon reserved, and likewise dis-heartning others (that is to say) some from suing forth the Licences for which they have respectively contracted, others from contracting with Our Agents appointed in that behalf; and the better to colour their practises, have spread abroad, especially within Our City of London, and the parts adjacent, false reports and rumours, as if We intended to desist from Our aforesaid course of reformation: which their practises and bold attempts We have just cause to take in ill part, and not to suffer the same to passe unpunished.

Yet because some of Our Subjects, through the false reports and rumours so spread abroad, as aforesaid, may make some doubt of Our Royall intention in the Premisses, therefore We have thought meet hereby to declare and publish to all Our people, that We will not leave unfinished so great a work begun with such advice and care, and so much tending to their health and welfare, neither will We suffer Our Revenue in any part thereof by the wilfull opposition of some few refractory persons to be impaired.

And therefore We do hereby straitly charge and command all Our loving Subjects, that none of them do from henceforth presume directly or indirectly, to sell, utter, or deliver any Tobacco by Retail, in any place or places within Our said Kingdom of England, Dominion of Wales, and Town of Barwick, or any of them, without Our speciall Licence under Our great Seal of England, to be obtained in that behalf.

And We do likewise will and command all Pedlers who wander up and down, not making their constant abode in any one place, and all and every other Interloper or Interlopers whatsoever, that none of them do from henceforth directly or indirectly, sell, utter, or deliver any Tobacco by Retail, or under colour or pretext of giving Tobacco, do by themselves, or any other, take or receive any recompence for the same.

And whereas divers of Our Subjects, who are licensed to retail Tobacco in their own houses onely, do notwithstanding retail Tobacco in Fairs and Markets abroad, to the prejudice of such persons as are licensed to sell Tobacco in those places, Our will and pleasure is, and We do hereby straitly charge and command that from henceforth they and every of them do forbear to sell, utter, or deliver Tobacco by Retail, in any other places then according to the purport and true meaning of their respective Licences under Our great Seal.

And whereas We are informed that much English Tobacco, which through the coldnesse of the climate and unaptnesse of the soil not coming to perfect maturity, is altogether unwholsome to be taken, and other Tobacco adulterate and mixed with rotten fruits and other corrupt ingredients is dayly sold and uttered to Our people; We do hereby charge and straitly command, that no person whatsoever within Our said Kingdom of England and Ireland, Dominion of Wales, and Town of Barwick, or any of them, do from henceforth presume to buy, sell, or utter, directly or indirectly, any Tobacco of the growth of Our Kingdoms of England and Ireland, Dominion of Wales, and Town of Barwick, Islands of Jersey, Garnsey, and

Man, or any of them, or any mixed or adulterate Tobacco whatsoever: And the better to prevent the great abuse offered and done to Our loving Subjects in the sale of English Tobacco, We do also straitly charge and command that no person whatsoever do at any time hereafter plant, or cause to be planted, any Tobacco within Our Kingdoms of England and Ireland, or either of them, or within Our Dominion of Wales, or Town of Barwick, or within Our Islands of Jersey, Garnsey and Man, or any of them, and that all Tobacco already planted, and now growing there, be presently displanted and utterly destroyed.

And to the end the doing hereof be not in any wise omitted or neglected, We do charge and command all Constables, Tithingmen, Headboroughs, and other Officers within their severall limits and jurisdictions, carefully to see the same executed accordingly.

And further, We do will and command all Justices of Peace, Maiors, Sheriffs, and other principall Officers in their severall places, within the compasse of their severall jurisdictions and authorities, upon complaint to them made, to cause the same to be duly performed without partiality, as they and every of them will answer their contempts at their perils.

And We do further will and command, that no Tobacco whatsoever be from henceforth imported, landed, or unladed to, in, or at any other Port, Haven, Creek, or place within Our Kingdom of England, Dominion of Wales, and Port and Town of Barwick, or any of them, then to, in, or at Our Port of London, without speciall warrant to be obtained from Our Lord high Treasurer of England for the time being in that behalf: And that all Merchants, Masters, and Owners of any Ship or Ships, and other persons whatsoever within or under Our obedience, do take notice of Our Royall command and pleasure herein, and do carefully and duly observe the same accordingly.

And We do hereby straitly charge and command all Our Subjects to yeeld their due obedience in all and singular the Premisses, as they tender Our pleasure, and will answer the contrary at their perill.

Given at Our Court at Whitehall the five and twentieth day of March, in the fourteenth yeer of Our Reign.

GOD SAVE THE KING.

Imprinted at London by Robert Barker, Printer to the Kings most Excellent Majestie: And by the Assignes of John Bill. 1638.

3 pp. folio. There are two issues, varying only in the spelling of "thorow" and "through" in the first line. Copies in Antiq., Bodl., and Crawf. Entered on Patent Rolls.

1639, AUGUST 19.

[LICENSING OF TOBACCONISTS.]

BY THE KING.

A Proclamation declaring His Majesties pleasure to continue His Commission, and Letters Patents for licensing Retailors of Tobacco.

Whereas by His Majesties Proclamation dated at York the ninth day of April last, it was declared, That (amongst sundry other Commissions and Grants obtained upon untrue surmises) a Commission for compounding with Offendors touching Tobacco, was thereby revoked and determined;[29] under colour whereof, and by a wilfull mistaking of His Majesties said Proclamation, sundry persons have pretended, that His Majesties Commission to the Lord Goring, and others, for licensing Retailors of Tobacco within England, Wales, and Barwick, was thereby called in: And thereupon His Majesties Commissioners have been interrupted in their proceedings in that service for His Majesty; Tobacco in divers parts of the kingdome (contrary to His Majesties Proclamation of the five and twentieth of March last) hath been retailed without His Majesties Licence; and many of those persons who have Licences have forborn to make paiment of their Rents: His Majesty therefore, to remove all doubts and questions touching the Premisses, Hath thought fit (with the advice of His Councell) to make publike declaration of His Royall intention and meaning therein, which was, That His Majesties Letters Patents, and Commission to the Lord Goring, and others, concerning the licensing of Retailors of Tobacco, was not impeached, or meant to be impeached by His Majesties said Proclamation of the ninth of April last; But that the same Letters Patents and Commission are still in force, and no way infringed or restrained thereby, but are still to be proceeded in and executed according to the tenour and true meaning thereof. And His Majesty doth further declare hereby, That His Majesty by His said Proclamation in April last, did repeal and determine a Commission to Lawrence Louns, and others, to compound with such, as from the ninth of April in the first yeer of His Majesties reign, untill the date of that Commission, had offended in defrauding His Majestie of His Customes and other duties for Tobacco imported, or in planting Tobacco in England, or Ireland, or by importing Tobacco of the growth of other forraign parts, or in greater quantities then were limitted, or in buying or selling the same contrary to His Majesties Proclamations before

[29] The proclamation of April 9, 1639, revoked, among many other grants, licenses, and commissions, the "Commission for compounding with Offenders touching Tobacco." This proclamation is printed in Rymer's *Fœdera*, xx, 340, and in Rushworth's *Historical Collections*, ii, 915.

that time published, and none other Commission touching Tobacco. And therefore His Majesty doth hereby require and command all manner of persons whatsoever whom it may concern, to take knowledge of this His Majesties Declaration and Confirmation of His said Letters Patents and Commission to the Lord Goring, and others, for the licensing Retailors of Tobacco, and that accordingly they yeeld all conformity thereunto as is meet, upon pain of His Majesties high displeasure, and such punishments as their contempt or neglect of His Majesties Royall commands herein shall deserve. And lastly, His Majesty doth hereby require and command all Justices of Peace, Mayors, Sheriffs, Bailiffs, Constables, Headboroughs, and all others His Officers and Ministers whatsoever, to be aiding and assisting in the full accomplishment and execution of His Majesties Royall pleasure herein declared.

Given at His Majesties Court at Whitehall the nineteenth day of August, in the fifteenth yeer of His Majesties Reign.

GOD SAVE THE KING.

Imprinted at London, by Robert Barker, Printer to the Kings most Excellent Majesty: And by the Assignes of John Bill. 1639.

1 p. folio. Copies in Bodl., and Crawf. Entered on Patent Rolls. Printed in Rymer's "Fœdera," xx, 348.

1643, NOVEMBER 24.

[REQUIRING LOYALTY FROM AMERICA.]

BY THE KING.

A Proclamation to give Assurance unto all His Majesties Subjects in the Islands and Continent of America, of His Majesties Royall Care over them, and to preserve them in their due Obedience.

Charles, by the grace of God, King of England, Scotland, France and Ireland, Defendor of the Faith, etc. Whereas We have seen a Paper, called an Ordinance of the pretended Houses of the Lords and Commons in Parliament, ordered to be Printed the second day of this instant November,[30] Whereby Robert Earle of Warwick is made Governor in chiefe, and Lord High Admirall of all those Islands and other Plantations inhabited, Planted, or belonging to any of Our Subjects within the Bounds, and upon the Coasts of America, and a Committee appoynted to be assisting unto him in the Government thereof: The intention of which Ordinance cannot reasonably be conceived to be other, then to spread the contagion of this horrid Rebellion, even unto those remoter parts, and that the continuers thereof (foreseeing how little prosperous their wicked Designes are likely to prove here in Our Realme of England) may provide for themselves a place of Retreat and Security in those Westerne Countries: The consequences whereof would be the disturbance of that quiet, which those Our Subjects in America doe yet injoy under Our Government, and instead of Peace, to introduce amongst them the like Oppressions, Bloodshed, Rapine, Disorders and Confusion in Church and State, as they have brought already into some parts of this Our Kingdome, and would have gone farther on, if the Goodnesse of Almighty God, giving strength to Our Forces, and successe to Our Enterprises, had not given a stop to their Malitious and Rebellious attempts. To prevent which inconveniences from those Westerne parts, out of Our Royall care of Our good Subjects there, We have thought good hereby to give timely notice unto them, not only that the said Ordinance was made without Our Royall assent, and therefore that it ought not to bind any of Our Subjects, but also that the said Earle of Warwick: hath been justly Proclaimed a Traitor by Us, and that he still persists in his Treason and Rebellion against Us; and therefore We doe require and Command all Our Subjects whatsoever, That they doe not give obedience to the said Ordinance, nor unto him the said Earle, as their Governor, or Admirall, nor to any other by pretence of any Authority from him, or from any

[30] This ordinance, appointing the Earl of Warwick governor of the Plantations, is printed in the *Journal of the House of Lords*, vi, 291, and in Husband's *Collection of Orders, Ordinances and Declarations*, p. 378.

of the said Committee, but that they shall endeavour the suppression of all such Rebellious Attempts, as they shall have means and Opportunity to doe it. And We doe farther declare, That as We have given unto all Our faithfull Subjects in generall all possible testimonies and assurances of Our care of their wellfare and happinesse, in preservation of the true Protestant Religion established by the Lawes, the Liberty of their Persons, the Propriety of their Goods, and the just Priviledges of Parliaments, which We have done by such Professions before Almighty God, and such Acts of Grace, as have exceeded all the Precedents of former times: So shall Our Subjects in the said Islands, and Continent of America in particular, find the constant fruits and effects of Our gratious Government and Protection, and of those assurances, in as full and ample measure as any other Our Subjects whatsoever. And therefore We doe strictly charge and Command all Governors and Magistrates, who exercise any authority under Us in the said Islands and Plantations, That they doe not only publish unto Our good People there, these Our gratious intentions towards them, but that they let them feel the benefit thereof, by due administration of Justice amongst them, and by seasonable Provisions of all things needfull for their defence and prosperity. And We doe in like manner require all Our said Subjects, that they persist in their due Allegiance and Obedience unto Us, whereto they are obliged by all Lawes Divine and Humane; and that they receive not any Governors nor Commanders, or obey any Ordinances contrary to, or without Our Royall consent, but that they pursue and apprehend them as Traytors to Our Royall Person and Dignity; and that as they tender their duty to God, the avoyding of Our High Displeasure, and the preservation of their own Peace and Happinesse. Given at Our Court at Oxford, the Twenty fourth day of November, in the Nineteenth yeare of Our Raigne. 1643.

GOD SAVE THE KING.[31]

1 p. folio. Copy in Bodl.

---

[31] The imprint in the only known copy of the original is missing, but it was undoubtedly *"Oxford: L. Lichfield: 1643,"* as in proclamations immediately preceding and following this date.

1655, OCTOBER 10.

[ENCOURAGING SETTLING IN JAMAICA.]

BY THE PROTECTOR.

A PROCLAMATION

GIVING ENCOURAGEMENT TO SUCH AS SHALL TRANSPLANT THEMSELVES
TO JAMAICA.

Whereas the Island of Jamaica in America, is by the Providence of God, in the hands and possession of this State,[32] the Enemy which was found upon it, being fled into the Mountains with an intention to escape into other places, save such of them as do daily render themselves to our Commander in chief there, to be disposed of by him; and We being satisfied of the Goodness, Fertility, and Commodiousness for Trade and Commerce of that Island, Have resolved, by the blessing of God, to use Our best endeavours to secure and plant the same. For which end and purpose, We have thought it necessary to publish, and make known unto the People of this Commonwealth, and especially to those of the English Islands, Plantations and Colonies in America, our Resolutions and Intentions on that behalf, as also to declare unto them the Encouragements which We have thought fit to give unto such as shall remove themselves, and their habitations into the aforesaid Island of Jamaica, within the time mentioned and expressed in these Presents. And first, concerning the securing thereof against the Enemy, We have already upon the Island, which landed there in May last, above six thousand Souldiers, and the beginning of July after, we sent from hence a Regiment of eight hundred more, drawn out of Our old Regiments in England, with eight Ships of War, besides Victualers, to be added to twelve others, that were left there by General Pen, under the command of Captain Will. Goodson, all which are appointed to remain in those Seas for the Defence of the said Island; and We shall from time to time take care to send thither other, both Land and Sea Forces, that We may have alwaies in those parts, such a strength as may be able, through the blessing of God, to defend

---

[32] The English forces, soon after the declaration of war against Spain, sailed for the conquest of the Spanish West Indies. After an unsuccessful attack on Hispaniola, they landed at Jamaica and on May 10, 1655, took possession of the island. It now became the cherished plan of Cromwell to settle Jamaica, especially with the colonists of the other plantations in America. Numerous entries regarding Jamaican affairs are to be found in the records of the Council of State during this period. In the Interregnum Entry Book, p. 328, there is an order of October 10, 1655, approving the draft of this particular proclamation (*Cal. State Papers, Colonial, 1574-1660*, p. 431).

and secure it against any Attempt of the Enemy; that whereas the Planters in other Places have been at Great and vast expences at their first sitting down, and in the very beginning of their Plantations for their necessary defence, as well against the Natives of the Countrey as other Enemies, those who shall remove thither, will be under the immediate Protection of this State, and so eased both of the danger and charge which other Plantations are subject to, and shall have, for their further encouragement, the terms and conditions following.

1. Those who shall transport themselves as aforesaid shall have land set forth unto them, according to the proportion of twenty Acres, besides Lakes and Rivers, for every Male of twelve years old and upwards, and ten Acres for every other Male or Female, in some convenient place of the said Island; and in case any whole Plantation, That is to say, the Governours and greatest part of the people shall remove themselves, they shall be preferred in respect of the place of their sitting down, that it may be near some good Harbour commodious for Commerce and Navigation.

2. That the said Proportion of Land shall be set forth unto them, within six Weeks after notice given by them under their hands, or the hands of some of them on the behalf of the rest, unto his Highness Commander in chief, or Commissioners there, appointed for that purpose of their resolutions to remove, and of the time they intend to be upon the place.

3. That they shall have Liberty for the space of seaven years to hunt, take and dispose of to their own use such Horses, and other cattle as are, or shall be upon the said Island, the same not being marked by, or belonging to other Planters, subject nevertheless to such Rules and Directions as to their hunting, and taking of Horses, Cattle, and other Beasts out of their own bounds and limits, as shall from time to time be made by the Persons authorized by his Highnesse, for mannaging the affairs of the said Island.

4. That they shall hold the said Land with all Houses, Edifices, Woods, Trees, Profits and Advantages thereupon, to them and their Heirs for ever, to be held in free, and common Soccage, without any Rent for the first seven years, and then one penny an Acre, and by no other rent, tenure, or service whatsoever.

5. That after the said Proportions of Land are set forth as aforesaid, His Highness, or his Successors, upon the desire of the Owners thereof, shall by Letters Pattents, under the Great Seal of England, or by such other sure ways as shall be devised by their Counsel learned in the Law, give, grant, and confirm unto him or them, their heirs and assigns the said Proportions of Land, together with all and singular the Privileges, Jurisdictions, Profits and advantages which are intended hereby to be enjoied by them, with power to erect and create any Mannour or Mannors, with tenures in free and common Soccage within such Plantation, or Plantations, as shall be capable thereof.

6. That they shall hold and enjoy all, and singular Mines of Copper, Iron, Tin, or other Minerals whatsoever (excepting Gold, and Silver Mines) and all Mines of Quarries, Coal, Stone, Allum, or other Mines, whatsoever (except as aforesaid) within the circuit, Meets or bounds of the said several and respective proportions

of Land; and also all Fishings, and Piscaries whatsoever upon or within any of the Lakes, Streams or Rivers within their Meets, and bounds; and also full power, and authority to man, and send forth to Sea, and unto any the Coasts, and Shores, Roads, Harbours or Creeks within or near the said Island, any Ships, Boats or other Vessels to fish for, find out, or take any Pearls, precious Stones, or Jewels therein being, and to enjoy the same to his and their own use or uses, rendering and paying to the Governour of the said Island for the time being, or to such other person or persons, for the time being, as His Highnesse shall authorize to receive the same, to his Highness use, the full fifth part only, and no more of all such Pearls, precious Stones and Jewels as shall be got, found, and taken, as aforesaid; and also one tenth part of all such Mettal as shall be had, found, and gained in the Mines, granted hereby to the aforesaid Planters.

7. That no Custom, Excise, Impost, or other duty shall be set or imposed for the space of three years to be accounted from the 29. day of September, which shall be in the year of our Lord 1656. upon any of their Goods and Merchandizes of the growth, production or Manufacture of the said Island, which they shall transport into this Commonwealth: Nor shall they or their Servants, without their own consent, be drawn out into the Wars, unlesse it be in case of Invasion, or Rebellion, and for the defence of the Island.

8. That they shall have power to build Walls, and raise Bulwarks and Castles upon their own Land for the defence, and security of their own plantations, and also to arme themselves, and servants, and to lead, and conduct them against any Enemies, or Rebels within the said Island; Subject nevertheless to such Orders, and directions as they shall on this behalf receive from the Governour or Commander in chief of the said Island for the time being.

9. That all and every person and persons, that shall hereafter happen to be born within the said Island, shall be, and shall be deemed, and accounted to be free Denizons of England, and shall have and enjoy all and every such benefits, privileges, advantages and immunities whatsoever, as any of the Natives or People of England born in England now have and enjoy in England.

That all such professing the Protestant Religion, who shall transport themselves into the aforesaid Island within two years to be accounted from the said 29. day of September 1656. and shall make a beginning therein by transporting to the said Island one third part of their number before the 29. day of September next, shall have, and enjoy the aforesaid Privileges, and Advantages. And for the more certain carrying on of this businesse, and answering Our intentions herein, We do hereby authorize and require Our Commander in chief of the said Island, for the time being, and also the aforesaid Commissioners that they take notice of the Premisses, and cause a due and effectual execution of the same from time to time as there shall be occasion, according to the purport, et true meaning hereof, for which these presents shall be their sufficient warrant. Given at White-Hall the 10. of October 1655.

London, Printed by Henry Hills and John Field, Printers to His Highness, MD-CLV.

2 pp. folio. Copy in Guild. Manuscript draft in P. R. O., State Papers, Dom. Interreg. 76A, pp. 152-154. Printed in Thurloe's "State Papers," iii, 753, and in "Interesting Tracts relating to the Island of Jamaica," 1800, p. 1.

1658, MARCH 9.

[LIMITING GREENLAND TRADE TO MUSCOVY COMPANY.]

BY THE PROTECTOR.

A PROCLAMATION

DECLARING THE RIGHT OF THE FELLOWSHIP AND COMPANY OF ENGLISH MERCHANTS FOR DISCOVERY OF NEW TRADES (COMMONLY CALLED THE MUSCOVIA COMPANY) TO THE SOLE FISHING FOR WHALES UPON THE COASTS OF GREEN-LAND AND CHERY-ISLAND, AND FOR RESTRAINING AND PROHIBITING OF ALL OTHERS.

Whereas the Discovery of the Island called Chery-Island, and the Continent of Green-land, with the fishing for Whales upon the Seas and Coasts thereof, and of the Islands and places thereto adjacent, (having been made by the Fellowship of English Merchants, for Discovery of New Trades commonly called the Muscovia Company, and at their own great charges and hazards) hath by experience been found to be, and is a very great honour and advantage to this Nation and Commonwealth, aswel in the inlargement of the Dominions and Territories thereof, as also in the advancement and increase of Navigation, and the entring upon and gaining of the Trade of Whale-fishing, whereby great quantities of Whale-Oyl, Whale-Fins and other Commodities are yearly hither imported, to the enriching of this Nation, without the Exportation of any Commodities from hence: And whereas upon consideration of the Premises, and for recompence of the said charge and hazards in the said Discovery, and for the encouragement of the said Company and others in time to come, several Grants and Letters Patents under the Great Seal of England, have been heretofore made and granted to the said Fellowship, and particularly in the Raign of the late King Philip and Queen Mary, by which all main Lands, Isles, Havens, Ports, Creeks and Rivers, by the said Company then discovered or to be after discovered, were forbidden to be traffiqued unto, or visited by any the People of this Nation, without the License of the said Company; which Letters Patents were afterwards confirmed by Act of Parliament in the Eighth year of the Raign of the late Queen Elizabeth, under the penalty of forfeiting the Ships and Goods of any Trading thither without License, and with addition of divers others Priviledges and Liberties unto the said Fellowship and Company. And the late King James, for the further encouragement of the said Company, and preventing others to interrupt, distract or disturb their said Trade-fishing and Discoveries, did, in pursuance of the said Act of Parliament, and the true intent and meaning of the same, by his Letters Patents grant unto the said Fellowship, the sole Trading and Fishing in those Seas and places so discovered by them, And all others were forbidden to fish in those Seas and Coasts, or to sail thither for Trade without License of the said Company. Notwithstanding which, the said Company as We are given to understand, have of late received some disturbance by the interloping and intruding of some persons into the said Whale-fishing, upon those Seas and Coasts of Green-land and Chery-Island, whereupon the said Company having addressed their humble Petition unto Us, And the matter having been by Us referred to the consideration of our Privy Council, and fully heard and debated before a Committee of Our said Council, as well on behalf of the said particular Traders, as also on behalf of the said Fellowship and Company. And the Act of Parliament and the Grants and Charters made to the said Fellowship and Company shewed forth and read, and the whole matter having been fully considered, and thereupon made evident, that such particular fishing for Whales upon those Seas, Harbours and Coasts, by persons separate from the said Company, and trading therein by themselves apart, with like power and strength, did not onely disturb the main Trade of Fishing and taking of Whales by the Company, but did tend to the ruine and destruction of that Fishing, and unless prevented, might occasion Forraigners to come in and gain away that fishing and Trading from this Nation, which might tend to the great damage and dishonour of Us and this Nation, besides the particular damage of the said Company. And whereas the whole state of the matter having been again represented to Our said Privy Council and by them also fully considered, it was by them conceived to be for the good of this Nation, to encourage the carrying on of the said Whale-fishing and Trade, by the said Fellowship and Company onely, and to forbid all others, except such as the said Company should License, to intrude or meddle therein. And the said Company having further declared, that they appropriating those parts of the said Seas called Bell Sound, and Horn Sound, with such other places as they shall fish in, to themselves onely, were well contented, and do promise to grant Licenses gratis to all and every person of this Nation and Commonwealth, that shall or will but ask or desire to fish for Whales, or Trade in any other of the said Seas, or Coasts of Green-land, or Chery-Island, where they themselves fish not. We therefore taking the Premises into Our consideration (with the advice of Our said Privie Council) Do hereby publish and Declare, That the whole and sole Trade and fishing for Whales, and absolute fishing in and upon the said Seas, Coasts and parts of Green-land,[33] and Chery-Island, and in and upon the said Bell Sound, and Horn Sound, being part of the said Seas and Coasts, doth and ought to belong unto the said Fellowship of English Merchants for discovery of New Trades, commonly called the

---

[33] This name refers to Spitzbergen, which was then called Greenland, and which was thought by the voyagers of the day to be connected with Greenland proper. The early maps show Spitzbergen, which they term "Greenland or Spitzbergen," with Bell and Horn Sounds on the west coast and Cherie Island, named after Sir Francis Cherie, a few miles to the south. The country was also sometimes called East Greenland, while the modern Greenland was termed "Groenland." See especially the map of 1613 in *Amer. Antiquarian Society Transactions*, iv, 314; the map in Edward Pelham's *God's Power and Providence*, 1631, reproduced in *A Collection of Documents on Spitzbergen and Greenland* (Hakluyt Society), 1855; and map no. xiv in H. Moll's *World Described, 1708-20*.

Muscovia Company, and that no other Person or Persons of this Commonwealth (other then the said Fellowship of English Merchants for discovery of New Trades, called the Muscovia Company) shall fish for Whales in and upon the said Seas, Coasts of Green-land and Chery-Island, or in and upon the said Bell Sound and Horn Sound, being part of the said Seas and Coasts. Yet so, as nevertheless the said Company, upon their own offer and agreement aforesaid, be and shall be, and are hereby obliged to grant License and Licenses, to all and singular the People and Subjects of this Commonwealth, upon request in that behalf to be made (without delay or paying anything for the same) to fish for Whales, or trade or fish in all or any other parts or places, of the said Seas or Coasts of Greenland and Chery-Island, Except the Harbours and places of Bell Sound and Horn Sound aforesaid, or where the said Company shall set out Ships to fish, And We do hereby command, That all persons whatsoever (other then the said Fellowship and Company) do forbear to enter into the said Bell Sound or Horn Sound, or to fish or trade within Three Leagues of either of them, but clearly and absolutely leave the said Bell Sound and Horn Sound, and all the sole and whole fishing and trading thereof, unto the said Fellowship and Company, and their Ships and Agents, and such as shall be set forth, hired or imployed by them, without making any disturbance or interruption, or giving the said Company or their Ships or Vessels, any impediment or hinderance therein, under pain of Our high displeasure, and such other pains and penalties as by the Laws of this Land may be inflicted upon them for their disobedience and contempt therein, Leaving all other the People and Subjects of this Commonwealth free notwithstanding, to take Licenses from the said Company to trade or fish for Whales or otherwise, in and upon all other of the said Seas, Coasts and places, Except the said Bell Sound and Horn Sound, and such other places of Green-land, as the said Fellowship or their Agents shall fish in, as aforesaid. And We do hereby further will and command, aswel Our Generals at Sea, Admirals of Our Fleet, Vice-Admirals, Commanders of Squadrons, and other Commanders, Captains and Officers whatsoever, of any Our Ships, as also Our Judges of the High Court of Admiralty of England, and all other Our Officers and Ministers, in their several places to be aiding and assisting, unto the said Fellowship and Company, and all such as they shall set out and imploy in their said sole Trade and fishing, and in hindring all others hereby forbidden to use the said Trade and fishing, otherwise then as is before mentioned. And likewise to be aiding and assisting unto the said Fellowship and Company and their said Agents, in doing and executing of all and singular the premises. And lastly, We do hereby charge and Command the said Fellowship and Company, That in all Ships and Vessels which shall from time to time be sent out by them, or imployed under them, into or in the Seas and parts aforesaid, they do imploy for Harpineers, Steersmen and Mariners, the People and Subjects of this Commonwealth, and no other.

Given at Our Palace of Westminster the 9th day of March, in the year of Our Lord, 1657.

London, Printed by Henry Hills and John Field, Printers to His Highness, 1657.

3 pp. folio, pasted together to form one long sheet. Copy in B. M.

1660, SEPTEMBER 22.

[FOR APPREHENSION OF WHALLEY AND GOFFE.]

BY THE KING.

A PROCLAMATION

For Apprehension of Edward Whalley and William Goffe.

Charles R.

Forasmuch as Edward Whalley, commonly known by the name of Colonel Whalley, and William Goffe, commonly called Colonel Goffe, are, amongst others, by an Act of this present Parliament, Entituled, An Act of Free and General Pardon, Indempnity and Oblivion,[34] wholly excepted from Pardon, and left to be proceeded against as Traytors, for their execrable Treasons in sentencing to death, signing the Instrument for the horrid Murder, or being instrumental in taking away the precious Life of Our late dear Father of Blessed Memory.

And forasmuch as they the said Edward Whalley and William Goffe,[35] having absented and withdrawn themselves, as We have been informed, to the parts beyond the Seas, are now, as We certainly understand, lately returned into Our Kingdom of England, and do privately lurk and obscure themselves in places unknown; We therefore have thought fit, by, and with the Advice of Our Privy Council, to publish the same to all Our loving Subjects, not doubting of their Care and forwardness in their apprehension; And We do hereby Require and Command, as well all and singular Our Judges, Justices of the Peace, Mayors, Sheriffs, Bayliffs, Constables and Headboroughs, as also the Officers and Ministers of our Ports, and other Our Subjects whatsoever, within Our Realms of England, Scotland, Ireland, or Dominion of Wales, and all Our Dominions and Territories, to be diligent in Inquiring, Searching for, Seizing and Apprehending them, the said Edward Whalley, and William Goffe, in all places whatsoever, as wel within Liberties as without, whom if they shall happen to Take and Apprehend Our further Will and pleasure is, That they cause them and either of them so Apprehended, to be safely carried to the next Justice of the Peace, to the place where they or either of them shall be Arrested, whom We straitly Command to Commit them and either

---

[34] *Statutes of the Realm,* vol. 5, p. 226, 12 Chas. II, ch. 11.

[35] Several documents concerning the attempt to apprehend Whalley and Goffe are calendared in the *Cal. State Papers, Colonial, 1661-1668.* See also *Dictionary of National Biography* under Edward Whalley and William Goffe, and "Memoranda respecting Edward Whalley and William Goffe," by F. B. Dexter, in *New Haven Colony Historical Society Papers,* ii, 117.

of them to Prison, and presently Inform Us or Our Privy Council of their or either of their Apprehensions.

And We do hereby further Declare and Publish, That if any Person or Persons after this Our Proclamation published, shall Directly or Indirectly Conceal, Harbor, Keep, Retain, or Maintain the said Edward Whalley and William Goffe, or either of them, or shall Contrive or Connive at any means whereby they or either of them shall or may Escape from being Taken or Arrested, or shall not use their best Endeavor for their and either of their Apprehensions, as well by giving the Advertisement thereof to Our Officers, as by all other good means; We will (as there is Just Cause) proceed against them that shall so neglect this Our Commandment with all severity.

And lastly We do hereby Declare, That whosoever shall discover the said Edward Whalley or William Goffe, either within Our Kingdoms of England, Scotland, Ireland, or Dominions of Wales, or in any other our Dominions and Territories, or elsewhere, and shall cause them, or either of them, to be Apprehended, and brought in alive or dead, if they or either of them, attempting Resistance, happen to be slain, shall have a Reward of One hundred pounds in money for each of them so brought in, dead or alive, as aforesaid, to be forthwith paid unto him in recompence of such his Service.

Given at Our Court at Whitehall the Two and twentieth day of September, in the Twelfth year of Our Reign.

London, Printed by Christopher Barker and John Bill, Printers to the Kings most Excellent Majesty. 1660.

1 p. folio. Copies in Adv., Antiq., Bodl., B. M., Camb., Ch., Crawf., Dalk., Dubl., Guild., Hodg., P. R. O., Q. C., and T. C. D.; also in N. Y. Public Library. Entered on Patent Rolls. Abstract printed in "Parliamentary Intelligencer," Sept. 24, 1660, and in "Mercurius Publicus," Sept. 27. 1660.

1661, MARCH 29.

[PROHIBITING PLANTING OF TOBACCO IN ENGLAND.]

BY THE KING.

A PROCLAMATION

Prohibiting the Planting, Setting and Sowing of Tobacco in England and Ireland, according to an Act of Parliament herein specified.

Charles R.

Whereas by an Act of Parliament made in Our late Parliament begun and held at Westminster in the County of Middlesex, the Five and Twentieth day of April in the Twelfth year of Our Reign, for and upon the reasons and grounds therein expressed, it was Enacted by the Authority of the same Parliament, That no person or persons whatsoever should, or do from and after the First day of January, in the Year of our Lord One thousand six hundred and sixty, Set, plant, improve to grow, make or cure any Tobacco either in Seed, plant or otherwise, in or upon any ground, earth, field, or place within Our Kingdom of England, Dominion of Wales, Islands of Guernsey or Jersey or Town of Berwick upon Tweed, or in Our Kingdome of Ireland, under the penalty of the forfeiture of all such Tobacco, or the value thereof, or of the Sum of Forty shillings for every Rod or Pole of Ground so planted, set or sowen as aforesaid, and so proportionably for a greater or lesser quantity of ground, One moyety thereof to Us Our Heirs and Successors, and the other moyety to him or them that shall sue for the same to be recovered by Bill, Plaint or Information in any Court of Record, wherein no Essoign, protection or wager in Law shall be allowed: And it was thereby further enacted, That all Sheriffs, Justices of the peace, Mayors, Bailiffs, Constables, and every of them, upon information or complaint made unto them or any of them, by any the Officers of the Customes, or by any other person or persons whatsoever, that there was any Tobacco set, sown, planted, or growing within their jurisdictions or precincts contrary to the same Act should within ten dayes after such information or complaint cause to be burnt, plucked up, consumed, or utterly destroyed all such Tobacco so set, sowen, planted, or growing. And it was thereby further enacted, That in case any person or persons should resist or make forcible opposition against any person or persons in the due and through execution of the same Act, That every such person or persons for every such offence should forfeit the sum of Five pounds to be divided and recovered in manner aforesaid; And in case any person or persons should not pay the summs of money by them to be paid, by vertue of the same Act, that in every such case distress should be made and sale thereof, returning the overplus to the owners; And in case no distress shall be found, that then every such party should be committed to the common Gaol in the County where such offence should be committed, there to remain for the space of two moneths without Bail or Mainprise. Provided always, and it was thereby enacted, That the same Act nor any thing contained therein should extend to the hindering of the planting of Tobacco in any Physick-garden of either University, or in any other private garden for Physick or Chirurgery, only so as the quantity so planted exceed not one half of one pole in any one place or garden, as in et by the same Act it doth and may more fully appear.[36] Now to the end that all Our loving Subjects in all parts of Our said Kingdoms of England and Ireland, and Dominion of Wales, and in the said Islands of Guernsey and Jersey, and in our said Town of Berwick upon Twede, may the better take notice of and more duely observe the said Act, and not ignorantly offend against the same for the future, We have thought good to publish et declare the same to all Our loving Subjects by this Our Royal Proclamation, And do withall likewise signifie and declare, that for the future We shall expect, and do hereby require all dutiful observance thereof, and ready conformity thereunto, and that not onely upon the pains, penalties, and forfeitures therein expressed, but also of Our high indignation and displeasure, justly and deservedly to be inflicted upon all those that shall knowingly and presumptuously offend against so just and reasonable a Law. And we do hereby streightly charge and command all Our Judges of Assise and Commissioners of Oyer and Terminer in their several Circuits, and all Our Justices of Peace in their several and respective Quarter-Sessions, that they give the same Law in charge to the several et respective Juries in their several and respective Inquests before them, to the end that the offences and offenders against the same, both in the setting, planting, or sowing of Tobacco, contrary to the true intent and meaning of the same Act, and also all forcible opposition et resistance made or to be made against any person or persons in the due execution of the same Act, may be punished according to Law and the demerit of their offences in this behalf. And We do further command and require all Sheriffs, Justices of the peace, Mayors, Bayliffs, Constables, and all other Our Officers and ministers whatsoever whom the premisses shall or may concern, that they from time to time as occasion shall require, be diligent, circumspect, and careful in the due execution of the same Act in all things according to the true intent and meaning, thereof, as they will answer the contrary at their perils.

Given at Our Court at Whitehall, the Twenty ninth day of March, in the Thirteenth Year of Our Reign, One thousand six hundred sixty one.

GOD SAVE THE KING.

London, Printed by John Bill, Printer to the King's most Excellent Majesty,

---

[36] This act, entitled "An Act for Prohibiting the Planting Setting or Sowing of Tobaccho in England and Ireland," passed the House of Commons on December 17, 1660 (*Commons Journals*, viii, 212), the House of Lords on December 20 (*Lords Journals*, xi, 218), was read in Council on December 21 (*Acts of Privy Council*, i, 303), and is printed in *Statutes of the Realm*, 12 Chas. II, ch. 34, vol. 5, p. 297.

1661. At the King's Printing-House in Black-Friers.

2 pp. folio. Copies in Adv., Antiq., Bodl., B. M., Camb., Crawf., Dalk., Dubl., Guild., P. R. O., Q. C., and T. C. D. Abstract printed in "Kingdomes Intelligencer," April 8, 1661, and in "Mercurius Publicus," April 11, 1661.

1661, MAY 9.

[SUPPRESSING VAGRANCY.]

BY THE KING.

A PROCLAMATION

For the due Observation of certain Statutes made for the suppressing
of Rogues, Vagabonds, Beggers, and other idle disorderly Persons,
and for Relief of the Poore.

Charles R.

The Kings most Excellent Majesty being watchful for the publick good of his loving Subjects, and taking notice of the great and unusual resort of Rogues, Vagabonds, Beggers, and other idle Persons of all Ages and Sexes, from all parts of the Nation to the Cities of London and Westminster and the Suburbs of the same, where they make it their trade to beg and live idly, and to get their living by Begging, Stealing, and other wicked and lewd practises, to the great offence of Almighty God, and to the dishonour of His Majesties Royal Government; And his Majesty taking it into His Princely consideration, that this Realm is furnished with excellent Laws and Orders for redress of such Enormities, yet through negligence of Officers, and presumption of the Offenders, the same nevertheless do rather grow then abate. His Majesty hath therefore thought fit at this present by advice of his Privy Councel, to cause some necessary Laws formerly made for the reforming the Abuses aforesaid, to be duely executed and observed. And for that end, whereas by the Laws of this Land all Vagabonds, Beggers, and idle persons are to be sent to the place of their Birth, or of their last abode, there to be relieved and kept if they be impotent, or otherwise made to labour: His Majestie doth by this Proclamation publish and declare His Royal Pleasure and Commands, that all such Vagabonds, Beggers and Idle persons within the Cities of London and Westminster and the Suburbs of the same, which by Law are not there to be provided for (to the wrong of the native poor, and a burden to the several Parishes where now they are) but that they forthwith at their Perils depart from the same and speedily resort to the place of their Birth or last abode, that they may be there provided for as they ought to be. And if any such Vagabonds, Beggers, or idle persons shall or may be found within the Cities of London and Westminster, or in any of the Suburbs or Precincts of the same, or in the Borough of Southwark, or in any Town near adjoyning, upon the four and twentieth day of this moneth of May, His Majesty streightly chargeth and commandeth, as well the Lord Mayor, Recorder, Aldermen and Sheriffs of the said City of London, and all other Officers of the said City, and all other His Majesties Justices of the Peace, Magistrates and Officers whatsoever within the City of Westminster, Borough of Southwark, or within the County of Middlesex, to cause all such persons to be apprehended, and openly whipped, and sent away (except such as are willing to go to the English Plantations) And that in all things they do speedily execute, and cause to be put in execution the Statute made in the Thirty ninth yeare of Queene Elizabeth Chap. the 4th concerning the punishment of Rogues and Vagabonds: And to the end that all such persons may not only be setled and kept from wandring, but also made to labour and so kept from idleness, his Majesty doth streightly charge and command all and singular Sheriffs, Justices of the Peace, and other Officers and Ministers in the several Counties of this Realm, and all Mayors, Sheriffs, Bayliffs, Aldermen and other Magistrates, Officers and Ministers of all other Cities and Towns Corporate, that they and every of them within their several Limits and Jurisdictions respectively do carefully and diligently put in due and speedy Execution the same Statute of the Thirty ninth of Elizabeth, Chapter the Fourth, both for erecting houses of Correction, and for punishing such Vagabonds and idle persons; as also the Statutes of the I. Jacob. Chap. 7. made for the explanation of the said Statute made in the Seventh year of King James Chapter Fourth, for the ordering such houses of Correction. And to the end that not onely sturdy Rogues and Vagabonds may be duely kept from wandering and idleness, and held to labour, but that also poor and Fatherless Children and Widows, the Aged and Impotent may be also carefully provided for and relieved, and not permitted to wander and be in the Streets begging from door to door; It is His Majesties express Charge and Command to all Mayors, Sheriffs, Bayliffs, Justices of the Peace, Magistrates, Officers and Ministers in the several Counties of this Realm, and in all Cities and Towns Corporate, that they diligently and carefully put in execution that excellent Statute made in the Fourty third Year of Elizabeth, Chapter the second, concerning the Overseers of the Poor, and their duty for raising a Stock for maintenance of the Poor, and for binding forth Children Apprentices, which His Majesty commends in an especial manner to their Care: Their neglecting this so great a work, in not carefully providing for poor Fatherless Children and Infants for their teaching and instructing them, and for fitting them for Trades and Services, and in not binding them forth Apprentices; all which neglect is a great cause of poor childrens idleness, wandring, and wickedness in the whole course of their lives; And to the end that convenient Stocks may be raised in all Parishes, especially for the ends aforesaid, His Majesty requireth the several Overseers of the Poor to be diligent in raising such Stocks according to the Power given them, And also His Majesty requireth all Mayors, Bayliffs, Justices of the Peace, Magistrates and other Officers aforesaid, to be careful in putting in speedy and due Execution all the Statutes concerning Tipling and Drunkenness, and concerning unlawful or irregular Inns or Alehouses, and all other Statutes, the penalties whereof are disposed to the use of the Poor of the several Parishes; and to cause the said several penalties to be delivered to the Overseers of the Poor respectively for the increase of the said Stock, to buy materials to imploy the said Poor, and also to be careful in diligent calling to account the said Overseers, and to see the said sums so raised may be carefully imployed for the good education and instruction and binding out of such poor Infants and Fatherless Children, and providing for relief of the Poor aforesaid, which may in probability encourage some charitable and well disposed Persons voluntarily to contribute and add to such Stocks by their free and weekly contributions (which they dayly bestowed on idle begging Poor) or otherwise. His Majesty therefore expects all Mayors, Justices, Magistrates and other His Officers to whom the Execution of the Law aforesaid is particularly concerned, that they be very careful in the due and speedy execution of every one of them, as they will avoid His Majesties just indignation for their neglect of their duties in hindring this so great a National work, and for the Contempt of His Royal Commandments: His Majesty being resolved to have an account, both from the said Justices, and the several Judges of Assizes in their several Circuits, of the due observation hereof, until His Majesty shall take a further Course by the advice of His Parliament, which he determines to do, that no poor shall be permitted to be Vagrant or Begging, but all such as are Impotent and not able to work, may be provided for, so as to live comfortably, and yet be kept from profess'd idleness, and such as are able may have means provided to set them on work.

Given at Our Court at Whitehall, the Ninth day of May, One thousand six hundred sixty one, and in the Thirteenth year of His Majesties Reign.

God Save The King.

London, Printed by John Bill and Christopher Barker, Printers to the King's most Excellent Majesty, 1661. At the Kings Printing-House in Black-Friers.

3 pp. folio. Copies in Adv., Antiq., Bodl., B. M., Camb., Ch., Crawf., Dalk., Dubl., Guild., P. R. O., Q. C., and T. C. D. Abstract printed in "Mercurius Publicus," May 16, 1661, and in "Kingdomes Intelligencer," May 20, 1661.

1661, DECEMBER 14.

[ENCOURAGING SETTLING IN JAMAICA.]

BY THE KING.

A PROCLAMATION

For the encouraging of Planters in His Majesties Island of Jamaica
in the West-Indies.

Charles R.

We being fully satisfied, that Our Island of Jamaica, being a pleasant and most fertile soyl, and scituate commodiously for Trade and Commerce, is likely, through Gods blessing, to be a great Benefit and Advantage to this and other Our Kingdoms and Dominions, have thought fit, for encouraging of Our Subjects, as well such as are already upon the said Island, as all others that shall transport themselves thither, and Reside and Plant there, to declare and publish, And We do hereby declare and publish, That Thirty Acres of Improveable Lands shall be granted and allotted to every such Person, Male, or Female, being Twelve years old or upwards, who now Resides, or within Two years next ensuing, shall Reside upon the said Island, and that the same shall be assigned and set out by the Governor and Council within Six weeks next after notice shall be given in Writing, subscribed by such Planter or Planters, or some of them, in behalf of the rest, to the Governor, or such Officer as he shall appoint in that behalf, signifying their resolutions to Plant there, and when they intend to be on the place. And in case they do not go thither within Six moneths then next ensuing, the said Allotment shall be void, and free to be assigned to any other Planter; And that every person and persons to whom such Assignment shall be made, shall hold and enjoy the said Lands, so to be assigned, and all Houses, Edifices, Buildings, and Inclosures, thereupon to be built or made, to them and their Heirs for ever, be and under such Tenure as is usual in other Plantations subject unto Us. Nevertheless they are to be obliged to serve in Arms upon any Insurrection, Mutiny, or Foreign Invasion; and that the said Assignments and Allotments shall be made and confirmed under the publick Seal of the said Island, with power to create any Mannor or Mannors, and with such convenient and suitable Priviledges and Immunities as the Grantee shall reasonably devise and require; And a draught of such Assignments shall be prepared by Our Learned Council in the Law, and delivered to the Governor to that purpose; And that all Fishings and Piscaries, and all Copper, Lead, Tin, Iron, Coals, and all other Mines (except Gold and Silver) within such respective

Allotments, shall be enjoyed by the Grantees thereof, reserving only a Twentieth part of the Product of the said Mines to Our use. And we do further publish and declare, That all Children of any of Our Natural born Subjects of England to be born in Jamaica, shall from their respective Births be reputed to be, and shall be free Denizens of England, and shall have the same Priviledges to all Intents and Purposes as Our Free-born Subjects of England; And that all Free persons shall have liberty without Interruption, to transport themselves and their Families, and any their Goods (except only Coyn and Bullions) from any of Our Dominions and Territories to the said Island of Jamaica. And we do straitly charge and command all Planters, Soldiers, and others upon the said Island, to yield obedience to the lawful Commands of Our Right Trusty and Welbeloved Thomas Lord Windsor, now Our Governor of the said Island, and to every other Governor thereof for the time being, under pain of Our displeasure, and such penalties as may be inflicted thereupon.

Given at Our Court at Whitehal the Fourteenth day of December, 1661. In the Thirteenth year of Our Reign.[37]

GOD SAVE THE KING.

London, Printed by John Bill and Christopher Barker, Printers to the King's most Excellent Majesty. 1661.

2 pp. folio. There are two issues, varying slightly in set-up. Copies in Adv., Antiq., Bodl., B. M., Camb., Ch., Crawf., Dalk., Dubl., Guild., Hodg., P. R. O., Q. C., T. C. D., and in N. Y. Historical Society. Entered on Patent Rolls. Printed in "Interesting Tracts relating to the Island of Jamaica," 1800, pp. 135, 136, and in preface to "Laws of Jamaica," 1792.

---

[37] There is a series of documents in the Public Record Office regarding the publication of this proclamation in Barbadoes (see abstracts in *Cal. State Papers, Colonial, 1661-1668*, pp. 97, 103).

1667, AUGUST 23.

[RECALLING DISPENSATIONS OF NAVIGATION ACT.]

BY THE KING.

A PROCLAMATION

For recalling Dispensations, with some Clauses in the Acts for
Encouragement and Increasing of Shipping and Navigation,
and of Trade.

Charles R.

Whereas We by an Order in Council[38] of the Two and twentieth day of March,

---

[38] Since this order does not appear among the printed *Acts of the Privy Council, 1613-1680*, it is here noted. On March 22, 1665, it was ordered that the "Act for encouraging and encreasing of Shipping and Navigation" should be suspended so far as concerned commerce with Norway and the Baltic Sea, also with Germany, Flanders, or France, provided the merchants and owners were English natural-born subjects. The order further allowed the merchants of any nation in amity with England to import hemp, pitch, tar, masts, saltpeter, and copper, paying only such duties as were imposed by the Act of Tonnage and Poundage. The clauses relating to America follow:

"And His Majesty doth further Order, That notwithstanding the said Act for Encouraging and encreasing of Shipping and Navigation, and one other Act made in the said Parliament begun at Westminster the eighth day of May in the thirteenth year of His Majesties Reign, intituled [An Act for the Encouragement of Trade] or either of them, or any Clause or Clauses in them, or either of them to the contrary, It shall and may be lawful for any English Merchants, and they are hereby authorised, freely and without interruption, to make use of, and employ any Foreign Ships or Vessels whatsoever, Navigated by Mariners or Seamen of any Nation in Amity with His Majesty, for importing or exporting of Goods and Commodities, to or from any Port in England or Wales, to or from any of His Majesties Plantations.

"Provided, That no Goods or Commodities whatsoever, be by them imported into any of His Majesties said Plantations, but what shall be without fraud, Laden and Shipped in England or Wales, and thence directly carried, and from no other place to His Majesties said Plantations.

"Provided also, That such Goods and Commodities as shall be by them laden or taken on Board at His Majesties said Plantations, or any of them, be brought directly from thence to some of His Majesties said Ports in England or Wales. And all Governours, and Officers of the Customs are hereby charged and required, strictly to observe all Rules, Directions and Orders for taking of Bonds or other Securities, and exacting all Forfeitures, and Penal-

One thousand six hundred sixty four, have dispenced for some time with certain Clauses in the late Acts of Parliament for Encouraging and Increasing of Shipping and Navigation, and for the Encouragement of Trade; and therein also Declared, That when We should think fit to determine that Dispensation, We would by Our Royal Proclamation give Six moneths notice thereof, to the end no Merchant, or other Person therein concerned should be surprised. In order whereunto, We taking the same into consideration, have thought fit (with the advice of Our Privy Council) to publish this Our Royal Proclamation; and do hereby Declare, That the said Order of the Two and twentieth of March, One thousand six hundred sixty four, and all and every the Dispensations, Clauses, Matters, and things therein contained, shall from and after the end of six moneths next ensuing the Date of this Proclamation, Cease, Determine, and be Void to all intents and purposes whatsoever; Whereof all Persons concerned are to take notice, and to conform themselves accordingly.

Given at Our Court at Whitehall the 23. day of August, 1667. In the Nineteenth year of Our Reign.

GOD SAVE THE KING.

In the Savoy, Printed by the Assigns of John Bill and Christopher Barker, Printers to the Kings most Excellent Majesty. 1667.

1 p. folio. Copies in Antiq., Bodl., B. M., Camb., Ch., Crawf., Dalk., Guild., P. C., P. R. O., Q. C., and T. C. D. Entered on Patent Rolls.

---

ties by the said Acts or either of them required or enjoyned: save only in the Two Clauses concerning English Ships or English Mariners herein before dispensed with.

"And lastly, His Majesty doth declare, That this shall continue and be in force during His Majesties pleasure: And when His Majesty shall think fit to determine the Dispensation hereby granted, He will by His Royal Proclamation give six moneths notice thereof, To the end no Merchant or other person herein concerned, may be surprized."

This order in Council was printed as a broadside by John Bill and Christopher Barker, and copies of it are in Antiq., B. M., Crawf., P. R. O., and Q. C.

1671, DECEMBER 22.

[CONCERNING THE PLANTERS
AT ST. CHRISTOPHERS.]

BY THE KING.

A PROCLAMATION

Touching the Planters in the Island of Saint Christophers.

Charles R.

Whereas it hath been Our care before and since the Restitution of that part of the Island of Saint Christophers,[39] which formerly belonged to Us and Our Subjects, to provide for the Plantation and Improvement thereof, by giving all manner of Encouragements to Our good Subjects to return thither, and to Re-establish the former Trade and Commerce: In order whereunto We lately sent thither Sir Charles Wheeler Baronet, with Our Commission to be Our Lieutenant-General, and General Governour of Our Leeward Islands in America; and for the better execution of so important a Charge, gave him such Directions and Instructions as were most suitable to these Our Royal Intentions, and might best tend to the advancement of the general Good and Welfare of all Our Subjects there, so that We might reasonably have expected before this time, some Account of the good success of these Our endeavours in the happy and peaceable Settlement of Our Subjects in their former Proprieties and Possessions; nevertheless, to the utter disappointment of Our just expectations, and the general Discouragement of such of Our Subjects who formerly Inhabited that Island, We are given to understand, That on or about the Twenty fourth of August last past, Sir Charles Wheeler hath caused a certain Proclamation to be published in that Island, thereby endeavouring to oblige the former Inhabitants and Proprietors to appear before a certain Court of Claims by him there Erected, and to return with a Stock sufficient for the quantity of Land they Claim, on peril of losing such part of their Estates they shall not be able to Stock, which shall be given to them who are better able; And moreover, to be Contributory to all Levies to be made for satisfaction of the French

---

[39] Although the Island of St. Christophers, occupied by both the French and the English, was given to England in 1667 according to the seventh article of the Treaty of Breda, the next few years were filled with constant controversies in the effort to compose the differences between the two nations (see the *Calendar of State Papers, Colonial, 1669-1674*, and the *Acts of the Privy Council*, vol. 2). The above proclamation was reported as advisable by the Council for Plantations on December 7, 1671 (*Cal. State Papers*, p. 285).

Demand, upon any Article of the Peace at Breda, or for satisfaction of any other disbursments concerning Fortifications, or any other Publick Expences; with a further menacing intimation to all such as shall be found to have Acted or Counselled in the late Rendition of the Island to the French, or have been guilty of any Cowardise or Folly in that War, That they are not to expect the like advantages with the rest of Our Subjects: And a Declaration, That upon every mans Estate a Quit-Rent shall be reserved, greater or lesser, according to the merit or demerit of the person Restored, with an allowance of no longer time to such of Our Subjects who were in the Barbadoes and Caribee Islands, for putting in their Claims, then One Moneth, and but Three Moneths to those who were in any part of Europe, Virginia, Jamaica, Carolina, Bermuda's, or New England, Then which nothing could have been done more contrary to the Commission and Instructions We had given him, nor more repugnant to Our Royal Intentions, and the just Interests and Advantages of the antient Planters and Proprietors: Wherefore, and for the better prevention of the ill consequences which might otherwise ensue upon that Proclamation so issued out by the said Sir Charles Wheeler, if the same should be allowed to have any force or effect, We have thought fit, by Advice of Our Council, to Publish this Our Royal Proclamation, and do hereby Declare Our Will and Pleasure, That the said Proclamation, and everything therein contained, is, and shall be null and void, to all intents and purposes whatsoever, as if the same had never been had nor made; And because the Return and Re-settlement of the antient Planters and Proprietors hath been many ways obstructed, not onely by the Severities of the said Illegal Proclamation, but by several accidents which for a long time did very much retard the Surrender of the said Island, We therefore out of the just sense We have of the great Sufferings of the said late Planters and Proprietors, do by these presents, for their ease, and in their favour, further Declare, That all and every the late Planters and Proprietors, their Heirs, Executors and Assigns, or their Agents respectively, shall be admitted to enjoy their several and respective Plantations, carrying with them such Stock onely as they are able, or can conveniently provide: Which Grace and Favour of Ours We would have to be understood with these Qualifications and Restrictions onely (That is to say) That such who have sold their Plantations to the French, or Claim under those who did Sell the same to the French, shall be obliged to re-imburse the Purchasers the Price or Money they or those under whom they Claim, did actually receive for their ·respective Possessions and Estates, within the space of one whole year, to be accounted from the Re-delivery of the English part of the said Island, which We are informed, was upon the 5/15 of July 1671. And all such who have not Sold to the French and their Heirs, Executors and Assigns, and their Agents respectively, shall be obliged to return unto the said Island before the Twenty fifth day of December, which shall be in the year of Our Lord, One thousand six hundred seventy two. And We do further Publish and Declare Our Royal Will and Pleasure, That no Taxes, Tallages, Aides, or other Impositions whatsoever, shall at any time hereafter be Assessed or Imposed, nor any Quit-Rents Reserved or Required, nor any Moneys Levied, nor any kind of Charge be laid upon, or raised out of any Lands or Tenements in the said Island, unless it be by vertue of some Publick Law made or to be made by the Assembly of the said Island, and with the consent of the Governour and Counsel there Assembled. And moreover, of Our further and more especial Clemency and Favour unto Our good Subjects in the said Island, We are Graciously pleased to Declare, That all and every the Inhabitants, Planters and Proprietors of the said Island, and all and every person and persons Claiming by, from, and under them, or any of them, and all other Our Subjects in the said Island, shall be, and are hereby Freed, Indempnified, and Discharged, as against Us, Our Heirs and Successors, of and from all Crimes, Offences, Miscarriages, and Misdemeanours whatsoever, which happened, and were committed in the said Island during the late War in the said Island, and of and from all Pains and Penalties incurred for or by reason of any matter or thing done, or omitted to be done during the said late War; And of and from all Prosecutions, Molestations, or Inquiries touching or concerning the same; All which matters and things shall be, and are hereby put into perpetual Oblivion, nor shall the same be ever mentioned to the prejudice of any of Our Subjects, either in their Persons, Estates, or Reputations. All which We Command to be Obeyed in all Our Dominions, and all Our Officers Civil and Military, to be Assisting in the Premises, as they will answer the contrary at their utmost perils.

Given at Our Court at Whitehall the Two and twentieth day of December 1671. in the Twenty third year of Our Reign, 1671.

GOD SAVE THE KING.

In the Savoy, Printed by the Assigns of John Bill and Christopher Barker, Printers to the Kings most Excellent Majesty, 1671.

2 pp. folio. Copies in Antiq., Bodl., B. M., Crawf., Guild., P. C., P. R. O., Q. C., and T. C. D. Abstract printed in "London Gazette," Dec. 28, 1671.

1674, MARCH 11.

[RECALLING DISPENSATIONS OF NAVIGATION ACT.]

BY THE KING.

A PROCLAMATION

FOR RECALLING DISPENSATIONS WITH SOME CLAUSES IN THE ACTS FOR ENCOURAGEMENT AND INCREASING OF SHIPPING AND NAVIGATION, AND OF TRADE.

CHARLES R.

Whereas We by an Order in Council of the Tenth day of May One thousand six hundred seventy two,[40] have Dispensed for sometime with certain Clauses in the late Acts of Parliament for Encouraging and Increasing of Shipping and Navigation, and for the Encouragement of Trade; And therein also Declared, That when We should think fit to determine that Dispensation, We would by Our Royal Proclamation give Six Moneths notice thereof, to the end no Merchant, or other Person therein concerned should be Surprized. In order whereunto, We taking the same into Consideration, have thought fit (with the Advice of Our Privy Council) to Publish this Our Royal Proclamation; And do hereby Declare, That the said Order of the Tenth of May One thousand six hundred seventy two, and all and every the Dispensations, Clauses, Matters and Things therein contained, shall from and after the end of Six moneths next ensuing the Date of this Proclamation, cease, determine, and be void to all intents and purposes whatsoever: Whereof all Persons concerned are to take notice, and to conform themselves accordingly.

Given at our Court at Whitehall the Eleventh day of March 1673/4 in the Six and twentieth year of Our Reign.

GOD SAVE THE KING.

London, Printed by the Assigns of John Bill and Christopher Barker, Printers to the Kings most Excellent Majesty, 1673/4.

1 p. folio. Copies in Antiq., Bodl., B. M., Camb., Crawf., Dalk., Guild., P. R. O., Q. C., and T. C. D. Entered on Patent Rolls.

---

[40] See *Acts of Privy Council, Colonial,* 1613-1680, p. 576.

1674, NOVEMBER 30.

[PROHIBITING AFRICAN TRADE TO PLANTATIONS.]

BY THE KING.

A PROCLAMATION

CHARLES R.

Whereas it is found by Experience, That Traffique with Infidels and Barbarous Nations not in Amity with Us, and who are not holden by any League or Treaty, cannot be carried on without the Establishment of Forts and Factories in places convenient, the maintenance whereof requires so great and constant Expence, that it cannot be otherwise defrayed, then by Managing the whole Trade by a Joynt Stock; We in Our Royal Wisdom taking the same into Our serious Consideration, and more especially having found by experience, That the whole Trade of the Coast of Guiny, Buiny and Angola, and other parts and places of Africa, so much importing our Service, and the Enriching of this Our Kingdom, was very much abated, and attempted to be Ingrossed by Foreigners, and in eminent danger to be utterly lost, and taken from Us, and Our loving Subjects, not onely by Foreign Force, but by the Violence and Inconstancy of the Heathen Natives: For the Recovery and Preservation whereof, We were Graciously pleased to encourage and invite Our loving Subjects to Raise a Joynt Stock to be used and imployed therein: And in consideration thereof, and for the better Securing of such as should come in and be concerned in the said Joynt Stock and Trade, We did by Our Letters Patents under Our Great Seal of England, bearing date the Seven and twentieth day of September, in the Four and twentieth year of Our Reign,[41] Grant unto several of Our loving Subjects, the whole entire and onely Trade into and from Africa, from the Port of Sally in South Barbary inclusive, to the Cape de Bona Esperanza inclusive, with all the Islands near adjoyning to those Coasts, and comprehended within the Limits aforesaid, and did Incorporate them by the name of The Royal African Company of England; And the said Company having raised a very great Stock sufficient to Manage the Trade thereof, have since, at their great Expence and Charge, Fortified and Setled divers Garisons, Forts and Factories, by which means they have so Secured the said Trade, that the same doth now begin to flourish, and if not disturbed, is likely to be further improved to the great benefit of this <u>Our Kingdom;</u> Nevertheless, We are Informed by the humble Petition of the said

[41] An abstract of this charter, dated September 27, 1672, is printed in the *Cal. State Papers, Colonial, 1669-1674*, p. 409.

Company, That divers of Our Subjects in several of Our Plantations in America, who are not Members of the said Company, nor any ways concerned in their Stock, do endeavour to reap the Benefit and Fruit thereof; and to that end have already sent several Ships into those parts to Trade, and are providing more, the which if it should be permitted, and not strictly and presently prevented, will disable the said Company from supporting the great Charge of maintaining the said Forts, Garisons and Factories, and consequently, unavoidably occasion the loss of the whole Trade of those Countreys: Wherefore for remedy thereof We have thought fit, with Advice of Our Privy Council,[42] to Publish and Declare Our Royal Will and Pleasure to be, And We do hereby strictly Prohibit and Forbid all and every of Our Subjects whatsoever, Except the said Royal Company and their Successours, at any time or times hereafter, to send or Navigate any Ship or Ships, Vessel or Vessels, or Exercise any Trade from any of Our Plantations, Dominions, or Countreys in America, to any of the Parts or Coasts of Africa, from Sally to Cape de Bona Esperanza, or any of the Islands near thereunto, as aforesaid, or from thence to carry any Negro Servants, Gold, Elephants Teeth, or any other Goods or Merchandizes of the Product or Manufacture of the said Places, to any of Our American Dominions or Plantations, upon pain of Our high Displeasure, and the forfeiture and loss of the said Negros, Gold, Elephants Teeth, and all other Goods and Merchandizes, and the Ships or Vessels which shall bring or carry the same. And We do hereby also strictly Require and Command all Our Governours, Deputy-Governours, Admirals, Vice-Admirals, Generals, Judges of Our Courts of Admiralty, Commanders of Our Forts and Castles, Captains of Our Royal Ships, Justices of the Peace, Provost-Marshals, Marshals, Comptrollers, Collectors of Our Customs, Wayters, Searchers, and all other Our Officers and Ministers Civil and Military, by Sea or Land, in every of Our said American Dominions or Plantations, to take effectual care, That no person or persons whatsoever within their respective Limits or Jurisdictions (except the said Company and their Successours) do send or Navigate any Ships or Vessels, or Exercise any Trade from any of Our said Dominions or Plantations, to any part of the said Coast of Africa, within the Limits aforesaid, or from thence to Import any Negro Servants, Gold, Elephants Teeth, or other Goods of the Product of any of those Parts, into any of Our said Dominions or Plantations in America; And if any person or persons shall presume to act or do in any wise contrary to this Our Royal Proclamation, to the end Our Will and Pleasure herein may be the better observed, We do further Will, Require, and strictly Command all Our said Governours, Deputy-Governours, Admirals, Vice-Admirals, Generals, Judges of Our Court of Admiralty, Commanders of Our Forts and Castles, Captains of Our Royal Ships, Justices of the Peace, Provost-Marshals, Marshals, Comptrollers, Collectors of Our Customs, Wayters, Searchers, and all other Our Officers and Ministers Civil and Military, by Sea or Land, in every of Our said American Dominions and Plantations, That as often as need shall require, they be Aiding and Assisting to the said Royal African Company, their Successors, Fac-

[42] The action of the Privy Council, November 4, 1674, resulting from a petition of the Royal African Company that American interlopers be kept out of the African trade, is in the *Acts of the Privy Council*, i, 614. The proclamation was approved on November 25, and on December 2, letters were sent to the various colonial governors forwarding directions regarding it (*Idem*, pp. 615, 616).

tors, Deputies or Assigns, to Attach, Arrest, Take and Seize all such Ship or Ships, Vessel or Vessels, Negro Servants, Gold, Elephants Teeth, or Goods, Wares and Merchandizes, wheresoever they shall be found, for Our Use, according to Our Royal Charter Granted to the said Company, upon pain of Our high Displeasure, and as they will answer the contrary at their Perils.

Given at Our Court at Whitehall, the Thirtieth day of November, in the Six and twentieth year of Our Reign.

GOD SAVE THE KING.

London, Printed by the Assigns of John Bill and Christopher Barker, Printers to the Kings most Excellent Majesty. 1674.

2 pp. folio. Copies in Antiq., Bodl., B. M., Crawf., Dalk., P. C., P. R. O., Q. C., and N. Y. Historical Society. Entered on Patent Rolls. Abstract printed in "London Gazette," Dec. 10, 1674.

1675, OCTOBER 1.

[FOR APPREHENDING DON PHILIP HELLEN.]

BY THE KING.

A PROCLAMATION

For the Discovery and Apprehension of Captain Don Philip Hellen,
alias Fitz-gerald.

Charles R.

Whereas it hath been represented unto Us by the humble Petition of Martin Stamp, and due proof made by the Testimony of credible Witnesses, That Timothy Stamp, Brother of the said Martin, being a Merchant, was in December 1672, taken by a Spanish Man of War, and his Ship, called the Humility of London, and the Goods therein, to the value of Five thousand pounds, carried into the Port of Havana; But the Governour of the place not finding cause for the Detainer of the said Ship, restored the same, with promise of Satisfaction for the Damage sustained, and a Protection against all Spanish Ships; Yet during the restraint of the said Ship, a Man of War was fitted out under the Command of Don Philip Hellen, alias Fitz-gerald[43] (Our Natural born Subject) who retook the said Ship within Musquet shot of the Castle of Havana, and after Tortured and Murdered the said Timothy Stamp, and most of his men; some they hanged until they were half dead, and then cut them with their swords, afterwards hung them up again until they were almost dead, then cut them in pieces with an Ax; others had their Arms cut off, and were cleft down with Axes; And afterwards the said Don Philip Hellen, alias Fitz-gerald, and his Company shared the said Ship and Goods; And the like Barbarous cruelty the said Don Philip Hellen, alias Fitz-gerald, hath since exercised upon other Our Subjects: We have therefore thought fit (with the advice of Our Privy Council) to publish the same to all Our loving Subjects, and doubt not of their care and forwardness in the discovery and apprehension of the said Fitz-gerald: And We do by this Our Proclamation (whereof he ought and shall be presumed to take notice) Enjoyn and Command the said Don Philip Hellen, alias Fitz-gerald, within Six Moneths after the publication hereof, to render himself to one of Our Principal Secretaries of State, or to the chief Governour of the Island of Jamaica, or to the chief Governour of some other of Our Foreign Plantations, to receive and undergo such Order as shall be given concerning him. And We do here-

[43] For various documents regarding Fitz-gerald's piracies in the West Indies, see *Cal. State Papers, Colonial, 1669-1674*, pp. 505, 537, 557, 608; *Idem, 1675-1676*, pp. 205, 293; and *Acts of the Privy Council*, i, pp. 594, 595, 600, 613, 632.

by further publish and declare, That if the said Don Philip Hellen, alias Fitz-gerald, shall not within the time aforesaid, render himself accordingly, then if any person or persons whatsoever shall at any time after apprehend and bring him dead or alive to one of Our Principal Secretaries of State, or to the Governour of Our Island of Jamaica, or to the chief Governour of any other of Our Foreign Plantations, he or they so apprehending and bringing him, shall have a reward of One thousand pieces of Eight. And We do also strictly Charge and Command all Our Officers and Ministers, as well Military as Civil, and other Our Subjects whatsoever, to be diligent, and use their best endeavours to search for and apprehend the said Don Philip Hellen, alias Fitz-gerald, in all places whatsoever, as they will answer the neglect therof at their perils. And We do hereby further publish and declare, That if any of Our Subjects shall after the publication of this Our Proclamation, directly or indirectly conceal or harbour the said Don Philip Hellen, alias Fitz-gerald, or shall not use his or their best endeavours for his discovery and apprehension, as well by giving due advertisement to Our Officers, as by all other good means, We will (as there is just cause) proceed against them that shall so neglect this Our Command, with all severity.

Given at Our Court at Whitehall the First day of October 1675. In the Seven and twentieth year of Our Reign.

GOD SAVE THE KING.

London, Printed by the Assigns of John Bill and Christopher Barker, Printer to the Kings most Excellent Majesty. 1675.

2 pp. folio. Copies in Antiq., Bodl., B. M., Ch., Crawf., Dalk., P. C., P. R. O., T. C. D., and in N. Y. Historical Society. Entered on Patent Rolls. Printed in "London Gazette," Oct. 14, 1675.

1675, NOVEMBER 24.

[ENFORCING NAVIGATION ACTS.]

BY THE KING.

A PROCLAMATION

FOR PROHIBITING THE IMPORTATION OF COMMODITIES OF EUROPE INTO ANY OF HIS MAJESTIES PLANTATIONS IN AFRICA, ASIA, OR AMERICA, WHICH WERE NOT LADEN IN ENGLAND, AND FOR PUTTING ALL OTHER LAWS RELATING TO THE TRADE OF THE PLANTATIONS, IN EFFECTUAL EXECUTION.

CHARLES R.

Whereas by one Act of Parliament made in the Fifteenth year of His Majesties Reign, Entituled, (An Act for the Encouragement of Trade)[44] it is Enacted, That from and after the Twenty fifth day of March 1664, no Commodities of the growth, production or manufacture of Europe, shall be Imported into any Land, Island, Plantation, Colony, Territory or Place to His Majesty belonging, or which shall belong unto, or be in the possession of His Majesty, His Heirs or Successors, in Asia, Africa, or America, (Tanger onely excepted) but what shall be bona fide, and without fraud Laden and Shipped in England, Wales, or the Town of Berwick upon Tweed, and which shall be carried directly thence to the said Lands, Islands, Plantations, Colonies, Territories and Places, and from no other place whatsoever, any Law, Statute, or Usage to the contrary notwithstanding, under the Penalty of the Loss of all such Commodities of the Growth, Production or Manufacture of Europe, as shall be Imported into any of them, from any other place whatsoever, by Land, or by Water; and if by Water, of the Ship or Vessel also in which they were Imported, with all her Guns, Tackle, Furniture, Ammunition and Apparel; the said forfeitures to be disposed as by the said Act is directed: Provided, that it shall be lawful to Ship and Lade in such Ships, and so Navigated, as in the said Act is expressed, in any part of Europe, Salt for the Fisheries of New England and New-found-land; and to ship and lade in the Maderas, Wines of the growth thereof; and ship and lade in the Western Islands, or Azores, Wines of the growth of the said Islands; and to ship and take in Servants or Horses in Scotland or Ireland; and to ship or lade in Scotland, all sorts of victual of the growth or production of Scotland; and to ship or lade in Ireland, all sorts of victual of the growth or production of Ireland, and the same to transport into any of the said Lands, Islands, Planta-

---

[44] The second Navigation Act of 1663, cited as 15 Chas. II, ch. 7, printed in *Statutes of the Realm*, vol. 5, p. 449.

tions, Colonies, Territories, or Places; Any thing in the foregoing Clause to the contrary notwithstanding. And whereas His Majesty is well informed, that notwithstanding the said Act of Parliament, great quantities of other Commodities of the growth, production and manufacture of Europe (then what are by the said Act permitted) have been, and are daily Imported into several of His Colonies, Plantations, and Territories, in Asia, Africa and America, (besides Tanger;) and that His Majesties Subjects of some of His Colonies, and Plantations, have not onely supplied themselves with such Commodities not Shipped in England, Wales or Berwick, but have conveyed them by Land and Water, to other of His Majesties Colonies and Plantations, to the great prejudice of His Majesties Customs, and of the Trade and Navigation of this Kingdom: His Majesty therefore for the prevention thereof for the future, doth by this His Royal Proclamation, (with the Advice of His Privy Council)[45] Require and Command all and every his Subjects, that they do not for the future presume to Import any Commodities of the growth, production, or manufacture of Europe, (except what may be Imported by vertue of the Proviso aforesaid) by Land, or Water, into any Land, Island, Plantation, Colony, Territory or Place to His Majesty belonging, or which hereafter shall belong unto, or be in the possession of His Majesty, His Heirs and Successors, (Tanger onely excepted) but which shall be bona fide, and without fraud laden and Shipped in England, Wales, or the Town of Berwick, and carried directly from thence, according to the true meaning of the said Act; whereof all persons concerned are to take notice, and yield due obedience thereunto. And His Majesty doth further strictly direct and require all Governours of His Colonies, and Plantations, and of all Lands, Islands, and Places in His possession in Asia, Africa, and America, (Tanger onely excepted) to take care that this His Royal Proclamation be put in due Execution: and also that one Act made in the Twelfth Year of His Majesties Reign, Entituled, An Act for the Encouraging and Increase of Shipping and Navigation, and one Act made in the Two and twentieth and Three and twentieth years of His Reign, Entituled, (An Act for the Regulating the Plantation Trade,) and also one other Act made in the Five and twentieth year of His Majesties Reign, Entituled, (An Act for the better Securing the Plantation Trade)[46] together with all other the Laws of this His Kingdom of England, relating to the Trade of His Plantations, be duely observed and put in execution in their respective Governments; And His Majesty doth further require all His said Governours, and that they Command all Officers, Civil and Military

---

[45] Ordered published by the Council, November 24, 1675 (*Acts of Privy Council*, i, 638).

[46] The above three acts are (1) "An Act for the Encourageing and increasing of Shipping and Navigation," 12 Chas. II, ch. 18, of the year 1660, printed in *Statutes of the Realm*, v, 246; (2) "An Act to prevent the Planting of Tobacco in England, and for Regulating the Plantation Trade," 22-23 Chas. II, ch. 26, of the year 1670, printed in *Statutes of the Realm*, v, 747; and (3) "An Act for the incouragement of the Greeneland and Eastland Trades, and for the better secureing the Plantation Trade," 25 Chas. II, ch. 7, of the year 1672, printed in *Statutes of the Realm*, v, 792. For a general description of the Navigation Acts, see Channing, *History of the United States*, ii, 27; Channing's "Navigation Laws" in *Amer. Antiquarian Society Proceedings*, vi, 160; and Beer's "Commercial Policy of England toward the American Colonies," in *Columbia University Studies*, ii, pt. 2. The acts themselves are reprinted in MacDonald's *Select Charters*.

under their respective Commands, to be aiding and assisting therein, and to the Collectors and other Officers of His Majesties Customs under them, in the Execution of their respective Offices in order thereunto, as they and every of them will answer the contrary at their utmost perils.

Given at Our Court at Whitehall, the Twenty fourth day of November, In the Seven and twentieth year of Our Reign.

GOD SAVE THE KING.

London, Printed by the Assigns of John Bill and Christopher Barker, Printers to the Kings most Excellent Majesty. 1675.

2 pp. folio. Copies in Antiq., Bodl., B. M., Crawf., Dalk., Guild., P. C., P. R. O., Q. C., and T. C. D. Printed in "London Gazette," Dec. 6, 1675.

1676, APRIL 1.

[CONCERNING PASSES FOR SHIPS.]

BY THE KING.

A PROCLAMATION

Concerning Passes for Ships.

Charles R.

His Majesty (with the Advice of His Privy Council) doth by this His Royal Proclamation publish and declare, That all Passes for Ships Entred out for the East or West Indies, or the parts of Africa beyond Cape Verde, which were granted before the date hereof, shall determine upon their return, and being unladen in some Port of England or Wales, or at the Town of Berwick upon Tweed; And that all Passes by vertue of any other Treaties then those of Algiers, Tunis and Tripoly,[47] for Ships Entred for the Mediterranean Sea, or Trading there, granted before the 25th of March 1675, shall determine at Michaelmas 1676. And that all such Passes for such Ships, granted after the 25th of March 1675, and before the date of this Our Royal Proclamation, shall determine on the 25th day of March 1677. And that if any of the said Ships shall be in any Port of this Kingdom, or in any Member or Creek thereof, at the time of the publishing of this Our Royal Proclamation, their Passes shall be then void; And if any of the said Ships shall happen to come into any Port of England, after the publishing of this Our Royal Proclamation, and before the expiring of the said Periods, and unlade, their Passes shall thereupon determine; And also that all Passes granted to Ships Entred to any other part of the World, or Coastwise, such Passes shall determine on the 29th day of September 1676. And hereof all persons concerned are to take notice at their perils.

[47] Two treaties had been recently entered into, viz.: "Articles of Peace between Great Britain and Tunis, concluded October, 1662. Renewed and confirmed February 4, 1674/5," and "Capitulations and Articles of Peace between Great Britain and the Ottoman Empire, September, 1675" (*Several Treaties of Peace and Commerce*, London, 1686, pp. 157, 203. See also Playfair's *Scourge of Christendom*, pp. 115-119). One of the clauses of these treaties required that all Englishmen traveling in foreign ships should be provided with passports. A proclamation of December 22, 1675, ordered that all passes issued before 1675 should expire on May 1, 1676, and that all new passes, except those for Guinea or the East or West Indies, should be in force for only one year. Another proclamation of January 28, 1676, explained that the passes referred to as expiring on May 1 concerned only the Mediterranean trade (see proclamation calendared in Lord Crawford's *Tudor and Stuart Proclamations*). The proclamation above printed was issued to determine the expiration of passes granted for the English colonial trade.

Given at Our Court at Newmarket the First day of April 1676. In the Eight and twentieth year of Our Reign.

GOD SAVE THE KING.

London, Printed by the Assigns of John Bill and Christopher Barker, Printers to the Kings most Excellent Majesty. 1676.

1 p. folio. Copies in Antiq., Bodl., B. M., Crawf., Dalk., Guild., P. C., P. R. O., Q. C., and T. C. D. Printed in "London Gazette," No. 1084.

1676, OCTOBER 27.

[SUPPRESSING THE REBELLION IN VIRGINIA.]

BY THE KING.

A PROCLAMATION

For the Suppressing a Rebellion lately raised within the Plantation of Virginia.

Charles R.

Whereas Nathaniel Bacon[48] the Younger, of the Plantation of Virginia, and others his Adherents and Complices (being Persons of mean and desperate Fortunes) have lately in a Traiterous and Rebellious manner levyed War within the said Plantation, against the Kings most Excellent Majesty, and more particularly being Assembled in a Warlike manner to the number of about Five Hundred Persons, did in the Moneth of June last past, Inviron and Besiege the Governor and Assembly of the said Plantation (then met together about the Publique affairs of the same Plantation) and did by Menaces and Threats of present Death compel the said Governor and Assembly to pass divers pretended Acts: To the end therefore that the said Nathaniel Bacon and his Complices may suffer such punishment as for their Treason and Rebellion they have justly deserved; His Majesty doth (by this His Royal Proclamation) Publish and Declare, That the said Nathaniel Bacon, and all and every such Persons and Person, being His Majesties Subjects within the said Plantation, as have taken Arms under, willingly joyned with, or assisted, or shall hereafter take Arms under, willingly joyn with, or assist the said Nathaniel Bacon, in raising or carrying on the War (by him as aforesaid levyed) are and shall be guilty of the crime of High Treason. And His Majesty doth hereby strictly Charge and Command all His Loving Subjects, That they do use their utmost endeavour to Apprehend and Secure the Persons of the said Nathaniel Bacon, and of all and every the said Complices, in order to the bringing of them to their Legal Tryal. And for the better encouragement of His Majesties said Loving Subjects to Apprehend and bring to Justice the said Nathaniel Bacon (who hath been chief Contriver and Ring-leader of the said Rebellion) His Majesty doth hereby Declare, That such Person or Persons as shall Apprehend the said Nathaniel Bacon, and him shall bring before His Majesties Governor, Deputy Governor, or other Com-

[48] The most comprehensive account of Bacon's Rebellion is to be found in Osgood's *American Colonies*, iii, ch, 8. The above proclamation was ordered by the King in Council, Sept. 20, 1676, and altered and approved Oct. 25 (see *Cal. State Papers, Colonial, 1675-1676*, pp. 455, 474).

mander in Chief of His Majesties Forces within the said Plantation, shall have as a Reward from His Majesties Royal Bounty, the sum of Three Hundred Pounds Sterling, to be paid in Money by the Lieutenant Governor. And because it may be probable that many of the Adherents and Complices of the said Nathaniel Bacon may have been seduced by him into this said Rebellion, by specious, though false pretences; His Majesty out of His Royal Pity and Compassion to his seduced Subjects, doth hereby Declare, That if any of His Subjects who have or shall have ingaged with, or adhered to the said Nathaniel Bacon in the said Rebellion, shall within the space of Twenty days after the publishing of this His Royal Proclamation, submit himself to His Majesties Government, and before the Governor, Deputy Governor, or other Commander in Chief of His Majesties Forces within the said Plantation, take the Oath of Obedience mentioned in the Act of Parliament made in England in the Third year of the Reign of His Majesties Royal Grandfather, and give such Security for his future good behaviour, as the said Governor, Deputy Governor, or Commander in Chief shall approve of, That then such Person so submitting, taking such Oath, and giving such Security, is hereby pardoned and forgiven the Rebellion and Treason by him committed, and shall be free from all punishments and forfeitures for or by reason of the same. And His Majesty doth hereby further Declare, That if any of His Subjects who have engaged, or shall engage with, or have adhered, or shall adhere to the said Nathaniel Bacon in the said Rebellion, shall not accept of this His Majesties gracious offer of Pardon, but shall after the said Twenty days expired, persist and continue in the said Rebellion, That then such of the Servants or Slaves of such persons so persisting and continuing such Rebellion, as shall render themselves to, and take up Arms under His Majesties Governor, Deputy Governor, or other Commander in Chief of His Majesties Forces within the said Plantation, shall have their Liberty, and be for ever Discharged and Free from the Service of the said Offenders. And to the intent His Majesties Loving Subjects within the said Plantation may understand how desirous and careful His Majesty is to remove from them all just Grievances, His Majesty doth hereby make known to all His said Subjects, That he hath not only alrady given particular Instructions to His Governor, to reduce the Salaries of the Members of the Assembly to such moderate rates as may render them less burthensom to the Countrey, but hath also appointed and sent into the said Plantation, Herbert Jeffreys Esq; Sir John Berry Knight, and Francis Morison Esq; His Majesties Commissioners, to inquire into, and report to His Majesty all such other Grievances as His Majesties subjects within the said Plantation do at present lye under, to the end that such relief and redress may be made therein, as shall be agreeable to His Majesties Royal Wisdom and Compassion. And although the pretended Acts or Laws made in the said Assembly of June last (being in manner aforesaid obtained) are in themselves null and void, yet to the intent no Person may pretend ignorance, His Majesty hath thought fit hereby to Declare and Publish His Royal Pleasure to be, That all and every Acts and Act, made or pretended to be made by the said Governor and Assembly in the late Grand Assembly held at James City in the Moneth of June last past, shall be taken and held as null and void, and shall not for the future be observed or put in execution.

Given at Our Court at Whitehall this Seven and Twentieth day of October,

1676. In the Eight and twentieth year of Our Reign.

GOD SAVE THE KING.

London, Printed by the Assigns of John Bill and Christopher Barker, Printers to the Kings most Excellent Majesty, 1676.

2 pp. folio. Two copies in P. R. O.

1681, APRIL 2.

[GRANTING PENNSYLVANIA TO WILLIAM PENN.]

Charles R.

Whereas His Majesty, in consideration of the great Merit and Faithful Services of Sir William Penn deceased, and for divers other good Causes Him thereunto moving, hath been Graciously pleased by Letters Patents bearing Date the Fourth day of March last past,[49] to Give and Grant unto William Penn Esquire, Son and Heir of the said Sir William Penn, all that Tract of Land in America, called by the Name of Pennsilvania, as the same is Bounded on the East by Delaware River, from Twelve Miles distance Northwards of Newcastle Town, unto the Three and fourtieth Degree of Northern Latitude, if the said River doth extend so far Northwards, and if the said River shall not extend so far Northward, then by the said River so far as it doth extend: And from the Head of the said River, the Eastern Bounds to be determined by a Meridian Line to be Drawn from the Head of the said River, unto the said Three and fourtieth Degree, the said Province to extend Westward Five Degrees in Longitude, to be Computed from the said Eastern Bounds, and to be Bounded on the North, by the Beginning of the Three and fourtieth Degree of Northern Latitude, and on the south by a Circle Drawn at Twelve Miles distance from Newcastle Northwards, and Westwards unto the Beginning of the Fourtieth Degree of Northern Latitude, and then by a straight line Westwards to the limit of Longitude above mentioned, together with all Powers, Preheminencies and Jurisdictions necessary for the Government of the said Province, as by the said Letters Patents, Reference being thereunto had, doth more at large appear.

His Majesty doth therefore hereby Publish and Declare His Royal Will and Pleasure, That all Persons Settled or Inhabiting within the Limits of the said Province, do yield all Due Obedience to the said William Penn, His Heirs and Assigns, as absolute Proprietaries and Governours thereof, as also to the Deputy or Deputies, Agents or Lieutenants, Lawfully Commissionated by him or them, according to the Powers and Authorities Granted by the said Letters Patents; Wherewith His Majesty Expects and Requires a ready Complyance from all Persons whom it may concern, as they tender His Majesties Displeasure.

---

[49] The charter of Pennsylvania, March 4, 1681, is printed in the *Charter to William Penn, and Laws of the Province of Pennsylvania*, Harrisburg, 1879, where a fac-simile of the original document is also reproduced. In the Public Record Office is a draft of the charter, dated February 28, 1681, and signed by the clerk of the Chapel of the Rolls (*Cal. State Papers, Colonial, 1681-1685*, p. 14; see also *Acts of Privy Council*, ii, 17). For the founding of Pennsylvania, see Shepherd's *History of Proprietary Government in Pennsylvania*.

Given at the Court at Whitehall the Second day of April 1681. In the Three and thirtieth year of Our Reign.

To the Inhabitants and
     Planters of the Province of   By his Majesties Command,
     Pennsilvania.   CONWAY.

London, Printed by the Assigns of John Bill, Thomas Newcomb, and Henry Hills, Printers to the Kings most Excellent Majesty. 1681.

1 p. folio. Copy in B. M. Printed in "Charter to William Penn, and Laws of the Province of Pennsylvania," 1879, p. 466, from original in Land Office at Harrisburg. Reproduced in lithograph fac-simile in J. J. Smith's "American Historical and Literary Curiosities," 1860, series 2, pl. 43.

1685, FEBRUARY 6.

[CONTINUING OFFICERS IN THE COLONIES.]

BY THE KING.

A PROCLAMATION.

James R.

Forasmuch as it hath pleased Almighty God lately to call unto his infinite Mercy the most High and Mighty Prince, Charles the Second of most Blessed Memory, the Kings Majesties most Dear and most Entirely Beloved Brother, by whose Decease the Authority and Power of the most part of the Officers and Places of Jurisdiction and Government within his Majesties Dominions did cease and fail, the Soveraign Person failing, from whom the same were derived. The Kings most Excellent Majesty in His Princely Wisdom and Care of the State (reserving to His Own Judgment hereafter, the Reformation and Redress of any Abuses in Mis-government, upon due Knowledge and Examination thereof) is Pleased, and hath so expresly Signified, That all Persons that at the time of the Decease of the late Kings His dearly beloved Brother, were Duly and Lawfully Possessed of, or Invested in any Office, or Place of Authority or Government, either Civil or Military, within His Majesties Realm of England and Ireland, Islands of Jerzey and Guernsey, Sark or Alderney, or within His Majesties Colonies and Plantations in America; And namely, all Governors, Lieutenants or Deputy-Governors, Councellors, Judges, Justices, Provost-Marshals, Sheriffs, Justices of the Peace, and all others in place of Government, either Meaner or Superior, as aforesaid; And all other Officers and Ministers, whose Interests and Estates in their Offices are determined, shall be, and shall hold themselves continued in the said Places and Offices, under the same Condition as formerly they held and enjoyed the same, until His Majesties Pleasure be further known, or that other Provision be made pursuant to His late Majesties Commission and Instructions to His Governors and Officers of the Islands, Colonies and Plantations aforesaid. And that in the mean while, for the Preservation of the State, and necessary Proceedings in matters of Justice, and for the Safety and Service of the State; All the said Persons of whatsoever Degree or Condition may not fail, every one severally, according to his Place, Office or Charge, to proceed in the Performance of all Duties thereunto belonging, as formerly appertained unto them, while the late King was living. And further, His Majesty doth hereby Will and Command all and singular His Highnesses Subjects, of what Estate, Dignity, and Degree, they or any of them be, to be Aiding, Helping and Assisting, and at the Commandment of the said Officers and Ministers, in the Performance and

Execution of the said Offices and Places, as they and every of them Tender His Majesties Displeasure, and will answer the Contrary at their uttermost Perils. And further, His Majesty's Will and Pleasure and Express Commandment is, That all Orders and Directions Made or Given by the Late King, of most Blessed Memory, the Lords of His Privy-Council, or His Principal Secretaries of State, or other Legal Authority, derived from His said Majesty in His Lifetime, shall be Obeyed and Performed by all and every Person and Persons, and all and every Thing and Things to be done thereupon, shall Proceed as Fully and Amply as the same should have been Obeyed or Done, in the Life of the said Late King, His Majesty's most Dearly and most Entirely Beloved Brother, until His Majesties Pleasure be further known thereupon.[50]

Given at the Court at Whitehall, the Sixth Day of February, In the First Year of His Majesty's Reign of England, Scotland, France and Ireland, and other His Majesties Territories and Dominions.

GOD SAVE THE KING.

London, Printed by the Assigns of John Bill deceas'd: And by Henry Hills, and Thomas Newcomb, Printers to the Kings most Excellent Majesty. 1684.

1 p. folio. Copies in Bodl., B. M., Ch., Crawf., Dalk., Guild., P. C., Q. C., and T. C. D.; also in Mass. State Archives. Entered in Privy Council Register, II James, vol. 1, p. 6.

---

[50] A letter to the several Governors of the Plantations was drawn up in the Council, February 6, 1685, announcing the death of King Charles, ordering that the new King be proclaimed in the colonies, and transmitting the above proclamation (*Acts of Privy Council,* ii, 74; see also *Cal. State Papers, Colonial, 1685-1688*, p. 1).

1685, APRIL 1.

[PROHIBITING AFRICAN TRADE TO PLANTATIONS.]

BY THE KING.

A PROCLAMATION

To Prohibit His Majesties Subjects to Trade within the Limits
Assigned to the Royal African Company of England,
Except those of the Company.

James R.

Whereas Our Dearly Beloved Brother the late King of ever Blessed Memory,
for the Supporting and Managing of a Trade very beneficial to this Our Kingdom,
and Our Foreign Plantations upon the Coasts of Guiny, Buiny, Angola, and other
Parts and Places in Africa, from the Port of Sally in South-Barbary inclusive, to
the Cape De Bona Esperanza inclusive, by His Letters Patents under the Great
Seal of England, bearing Date the Twenty seventh day of September, in the Four
and twentieth year of His Reign, did Incorporate divers of His Loving Subjects,
by the Name of the Royal African Company of England;[51] and did thereby Grant
unto the said Company the whole, intire, and onely Trade into, and from Africa
aforesaid, and the Islands and Places near adjoyning to the Coast of Africa, and
comprehended within the Limits aforesaid, with Prohibition to all other His Majesties Subjects to Trade there: And that in pursuance to such Grant, the said Company have Raised a very Great Stock Sufficient to Manage the Trade thereof; and
have since been at great Charges and Expence in Fortifying and Settling divers
Garrisons, Forts and Factories for the better Securing of the said Trade, whereby
the same began to flourish, to the great Commodity of this Kingdom, and Our
Foreign Plantations, until of late disturbed by several ill disposed Persons, who
preferring their private profit before the Publick Good, have contrary to the said
Royal Grant, and the Express Proclamation of the King Our Dearly Beloved Brother, bearing Date the Thirtieth day of November, in the Six and twentieth year of
His Reign, in a Clandestine and Disorderly manner, Traded into those Parts, to the
apparent danger of the Decay and Destruction of the said Trade, and in manifest
Contempt and Violation of the undoubted Prerogative of the Crown, whose Right
it is by the known Laws of these Our Realms, to Limit and Regulate such Foreign
Trades into those Remote Parts of the World; We taking the same into Our Princely

---

[51] See *ante*, p. 121.

Consideration, Do not onely give Leave and Direct, That the Persons who have so Contemptuously Violated the said Companies Charter, and the said Proclamation, be Prosecuted in Our Name at Law, in order to their Condign Punishment according to their Demerits: But for the Prevention of the like evil Practices for the future, We have thought fit, with Advice of Our Privy Council, to Publish and Declare Our Royal Will and Pleasure to be, And We do hereby strictly Prohibit and Forbid all and every of Our Subjects whatsoever, except the said Royal Company and their Successors, and such as shall be Imployed or Licenced by them, at any time or times hereafter to Send or Navigate any Ship or Ships, Vessel or Vessels, or Exercise any Trade to or from any of the Parts or Coasts of Africa from Sally, to Cape De Bona Esperanza, or any of the Islands near adjoyning thereunto as aforesaid, or from thence to carry any Negro Servants, Gold, Elephants Teeth, or any other Goods and Merchandizes of the Product or Manufacture of the said Places upon Pain of Our High Displeasure, and the Forfeiture and Loss of the said Negroes, Gold, Elephants Teeth, and all other Goods and Merchandizes, and the Ships and Vessels which shall be taken or found Trading in any Place or Places upon the Coast of Africa aforesaid, within the Limits aforesaid: And We do hereby also strictly Require and Command all Our Governours, Deputy-Governours, Admirals, Vice-Admirals, Generals, Judges of Our Courts of Admiralty, Commanders of Our Forts and Castles, Captains of Our Royal Ships, Justices of the Peace, Provost-Marshals, Marshals, Comptrollers, Collectors of Our Customs, Waiters, Searchers, and all other Our Officers and Ministers Civil and Military, by Sea or Land, in every of Our said American Dominions or Plantations, to take effectual Care That no Person or Persons whatsoever, within their respective Limits or Jurisdictions, (except the said Company and their Successors, and such as shall be Employed or Licenced by them) do Send or Navigate any Ships or Vessels, or Exercise any Trade from any of Our said Dominions or Plantations, to any Part of the said Coast of Africa, within the Limits aforesaid; Or from thence to Import any Negro Servants, Gold, Elephants Teeth, or other Goods of the Product of any of those Parts, into any of Our said Dominions or Plantations in America; And if any Person or Persons shall presume to Act or Do in any wise Contrary to this Our Royal Proclamation, To the end Our Will and Pleasure herein may be the better Observed, We do further Will and Require and strictly Command all Our said Governours, Deputy-Governours, Admirals, Vice-Admirals, Generals, Judges of Our Court of Admiralty, Commanders of Our Forts and Castles, Captains of Our Royal Ships, Justices of the Peace, Provost Marshals, Marshals, Comptrollers, Collectors of Our Customs, Waiters, Searchers, and all other Our Officers and Ministers Civil and Military, by Sea or Land, in every of Our said American Dominions and Plantations, That as often as need shall require, They be Aiding and Assisting to the said Royal African Company, their Successors, Factors, Deputies or Assigns, to Attach, Arrest, Take, and Seize all such Ship or Ships, Vessel or Vessels, Negro Servants, Gold, Elephants Teeth, or Goods, Wares and Merchandizes wheresoever they shall be found, for Our use, according to Our Royal Charter Granted to the said Company, upon Pain of Our High Displeasure, and as they will Answer the Contrary at their Perils: And We do hereby Require and Command all and every of Our Subjects who are or reside in Africa aforesaid, within the Limits aforesaid, or who are upon the Sea in their Voyage thither, Except such who are Imployed or Licenced by the said Company, That they do within Four Months next ensuing the Date hereof, Depart thence, and Return into this Kingdom, upon Pain and Peril that may fall thereon.

Given at Our Court at Whitehall, the First Day of April, 1685. In the First Year of Our Reign.

GOD SAVE THE KING.

London, Printed by the Assigns of John Bill deceas'd: And by Henry Hills, and Thomas Newcomb, Printers to the Kings most Excellent Majesty, 1685.

1 p. folio. Copies in Bodl., B. M., Ch., Crawf., Guild., P. C., Q. C., and T. C. D. Entered on Patent Rolls; entered in Privy Council Register, II James, vol. 1, p. 55. Noted in "London Gazette," April 9, 1685.

1688, JANUARY 20.

[SUPPRESSING PIRATES IN AMERICA.]

BY THE KING.

A PROCLAMATION

FOR THE MORE EFFECTUAL REDUCING AND SUPPRESSING OF PIRATES
AND PRIVATEERS IN AMERICA.

JAMES R.

Whereas frequent Robberies and Piracies have been, and are daily committed by great numbers of Pirates and Privateers as well on the Seas as on the Land of and in America, which hath occasioned a great prejudice and obstruction to the Trade and Commerce as well of Our Subjects, as of the Subjects of Our Allies, and hath given a great Scandal and Disturbance to Our Government in those Parts. And whereas We being resolved to take some effectual course for the putting an end to all such Outragious Insolencies, have therefore thought it requisite to send a Squadron of Ships into the Parts aforesaid, under the Command of Our Trusty and Welbeloved Servant Sir Robert Holmes,[52] Knight, Our Governor of Our Isle of Wight, and have otherwise given him all necessary Powers for Suppressing of the said Pirates and Privateers, either by force, or assurance of Pardon, and have Constituted and Appointed the said Sir Robert Holmes Our Sole Commissioner in that Affair; Now to the end that this Our Royal Purpose may be the better put in Execution, and that none of the said Offenders may have any cause of excuse or pretence left for want of a due Advertisement of Our Intended Mercy and Clemency towards them, upon their withdrawing themselves from their said wicked and Piratical courses for the future: We are Graciously pleased hereby to Promise and Declare, That in case any such Pirate or Privateer Pirates or Privateers shall within the space of Twelve months next ensuing the Date of this Our Proclamation, either in Person, or by their Agents Surrender, or become obliged to Surrender him or themselves unto the said Sir Robert Holmes, or any other person or persons appointed by him, or such other person or persons as in case of his Death shall be further Constituted and Appointed by Us, within any of Our said Islands, Planta-

---

[52] Holmes was commissioned by the King, August 21, 1687, to command a squadron to be sent to the West Indies for the suppression of pirates. On November 12, letters patent were issued granting to him all goods that he should take from the pirates for three years (*Cal. State Papers, Colonial, 1685-1688*, pp. 421, 467). In the Colonial Entry Books in the Public Record Office are entered the orders from the King to the Governors of the various colonies requiring the publication of this proclamation (*Idem*, p. 488).

tions, Colonies, or other Places on the Sea or Land, lying between the Tropiques of Cancer and Capricorn in America, and in case any Pirate or Privateer, Pirates or Privateers shall within the space of Fifteen months next ensuing the Date of these Presents, Surrender, or become obliged to Surrender him or themselves to the said Sir Robert Holmes, or any others Appointed as aforesaid, in any other parts of America, or within Our Kingdom of England, and shall give sufficient Security to be approved of by the said Sir Robert Holmes, or in case of his Death, by such other person or persons as shall be further Appointed by Us, for his or their future good Behaviour, We will, upon such humble Submission, and after such Security given, Grant unto such Pirate or Pirates, Privateer or Privateers, Our Gracious, Full and Ample Pardon for all Piracies or Robberies committed by him or them upon the Sea or Land before the Date of these Presents. And we do hereby straightly Charge and Command all and singular Our Admirals, Vice-Admirals, Chief Governours, Captains, Commanders, Mariners, Seamen, and all Our Officers and Ministers of and in all and every Our said Islands, Plantations, Colonies, and Territories whatsoever, and of all and every Our Ships of War and other Vessels, and all other Our Officers and Subjects whatsoever, not only to be Aiding, Favouring and Assisting in their several Places and Stations, unto the said Sir Robert Holmes, and such other Person or Persons as shall be appointed as aforesaid in and for the more effectual Reducing and Suppressing of all manner of Pirates and Privateers within the Limits and Parts aforesaid, or any of them, but also (upon the producing a Certificate or Instrument under the Hand and Seal of the said Sir Robert Holmes, or such other Person as in case of his Death shall be further Appointed by Us, signifying that any Pirate or Privateer, Pirates or Privateers hath or have Surrendered him or themselves unto the said Sir Robert Holmes, or such other Person or Persons appointed as aforesaid, and given Security for their future good Behaviour according to the Tenor of these Presents) to permit and suffer the said person or persons lawfully to Pass and Travel either by Sea or Land, without any Let, Hindrance or Molestation whatsoever, to or from any of Our said Islands, Plantations or Colonies, or into Our Kingdom of England, as soon as conveniently may be, in Order to his or their receiving Our full and Gracious Pardon as aforesaid, and that in the meantime no Indictment, Process, or other Proceeding shall be had in any of Our Courts of Record, or elsewhere, against any such person or persons producing such Certificate or Instrument, for any Piracy or Robbery by him or them committed as aforesaid, before the Date of these Presents. Provided always, That if any of the said Offender or Offenders whatsoever shall after the Publishing of this Our Proclamation, in contempt thereof, and of Our Princely Mercy and Clemency to them hereby offered, wilfully and obstinately persist in their Piracies, Robberies and Outragious Practices, or shall not Surrender themselves in manner aforesaid; Then We do hereby expressly Direct and Command, That all and every such person and persons shall be pursued with the utmost Severity, and with the greatest Rigour that may be, until they and every of them be utterly Suppressed and Destroyed; We Declaring it to be Our Royal Purpose and Resolution, That they and every of them shall from thenceforth be finally Excluded and Debarr'd from receiving any further Favour or Mercy. And lastly We do hereby Revoke, Annul and make void all Proclamations by Us formerly Issued touching the Premisses herein above mentioned, or any of them.

Given at Our Court at Whitehall this Twentieth Day of January, 168⅞. In the Third Year of Our Reign.

God Save The King.

London, Printed by Charles Bill, Henry Hills, and Thomas Newcomb, Printers to the Kings most Excellent Majesty. 168⅞.

2 pp. folio. Copies in Antiq., Bodl., B. M., Ch., Crawf., Dalk., Guild., P. C., Q. C., and T. C. D.; also in John Carter Brown Library. Entered on Patent Rolls; entered in Privy Council Register, II James, vol. 2, p. 577. Printed in "London Gazette," January 26, 1688.

1688, MARCH 31.

[PROHIBITING GENERAL TRADING
AT HUDSON'S BAY.]

BY THE KING.

A PROCLAMATION

Prohibiting His Majesties Subjects to Trade within the Limits
Assigned to the Governour and Company of Adventurers of England,
Trading into Hudson's Bay, except those of the Company.

James R.

Whereas Our Dearest Brother King Charles the Second of blessed Memory, did by His Letters Patents under the Great Seal of England, bearing Date the Second day of May, in the Two and twentieth Year of His Reign,[53] Incorporate a Governour and Company for carrying on a Trade in the North-west parts of America within the Streights and Bay, commonly called Hudson's Streights; and did Grant unto them and their Successors, the Sole Trade and Commerce of all those Seas, Streights, Bayes, Rivers, Lakes, Creeks, and Sounds in whatsoever Latitude they should be, lying within the Entrance of the Streights commonly called Hudson's Streights, together with all the Lands, Countreys, and Territories upon the Coasts and Confines of the Seas, Bayes, Lakes, Rivers, Creeks and Sounds aforesaid, which were not then Possessed by, or Granted to any of the Subjects of Our said Royal Brother, or Possessed by the Subjects of any other Christian Prince or State, Thereby Creating and Constituting the said Governour and Company for the time being, and their Successors, the true and absolute Lords and Proprietors of the same Territories, Limits and Places aforesaid, and of all other the Premisses, with express Prohibition to all other the Subjects of Our said Royal Brother to Trade to the Parts aforesaid. And whereas We are satisfied that the said Company hath for many years with great Industry, and at a very great Charge and Expense, Settled divers Factories, Erected several Fortifications, and maintained the Trade in the Parts aforesaid, to the great Honour and Profit of this Our Kingdom, until of late several ill-disposed Persons not being Members of the said Company, nor Licensed by them, preferring their private profit before the publick good, have contrary to the said Royal Grant, in a clandestine and disorderly manner, Traded into those

---

[53] The charter of May 2, 1670 is printed in Dobbs', *Account of the Countries adjoining to Hudson's Bay*, p. 171, and elsewhere. For the literature regarding the founding of this Company, see Winsor's *Narrative and Critical History*, viii, 65.

parts, to the apparent prejudice, if not destruction, of the Trade aforesaid, and in manifest Contempt of Our Prerogative Royal; and the better to colour their evil practices, do frame Designs to Hire, or do Hire themselves out in the Service of, or in conjunction with Foreigners to Sail to the Parts aforesaid, to undermine and destroy the said Companies Trade.[54] We, taking the Premisses into Our Princely Consideration, do not only give Leave and Direct, That the Persons who have so contemptuously violated the said Companies Charter, be Prosecuted in Our Name at Law, in order to their condign Punishment according to their demerits; But for prevention of the like evil practices for the future, We have thought fit, with the Advice of Our Privy Council, to Publish and Declare Our Royal Will and Pleasure to be, and We do hereby strictly Prohibit and Forbid that none of Our Subjects whatsoever, except the said Governour and Company and their Successors, and such as shall be duly Licensed by them at any time or times hereafter do presume to send or Navigate any Ship or Ships, Vessel or Vessels, or exercise any Trade whatsoever directly or indirectly on their own accounts, or in the Service of, or in conjunction with any Foreigner or Foreigners whatsoever, to, in or from the said Streights and Bay, called Hudson's Streights, or to, in or from any Bayes, Rivers, Creeks or Places whatsoever, by what names or denominations soever they or any of them have been heretofore, or shall hereafter be called or distinguished, that now are or lie within the Entrance of Hudson's Streights aforesaid, in what Latitude or Longitude soever the same or any of them do, doth or shall lie, remain or be within the Liberties, Territories, or Priviledges of the said Company, upon pain of Our high Displeasure, and the forfeiture and loss of the Goods, Merchandizes, Ships and Vessels which shall be taken or found Trading in any the Place or Places aforesaid, or within the Limits aforesaid. And We do hereby strictly Charge and Command all and every Our Subjects of what degree or quality soever, now Trading or Traffiquing, or designing to Trade or Traffique to or from the Parts aforesaid, or any of them, contrary to the true meaning of the said Companies Charter, That they forthwith do cease and forbear such their Trade and Traffique, and withdraw themselves from the parts aforesaid. And We do further hereby streightly Require and Command all and singular Our Governours, Lieutenant-Governours, Admirals, Vice-Admirals, Generals, Judges of all Our Courts of Admiralty, Commanders of our Forts and Castles, Captains of Our Royal Ships, Justices of the Peace, Provost-Marshals, Marshals, Comptrollers, Collectors of Our Customs, Wayters, Searchers, and all other Our Officers and Ministers Civil and Military by Sea or Land, in all and every of Our Dominions or Plantations, and all other Our Subjects whatsoever and wheresoever, to take effectual care that no person or persons whatsoever (except the said Company and their Successors, and such as shall be duly Licensed) do send or Navigate any Ships or Vessels, or exercise any Trade directly or indirectly from any of Our Kingdoms, Dominions or Plantations whatsoever, contrary to the said Charter granted to the said Company as aforesaid, to any the Places or Limits aforesaid, or from thence to any of Our said Kingdoms, Dominions, Plantations, or other Places; And if any person or persons

---

[54] The Hudson Bay Company had petitioned for relief from interruptions to their trade as early as July 13, 1682 (*Acts of Privy Council,* ii, 37). The Council order approving the above Proclamation was made March 30, 1688 (*Idem,* p. 108).

shall presume to act or do in any wise contrary to this Our Royal Proclamation, We do Will, Require and streightly Command all and singular Our said Governours, Lieutenant-Governours, Admirals, Vice-Admirals, Generals, Judges of Our Courts of Admiralty, Commanders of Our Forts and Castles, Captains of Our Royal Ships, Justices of the Peace, Provost-Marshals, Marshals, Sheriffs, Comptrollers, Collectors of Our Customs, Wayters, Searchers, and all other Our Officers and Ministers Civil and Military by Sea or Land in every of Our said Dominions and Plantations, and all other Our Officers, Ministers and Subjects whatsoever and wheresoever, that as often as need shall require, they and every of them respectively be Aiding and Assisting to the said Company, their Factors, Deputies, or Assigns, to Attach, Arrest, Take and Seize all such Ship or Ships, Vessel or Vessels, Goods, Wares and Merchandizes of such Person or Persons as shall be Used, Employed, or Traded in contrary to the Charter Granted to the said Company, wheresoever they shall be found, for Our Use, upon pain of Our high Displeasure, and as they will answer the contrary at their Perils.

Given at Our Court at Whitehall the One and thirtieth day of March 1688. In the Fourth Year of Our Reign.

GOD SAVE THE KING.

London, Printed by Charles Bill, Henry Hills, and Thomas Newcomb, Printers to the Kings most Excellent Majesty, 1688.

1 p. folio. Copies in Bodl., B. M., Crawf., Guild., P. C., Q. C., and T. C. D.; also in John Carter Brown Library. Entered on Patent Rolls; entered in Privy Council Register, II James, vol. 2, p. 641. Printed in "London Gazette," April 9, 1688.

1689, FEBRUARY 19.

[CONTINUING OFFICERS IN THE COLONIES.]

BY THE KING AND QUEEN.

A PROCLAMATION

WILLIAM R.

Forasmuch as it hath pleased God to call Us to the Throne, And that thereby it is incumbent upon Us to prevent any Inconvenience to Our Subjects that may arise by not executing the Laws necessary or conducing to the Peace and good Government of Our People, Wee therefore do hereby Declare Our Royall Pleasure That all Persons being Protestants, who at the time of the Receipt of these presents shalbe duly and lawfully possessed of, or invested in any office or Place of Authority or Governm^t either Civill or Military within Our Island of [blank left in text] in America, And namely all Governors, Lieutenants, or Deputy Governors, Councellors, Justices, Provost Marshalls, Sherifs, Justices of the Peace, and all others in Place of Governm^t either meaner or superior as aforesaid. And all other Officers and Ministers whose Interests and Estates in their offices are determined, shall be, and shall hold themselves continued in the said Places and offices under the same condition as formerly they held and enjoyed the same,[55] untill Our Pleasure be further known, or that other Provision be made pursuant to his late Ma^{ys} Commission and Instructions to [blank left in text] aforesaid, Which Wee do hereby Declare to be in full force untill further Order from Us. And that in the mean while for the Preservation of the State, all the said Persons of whatsoever Degree or Condition do not fail every one severally according to his Place Office or Charge, to proceed in the performance of all Dutys thereunto belonging as formerly apperteyned unto them. And further Wee do hereby will and command all and singular Our Subjects of what Estate, Dignity and Degree they or any of them be, to be aiding, helping and assisting, and at the Commandment of the said Officers and Ministers in the Performance and Execution of the said Offices and Places, as they and every of them tender Our Displeasure, and will answer the contrary at their Perills.

Provided alwaies, that nothing herein shalbe Construed or taken to Extend to give or continue any Authority, Priviledge, Jurisdiction or Command to any Papist or Papists with the said [blank left in text].

---

[55] The Prince of Orange issued a circular to the Governors of the Colonies, ordering all officers to be continued, on January 12, 1689, but it was not until February 19, that the proclamation was approved (*Cal. State Papers, Colonial, 1689-1692*, pp. 4, 7; *Acts of Privy Council*, ii, 122).

Given at Our Court at Whitehall this 19th day of February 1688. in the first year of Our Reigne.

G OD SAVE K ING W ILLIAM AND Q UEEN M ARY.

No printed copy found. Entered in Privy Council Register, III William, vol. 1, p. 13.

1689, MAY 7.

[DECLARATION OF WAR AGAINST FRANCE.]

THEIR MAJESTIES

DECLARATION

AGAINST THE FRENCH KING.

WILLIAM R.

It having pleased Almighty God to make Us the happy Instruments of Rescuing these Nations from Great and Imminent Dangers, and to place Us upon the Throne of these Kingdoms, We think Our Selves obliged to endeavour to the uttermost to Promote the Welfare of Our People, which can never be effectually secured, but by preventing the Miseries that threaten them from Abroad.

When we consider the many unjust Methods the French King hath of late Years taken to gratifie his Ambition, that he has not only Invaded the Territories of the Emperor, and of the Empire now in Amity with Us, laying Waste whole Countries, and destroying the Inhabitants by his Armies, but Declared War against Our Allies without any Provocation, in manifest Violation of the Treaties Confirmed by the Guaranty of the Crown of England; We can do no less then Joyn with Our Allies in opposing the Designs of the French King, as the Disturber of the Peace, and the Common Enemy of the Christian World.

And besides the Obligations We lie under by Treaties with Our Allies, which are a sufficient Justification of Us for taking up Arms at this time, since they have called upon Us so to do, the many Injuries done to Us and to Our Subjects, without any Reparation, by the French King, are such, that (however of late Years they were not taken Notice of, for Reasons well known to the World, nevertheless) We will not pass them over without a Publick and Just Resentment of such Outrages.

It is not long since the French took Licences from the English Governor of New-found-Land, to Fish in the Seas upon that Coast, and paid a Tribute for such Licences, as an Acknowledgment of the sole Right of the Crown of England to that Island; and yet of late, the Encroachments of the French upon Our said Island, and Our Subjects Trade and Fishery, have been more like the Invasions of an Enemy, then becoming Friends, who enjoy'd the Advantages of that Trade only by Permission.

But that the French King should Invade Our Charibbee Islands, and possess himself of Our Territories of the Province of New-York and of Hudson's-Bay in a

Hostile manner, seizing Our Forts, burning Our Subjects Houses, and enriching his People with the Spoil of their Goods and Merchandizes, detaining some of Our Subjects under the Hardship of Imprisonment, causing others to be inhumanely kill'd, and driving the rest to Sea in a Small Vessel, without Food and Necessaries to support them, are Actions not becoming even an Enemy; and yet he was so far from declaring himself so, that at that very time he was Negotiating here in England by his Ministers, a Treaty of Neutrality and good Correspondence in America.

The Proceedings of the French King against Our Subjects in Europe are so Notorious, that We shall not need to enlarge upon them; His countenancing the Seizure of English Ships by French Privateers, forbidding the Importation of great part of the Product and Manufactures of Our Kingdom, and imposing exorbitant Customs upon the rest, notwithstanding the vast Advantage he and the French Nation reap by their Commerce with England, are sufficient Evidences of his Designs to destroy the Trade, and consequently to ruine the Navigation, upon which the Wealth and Safety of this Nation very much depends.

The Right of the Flag, Inherent in the Crown of England, has been Disputed by his Orders in Violation of Our Sovereignty of the Narrow Seas, which in all Ages has been Asserted by Our Predecessors, and We are resolv'd to Maintain for the Honour of Our Crown, and of the English Nation.

But that which must nearly touch Us, is his unchristian Prosecution of many of Our English Protestant Subjects in France, for matters of Religion, contrary to the Law of Nations, and express Treaties, forcing them to abjure their Religion by strange and unusual Cruelties, and Imprisoning some of the Masters and Seamen of Our Merchant Ships, and Condemning others to the Gallies, upon pretence of having on Board, either some of his own miserable Protestant Subjects, or their Effects; And Lastly, as he has for some years last past, endeavoured by Insinuations and Promises of Assistance to overthrow the Government of England; So now by open and violent Methods, and the actual Invasion of Our Kingdom of Ireland, in support of Our Subjects in Arms, and in Rebellion against Us, he is promoting the utter Extirpation of Our good and Loyal Subjects in that Our Kingdom.

Being therefore thus necessitated to take up Arms, and Relying on the help of Almighty God in Our just undertaking, We have thought fit to Declare, and do hereby Declare War against the French King, and that We will in Conjunction with Our Allies, Vigorously Prosecute the same by Sea and Land (since he hath so unrighteously begun it) being assured of the hearty Concurrence and Assistance of Our Subjects in support of so good a Cause; Hereby Willing and Requiring Our General of Our Forces, Our Commissioners for Executing the Office of High Admiral, Our Lieutenants of Our several Counties, Governours of Our Forts and Garisons, and all other Officers and Soldiers under them, by Sea and Land, to do, and execute all acts of Hostility in the Prosecution of this War against the French King, his Vassals and Subjects, and to oppose their Attempts, Willing and Requiring all Our Subjects to take Notice of the same, whom We henceforth strictly forbid to hold any Correspondence or Communication with the said French King, or his Subjects; And because there are remaining in Our Kingdoms many of the Subjects of the French King; We do Declare and give Our Royal Word, that all such of the French Nation as shall demean themselves dutifully towards Us, and not Correspond with Our Enemies, shall be safe in their Persons and Estates, and free from all molestation and trouble of any Kind.

Given at Our Court at Hampton-Court, the Seventh Day of May, 1689. In the First Year of Our Reign.

God Save King William and Queen Mary.

London, Printed by Charles Bill, and Thomas Newcomb, Printers to the King and Queen's most Excellent Majesties, 1689.

1 p. folio. There are three issues, varying slightly in set-up. Copies in Antiq., Bodl., B. M., Ch., Crawf., Dalk., Guild., P. C., P. R. O., and Q. C.; also in John Carter Brown Library. Printed in "London Gazette," no. 2452.

1690, JULY 14.

[FOR APPREHENDING WILLIAM PENN.]

BY THE KING AND QUEEN.

A PROCLAMATION.

Marie R.

Whereas Their Majesties have received Information That the Persons herein after particularly Named have Conspired together, and with divers other disaffected Persons, to Disturb and destroy Their Government, and for that purpose have Abetted and Adhered to Their Majesties Enemies in the present Invasion, for which cause several Warrants for High Treason have lately been Issued out against them, but they have withdrawn themselves from their usual places of Abode, and are fled from Justice; Their Majesties therefore have thought fit by the Advice of Their Privy Council, to Issue this Their Royal Proclamation: And Their Majesties do hereby Command and Require all Their Loving Subjects to Discover, Take and Apprehend Edward Henry Earl of Litchfeild, Thomas Earl of Aylesbury, William Lord Montgomery, Roger Earl of Castlemaine, Richard Viscount Preston, Henry Lord Belasyse, Sir Edward Hales, Sir Robert Thorold, Sir Robert Hamilton, Sir Theophilus Oglethorp, Colonel Edward Sackvile, Lieutenant Colonel Duncan Abercromy, Lieutenant Colonel William Richardson, Major Thomas Soaper, Captain David Lloyd, William Pen[56] Esq; Edmund Elliot Esq; Marmaduke Langdale Esq; and Edward Rutter wherever they may be found, and to carry them before the next Justice of the Peace, or Chief Magistrate; who is hereby Required to Commit them to the next Goal, there to remain until they be thence delivered by due Course of Law: And Their Majesties do hereby Require the said Justice or other Magistrate immediately to give Notice thereof to Them or Their Privy Council: And Their Majesties do hereby Publish and Declare to all Persons that shall Conceal the Persons above named, or any of them, or be Aiding or Assisting in the Concealing of them, or furthering their Escape, that they shall be proceeded against for such their Offence with the utmost Severity according to Law.

[56] Because of his friendship for James II, William Penn fell under suspicion when William III came to the throne. On February 27, 1689, a warrant was issued by the Privy Council for his arrest upon suspicion of high treason (Privy Council Register, III William, vol. 1, p. 24). In June 1690 the interception of a letter written to him by James II caused him to be brought before the Privy Council. Upon receiving the news of the proclamation including him among the King's enemies, he at once surrenderd himself, but no evidence appearing against him, he was discharged by the court of King's bench on November 28. (*Dict. of National Biography*, xliv, 315).

Given at Our Court at Whitehall the Fourteenth Day of July, 1690.[57] In the Second Year of Our Reign.

GOD SAVE KING WILLIAM AND QUEEN MARY.

London, Printed by Charles Bill and Thomas Newcomb, Printers to the King and Queens most Excellent Majesties. 1690.

1 p. folio. There are two issues, varying slightly in set-up and in the cut of the royal arms. Copies in Antiq., B. M., Crawf., Dalk., D. H., Guild., P. C., P. R. O., and Q. C. Entered on Patent Rolls; entered in Privy Council Register, III William, vol. 1, p. 479. Printed in "London Gazette," July 17, 1690; reproduced in January 1909 number of the "Journal of the Friends Historical Society."

---

[57] Dixon, in his *William Penn* (1872 ed., p. 275), is evidently in error in referring to this proclamation as issued on June 24. J. M. Rigg, in his article on Penn in the *Dictionary of National Biography*, gives the date as July 17, possibly because on one of the two copies of the proclamation in the British Museum someone has written this date, or because it was printed in the *London Gazette* on that day.

1691, FEBRUARY 5.

[FOR APPREHENDING WILLIAM PENN.]

BY THE KING AND QUEEN.

A PROCLAMATION

For Discovering and Apprehending the late Bishop of Ely, William Penn, and James Grahme.

Marie R.

Whereas Their Majesties have received Information, That Francis late Bishop of Ely, William Penn Esquire, and James Grahme Esquire, with other Ill-affected Persons, have Designed and Endeavoured to Depose Their Majesties, and Subvert the Government of this Kingdom, by procuring an Invasion of the same by the French, and other Treasonable Practices, and have to that end held Correspondence, and Conspired with divers Enemies and Traitors, and particularly with Sir Richard Grahme Baronet, (Viscount Preston in the Kingdom of Scotland) and John Ashton Gent. lately Attainted of High Treason; For which Cause several Warrants for High Treason have been Issued out against them, but they have withdrawn themselves from their usual Places of Abode, and are fled from Justice: Their Majesties therefore have thought fit, by and with the Advice of Their Privy Council, to Issue this Their Royal Proclamation; And Their Majesties do hereby Command and Require all Their Loving Subjects to Discover, Take and Apprehend the said Francis late Bishop of Ely, William Penn and James Grahme, wherever they may be found, and to carry them before the next Justice of the Peace, or Chief Magistrate, who is hereby Required to Commit them to the next Goal, there to remain until they be thence Delivered by due Course of Law; And Their Majesties do hereby Require the said Justice or other Magistrate, immediately to give Notice thereof to Them or Their Privy Council. And Their Majesties do hereby Publish and Declare to all Persons that shall Conceal the Persons above named, or any of them, or be Aiding or Assisting in the Concealing of them, or furthering their Escape, that they shall be Proceeded against for such their Offence with the utmost Severity according to Law.

Given at Our Court at Whitehall the Fifth Day of February, 169%1. In the Second Year of Our Reign.

God save King William and Queen Mary.

London, Printed by Charles Bill and Thomas Newcomb, Printers to the King and Queens most Excellent Majesties. 1690.

1 p. folio. There are two issues, varying slightly in set-up and in the cut of the royal arms. Copies in Adv., B. M., Crawf., Dalk., D. H., Guild., P. C., P. R. O., and T. C. D. Entered on Patent Rolls; entered in Privy Council Register, III William, vol. 2, p. 112. Printed in "London Gazette," February 7, 1691; reproduced in the January number of the "Journal of the Friends Historical Society."

1700, JANUARY 29.

[FOR APPREHENDING AUTHOR OF DARIEN LIBEL.]

BY THE KING.

A PROCLAMATION.

WILLIAM R.

Whereas We have been Informed, That a False, Scandalous, and Traiterous Libel, Intituled, An Inquiry into the Causes of the Miscarriage of the Scotch-Colony at Darien, or, An Answer to a Libel, Intituled, A Defence of the Scots Abdicating Darien,[58] has been Printed and Dispersed, the Design of which libel was to Create a Misunderstanding between Our good Subjects of England and Scotland, and to Stir up Sedition and Rebellion, and is Injurious to, and Reflects on the Honour of both Nations: And whereas the Knights, Citizens and Burgesses in Parliament Assembled, have humbly besought Us,[59] to Issue Our Royal Proclamation for Discovering and Apprehending of the Author and Printer of the said Libel; We therefore (with the Advice of Our Privy Council) have thought fit to Issue this Our Royal Proclamation, hereby Requiring and Commanding all Our Loving Subjects whatsoever, to Discover and Apprehend the Author and Printer of the said Libel, to the end they may be dealt withal and proceeded against according to Law. And We do hereby Promise and Declare, That whosoever shall Discover or Apprehend the Author of the said Libel, so as he may be brought to Justice, shall Have and Receive, as a Reward for such Discovery and Apprehending, the Sum of Five hundred Pounds: And that whosoever shall Discover or Apprehend the Printer thereof, so as he may be brought to Justice, shall Have and Receive, as a Reward for such Discovery or Apprehending, the Sum of Two hundred Pounds; Which said respective Sums of Five hundred Pounds and Two hundred Pounds, the Commissioners of Our Treasury are hereby Required and Directed to Pay accordingly.

---

[58] The tract with this title was published with no place of imprint, 1699, pp. 84, and in another edition with the imprint, Glascow, 1700, pp. 112. *A Defence of the Scots abdicating Darien*, pp. 50, has 1700 as the date of imprint. A copy of the first tract is in the Library of Congress, and copies of the last two tracts are in the American Antiquarian Society and John Carter Brown Library.

[59] The House of Commons, on January 15, 1700, resolved that the book was "a false, scandalous, and traitorous libel," that it should be burned by the common hangman, and that an address should be presented to the King seeking a proclamation to apprehend the author of the book (*Commons Journals*, xiii, 123).

And We do hereby further Promise and Declare, That if any Person (other than the Author himself) who was any ways Privy to, or Instrumental in the Printing and Dispersing the said Libel, shall Discover or Apprehend the Author thereof, the Person making such Discovery, or Apprehending the said Author, shall not only have the said Sum of Five hundred Pounds, as aforesaid, but also Our Gracious Pardon for his Offence. And We do hereby strictly Charge and Command all Our Loving Subjects (as they will answer the contrary at their Perils) that they do not any ways Conceal, but Discover and Apprehend the Author and Printer of the said Libel, to the end they may be Proceeded against with the utmost Severity according to Law.

Given at Our Court at Kensington the Twenty ninth Day of January, 1699. In the Eleventh Year of Our Reign.

GOD SAVE THE KING.

London, Printed by Charles Bill, and the Executrix of Thomas Newcomb, deceas'd, Printers to the Kings most Excellent Majesty. 1699.

1 p. folio. There are two issues varying slightly in set-up and in the cut of the royal arms. Copies in Antiq., B. M., Dalk., and P. R. O.; also in John Carter Brown Library. There is also a manuscript draft of this proclamation in British Museum Additional MSS., 21136, fol. 63. Entered on Patent Rolls; entered in Privy Council Register, III William, vol. 5, p. 412. Printed in "London Gazette," February 1, 1700.

1701, MARCH 6.

[FOR THE APPREHENSION OF PIRATES.]

BY THE KING.

A PROCLAMATION.

WILLIAM R.

Whereas We have received Information, That notwithstanding the great Care that hitherto hath been taken to Prevent Piracies, divers Pirates do continue to Infest the Seas wherein Our Subjects Trade, to the great Damage of the Merchants, and Discouragement of Navigation;[60] We therefore (with the Advice of Our Privy Council) have thought fit to Issue this Our Royal Proclamation;[61] And We do hereby Promise and Declare, That if any Person or Persons belonging to the Company or Ships Crew of any Pirate Ship or Vessel, shall at any time, after the Date hereof, Seize, or cause to be Seized, the Person Commanding such Ship or Vessel, and any one or more Persons belonging to such Ship or Vessel, together with the said Ship or Vessel, and Goods, and Deliver them into the Custody of the Chief Magistrate of any of our Ports in Our Kingdoms of England or Ireland; Or in America, into the Custody of Our Governors, or Commanders in Chief of Our Islands, Colonies, or Plantations of Barbados, the Leeward Islands, Jamaica, Bermudos, Virginia, Maryland, New yorke or the Massachusetts Bay in New England, or of the Commander in Chief of Our Ships of War at Newfound Land, for the time being; Or in Africa, into the Custody of the Chief or Chiefs of the Royal African Company at Cape Corfe Castle, on the Gold Coast, at James Fort in the River of Gambia, or at Whiddah in the South-part of Guinea, for the time being; And shall give Evidence against the Persons so Seized and Secured, so as they may be Convicted of Piracy, the Person or Persons so Seizing, or causing to be Seized, such Pirate or Pirates, and Securing such Ship or Vessel, and Goods, as aforesaid, shall not only have Our most Gracious Pardon for the Piracies before that time Committed by him or them, but also, upon the Conviction of such Pirate or Pirates, receive as a Reward for his or their good Service, one moiety of Our Thirds of such Ship or Vessel, and Goods, where no more than those Thirds shall be by Us claimed; But if the whole Ship and

---

[60] The prevalence of piracy in American waters can best be traced in the documents listed in the *Calendars of State Papers, Colonial,* for the last decade of the 17th century.

[61] The draft of this proclamation was referred to the Admiralty, January 23, 1701, to propose the amount of the rewards to be offered, and was sent to the Board of Trade, February 20, 1701, to fix the time when pirates should be allowed to make confessions (*Acts of Privy Council*, ii, 342).

Goods shall belong to Us, for want of a timely and legal Demand thereof by the first Proprietor, then such Person or Persons shall Receive, as a Reward, the Sum of Twenty five Pound for every Hundred Pounds Value of such Ship or Vessel, and Goods; to be paid unto them by such Chief Magistrate, Governor, Commander, or other Persons aforesaid, in the Places where such Seizure and Conviction shall be made; who are hereby Required to Pay the same, upon the Parties producing a Certificate of such Seizure and Conviction made, and Ship or Vessel, and Goods Secured, under the Hands and Seals of the Persons, or the Major Part of them, before whom such Pirates have been Convicted (which Persons are hereby Required to give such Certificate, gratis, on Demand) and upon Producing of which Certificate, We do hereby Require our Judge or Judges of Admiralty in England, or elsewhere, and all other Persons impowered by Commission to Hear and Determine Piracies in Europe, Africa and America, to Stay any further Proceedings against such Person or Persons, who shall produce such Certificate, until he or they can obtain Our most Gracious Pardon. And We do hereby further Declare, That if any Person or Persons, belonging to any Pirate Ship or Vessel, shall Seize and Apprehend the Commanding Officer of any Pirate Ship or Vessel, or any of the Crew belonging to such Ship or Vessel, and shall give Evidence against him or them, as before Directed, so that the said Pirate or Pirates be Convicted, and shall have a Certificate thereof, as aforesaid, though such Person or Persons do not Take or Seize the Ship and Goods, yet such Person or Persons shall have Our most Gracious Pardon for any Piracies before that time by him or them Committed, and shall also have and receive, upon the Conviction of such Commanding Officer, or any of the said Crew of such Pirate Ship, the respective Rewards hereafter mentioned; viz. One Hundred Pounds for the Commanding Officer of such Pirate Ship or Vessel, and Twenty Pounds for every Inferiour Person thereunto belonging, that shall be so Seized and Apprehended, as aforesaid; which Sum or Sums shall be paid to him or them by the Governors or other Persons before mentioned. And for the greater Encouragement of those Persons belonging to any Pirate Ship or Vessel, who shall Seize and Apprehend any Commanding Officer, or any of the Crew belonging to such Ship or Vessel, and shall give Evidence against them, in order to their Conviction, and cause the said Ship or Vessel, and Goods to be Secured, as aforesaid, We do hereby Direct and Require the Commanders of all and every Our Ships of War, That upon any Person or Persons producing to them an Authentick Certificate of his or their having made such Seizure, and of the Conviction of such Commander or others of the said Ships Crew, so Seized by him or them, as aforesaid, or of his or their having Secured the Ship or Vessel, and Goods, as aforesaid, under the Hands and Seals of the Persons, or the Major part of them, before whom such Conviction shall have been made (which Certificate the said Persons are in like manner hereby Required to give, gratis, on Demand) and Desiring to be Entertained in Our Service, to Enter them on Board their Ships, for Victuals and Wages, and to Discharge them again when they shall Desire it. And whereas We are inclined to Believe, That many ignorant Persons have been drawn into this wicked Course of Life, and that they would willingly imbrace all Opportunities of freeing themselves therefrom provided they could be Secure of Pardon, We do hereby Promise and Declare, That if any Person or Persons, Serving on Board any Pirate Ship or Vessel, shall at any time, within Twelve Months after the Date hereof, leave the same, and repair to any of Our Chief Magistrates, Governors, Commanders, or other Persons aforesaid, and before them make Affidavit of the Piracies Committed by the Ship or Vessel whereto they did belong, the Person or Persons, so Leaving such Ship, and making Affidavit, shall have Our Gracious Pardon for the Piracies Committed by him or them before the Twenty fourth Day of June, Seventeen hundred and one, and upon a Certificate of his or their Surrender, and being so Intituled to this Our Gracious Pardon, under the Hands and Seals of any of Our Chief Magistrates, Governors, Commanders, or other Persons aforementioned (which Certificate the said Chief Magistrates, Governors, Commanders, and other Persons are hereby Required to give, gratis, on Demand) the Person or Persons, so leaving such Ship, and making Affidavit, shall in like manner be Intituled to the Advantage of being Entertained on Board any of Our Ships, for Victuals and Wages, as aforesaid. And We do hereby further Publish and Declare, That all such Persons who shall neglect to lay hold of these Our Gracious Offers of Mercy, or who by Complying herewith shall be Pardoned for the Piracies by them Committed to the time of such Pardon, and after such Pardon relapse into the like Evil Practices, shall immediately upon their being Seized (for which all possible Care and Diligence shall be taken) be brought to Tryal, and be Proceeded against with the utmost Severity of Law; We having in pursuance of a late Act of Parliament for that purpose, sent Commissions under Our Great Seal into the East and West Indies, for the speedy Tryal, Condemnation and Execution of all Pirates and Robbers upon the High Seas. Provided always, that nothing herein contained shall extend to the Pardoning of any Person or Persons that shall go out of Europe, or that shall Commit Piracy upon the Seas in Europe, from and after the Date of these Presents, nor to the Pardoning of such as shall Commit Piracy in any Place whatsoever, after notice of this Our Gracious Offer of Pardon, or of Henry Every,[62] alias, Bridgeman.

Given at Our Court at Kensington, the Sixth Day of March, 170⁹⁄₁. In the Thirteenth Year of Our Reign.

GOD SAVE THE KING.

London, Printed by Charles Bill, and the Executrix of Thomas Newcomb, deceas'd, Printers to the Kings most Excellent Majesty. 170⁹⁄₁.

1 p. folio. Copies in Antiq., B. M., P. C., and P. R. O. Entered on Patent Rolls; entered in Privy Council Register, III William, vol. 6, p. 162. Printed in "London Gazette," March 17, 1701.

---

[62] Two proclamations, dated July 17 and August 10, 1696, had been issued offering a reward for the capture of Every for having committed piracies in the seas of India and Persia (*Acts of Privy Council*, ii, 300).

1702, MARCH 9.

[CONTINUING OFFICERS IN THE COLONIES.]

BY THE QUEEN.

A PROCLAMATION.

ANNE R.

Forasmuch as it has Pleased Almighty God, lately to Call unto His Infinite Mercy, the most High and Mighty Prince William the Third, of most Blessed Memory; And whereas by an Act of Parliament made in the Seventh Year of the Reign of the said late King, It is Enacted, That no Commission, either Civil or Military, should Cease, Determine or be Void by reason of the Death or Demise of His said late Majesty, or of any of His Heirs or Successors, Kings or Queens of this Realm, but that every such Commission should Be, Continue and Remain in full Force and Virtue, for the Space of Six Months next after any such Death or Demise, unless in the mean time Superseeded, Determined or made Void by the next and immediate Successor, to whom the Imperial Crown of this Realm, according to the Act of Settlement therein mentioned is Limited and Appointed to Go, Remain and Descend; The Queens most Excellent Majesty,[63] in Her Princely Wisdom and Care of the State, (Reserving to Her Own Judgment hereafter, the Reformation and Redress of any Abuses in Misgovernment, upon due Knowledge and Examination thereof) is Pleased, and doth hereby Signifie and Declare, That all Commissions, both Civil and Military, Granted by His said late Majesty, and in Force at the time of His Death, shall Be, Continue and Remain in full Force and Virtue: And that all Persons, that at the time of the Decease of the late King, were Duly and Lawfully Possessed of, or Invested in any Office or Place of Authority or Government, either Civil or Military, within His Majesties Realms of England, Ireland, the Islands of Jersey and Guernsey, Sark or Alderney, or within His Majesties Colonies and Plantations in America; and Namely all Governors, Lieutenants or Deputy Governors, Counsellors, Judges, Justices, Provost-Marshals, Sheriffs, Justices of the Peace, and all others in Place of Government either Meaner or Superior, as aforesaid, and all other Officers and Ministers shall Be, and hold themselves Continued in the said

---

[63] A form of proclamation of the accession of Queen Anne was provided for the American colonies. It was sent over as a printed sheet, with blanks for the name of the colony and the body issuing the proclamation. Copies of this printed form are in the British Museum and the Public Record Office. A similar form was provided for previous accessions, but does not seem to have been printed, being found in the manuscript Registers of the Privy Council.

Places and Offices, under the same Condition as formerly they Held and Enjoyed the same, until Her Majesties Pleasure be further Known, or that other Provision be made, pursuant to His late Majesties Commissions and Instructions to His Governors and Officers of the Islands, Colonies, and Plantations aforesaid; And that in the meanwhile, for the Preservation of the State, and Necessary Proceedings in Matters of Justice, and for the Safety and Service of the State, all the said Persons, of whatsoever Degree or Condition, may not fail every one severally according to his Place, Office or Charge, to Proceed in the Performance of all Duties thereunto belonging, as formerly Appertained unto them while the late King was Living; And further Her Majesty doth hereby Will and Command all and singular Her Highness Subjects, of what Estate, Dignity or Degree they or any of them be, to be Aiding, Helping and Assisting, and at the Commandment of the said Officers and Ministers, in the Performance and Execution of the said Offices and Places, as they and every of them tender Her Majesties Pleasure, and will answer the contrary at their utmost Perils. And further Her Majesties Will and Pleasure, and Express Command is, That all Orders or Directions Made or Given by the late King of most Blessed Memory the Lords of His Privy Council, or His late Majesties Principal Secretaries of State, or other Legal Authority Derived from His said Majesty in His Life time, shall be Obeyed and Performed by all and every Person and Persons, and all and every Thing and Things to be done thereupon, shall Proceed as Fully and Amply as the same should have been Obeyed or Done in the Life of the said late King, until Her Majesties Pleasure be further Known thereupon.

Given at the Court at St. James's, the Ninth Day of March, In the First Year of Her Majesties Reign, of England, Scotland, France and Ireland, and other Her Majesties Territories and Dominions.

GOD SAVE THE QUEEN.

London, Printed by Charles Bill, and the Executrix of Thomas Newcomb, deceas'd; Printers to the Queens most Excellent Majesty. MDCCI.

1 p. folio. Copies in Antiq., B. M., Crawf., Dalk., P. C., and P. R. O. Entered on Patent Rolls; entered in Privy Council Register, Anne, vol. 1, p. 15.

1704, JUNE 18.

[RATES OF FOREIGN COINS IN PLANTATIONS.]

BY THE QUEEN.

A PROCLAMATION

For Settling and Ascertaining the Current Rates of Foreign Coins in Her Majesties Colonies and Plantations in America.

Anne R.

We having had under Our Consideration the different Rates at which the same Species of Foreign Coins do Pass in Our several Colonies and Plantations in America,[64] and the Inconveniencies thereof, by the indirect Practice of Drawing the Money from one Plantation to another, to the great Prejudice of the Trade of Our Subjects; And being Sensible, That the same cannot be otherwise Remedied, than by Reducing of all Foreign Coins to the same Current Rate within all our Dominions in America; And the Principal Officers of Our Mint having laid before Us a Table of the Value of the several Foreign Coins which usually Pass in Payments in Our said Plantations, according to their Weight, and the Assays made of them in Our Mint, thereby shewing the just Proportion which each Coin ought to have to the other, which is as followeth, viz. Sevill Pieces of Eight, Old Plate, Seventeen Peny-weight Twelve Grains, Four Shillings and Six Pence; Sevill Pieces of Eight, New Plate, Fourteen Peny-weight, Three Shillings Seven Pence One Farthing; Mexico Pieces of Eight, Seventeen Peny-weight Twelve Grains, Four Shillings and Six Pence; Pillar Pieces of Eight, Seventeen Peny-weight Twelve Grains, Four Shillings and Six Pence Three Farthings; Peru Pieces of Eight, Old Plate, Seventeen Peny-weight Twelve Grains, Four Shillings and Five Pence, or thereabouts; Cross Dol-

[64] The attention of the Council of Trade had been frequently called to the disorder in the currency in the Plantations (see *Cal. State Papers, Colonial, 1700*, pp. 108, 393; and Chalmers' *History of Currency in the British Colonies*, pp. 11-15). On November 18, 1703, the Privy Council referred to the Lord Treasurer a representation from the Board of Trade for settling the rates of foreign coins in America, upon which the Lord Treasurer, May 18, 1704, submitted a report from the Officers of the Mint with a table of the weights and values of foreign coins then current in the Plantations (*Acts of Privy Council*, ii, 452). The proclamation which followed was little observed, however, and after several reports on the subject had been rendered, an Act of Parliament was passed April 1, 1708, entitled "An Act for ascertaining the Rates of Foreign Coins in Her Majesty's Plantations in America." (*Statutes of the Realm*, viii, 792. See also *Lords Journals*, xviii, 486, 566; *Commons Journals*, xv, 635; *Acts of Privy Council*, ii, 452). For the action of Massachusetts upon this proclamation, see *Acts and Resolves of the Province of Massachusetts Bay*, viii, 471.

lars, Eighteen Peny-weight, Four Shillings and Four Pence Three Farthings; Duccatoons of Flanders, Twenty Peny-weight and Twenty one Grains, Five Shillings and Six Pence; Ecu's of France, or Silver Lewis, Seventeen Peny-weight Twelve Grains, Four Shillings and Six Pence, Crusadoes of Portugal, Eleven Peny-weight Four Grains, Two Shillings and Ten Pence One Farthing; Three Gilder Pieces of Holland, Twenty Peny-weight and Seven Grains, Five Shillings and Two Pence One Farthing; Old Rix Dollars of the Empire, Eighteen Peny-weight and Ten Grains, Four Shillings and Six Pence; The Half, Quarters and other parts in Proportion to their Denominations, and Light Pieces in Proportion to their Weight: We have therefore thought fit for Remedying the said Inconveniencies, by the Advice of Our Council, to Publish and Declare, That from and after the First Day of January next ensuing the Date hereof, no Sevill, Pillar, or Mexico Pieces of Eight, though of the full Weight of Seventeen Peny-weight and an half, shall be Accounted, Received, Taken, or Paid within any of Our said Colonies or Plantations, as well those under Proprietors and Charters, as under Our immediate Commission and Government, at above the Rate of Six Shillings per Piece Current Money, for the Discharge of any Contracts or Bargains to be made after the said First Day of January next, the Halfs, Quarters, and other lesser Pieces of the same Coins to be Accounted, Received, Taken, or Paid in the same Proportion: And the Currency of all Pieces of Eight of Peru, Dollars, and other Foreign Species of Silver Coins, whether of the same or Baser Alloy, shall, after the said First Day of January next, stand Regulated, according to their Weight and Fineness, according and in Proportion to the Rate before Limited and Set for the Pieces of Eight of Sevill, Pillar, and Mexico; So that no Foreign Silver Coin of any sort be permitted to Exceed the same Proportion upon any Account whatsoever. And We do hereby Require and Command all Our Governours, Lieutenant-Governours, Magistrates, Officers, and all other Our good Subjects, within Our said Colonies and Plantations, to Observe and Obey our Directions herein, as they Tender our Displeasure.

Given at Our Castle at Windsor, the Eighteenth Day of June, 1704. In the Third Year of Our Reign.

GOD SAVE THE QUEEN.

London, Printed by Charles Bill, and the Executrix of Thomas Newcomb, deceas'd; Printers to the Queens most Excellent Majesty. 1704.

1 p. folio. Copies in Antiq., B. M., Crawf., Dalk., P. C., P. R. O., and in N. Y. Historical Society. Entered in Privy Council Register, Anne, vol. 2, p. 132. Printed in "London Gazette," June 22, 1704; also in Boston News-Letter, Dec. 11, 1704.

1708, JUNE 26.

[ENCOURAGING TRADE TO NEWFOUNDLAND.]

BY THE QUEEN.

A PROCLAMATION.

ANNE R.

Whereas by Act of Parliament made in the Tenth and Eleventh Years of the Reign of the late King William the Third, Intituled, An Act to Encourage the Trade to Newfoundland;[65] It was, amongst other Things, Enacted, That from thenceforth all His Majesties Subjects of this Realm, or the Dominions thereto belonging, Trading to Newfoundland, should have Free Trade and Liberty to Take, Bait, and Fish in any the Rivers, Lakes, Creeks, Harbours, or Roads, in or about Newfoundland, the Seas, and Islands thereto adjacent, and to go on Shore on any Part of Newfoundland, or the said Islands, for the Curing, Salting, Drying, and Husbanding of their Fish, and Making Oyl, and to Cut down Wood for Building or Repairing of Stages, Ship-Rooms, Train-Fats, Hurdles, Ships, Boats, and other Necessaries; but that no Alien, or Stranger should Take any Bait, or Use any sort of Trade or Fishing whatsoever, in Newfoundland, or in any of the Places above-mentioned; and that after the Five and twentieth of March, One thousand seven hundred, no Balast, Prest, Stones, or other Things hurtful to the Harbours, should be Thrown out of any Ship or otherwise, but shall be Carried on Shore. And it is thereby further Enacted, That no Person should Destroy or Damage any such Stage or Cook-Room, or any Thing thereto belonging, but should be content with such Stage or Stages only as are needful for them, and leave the same Undamaged; and the same shall be Repaired with Timber fetcht out of the Woods there, and not by the Ruining of other Stages. And it is thereby further Enacted, That whoever should, after the said Five and twentieth Day of March, first Enter with his Fishing-Ship any Harbour or Creek in Newfoundland, should be for that Season Admiral of the said Harbour or Creek, and should Reserve so much Beech or Flakes as should be necessary for his Boats, and One over, as a Privilege for his first Coming thither; and the Master of the Second Fishing-Ship Entring such Harbour or Creek, shall be Vice-Admiral; and the Master of the Third Ship so Entring, Rear-Admiral for that Season; and that the Master of every Fishing-Ship there, shall take no more Beech

---

[65] *Statutes of the Realm*, 10 William III, ch. 14, vol. 7, p. 515. The House of Commons on March 31, 1708, petitioned the Queen that the laws regulating trade with Newfoundland should be enforced (*Commons Journals*, xv, 644, 648). A long address on the subject from the Privy Council to the Queen, May 20, 1708, is printed in the *Acts of the Privy Council*, ii, 553.

or Flakes than for necessary Use; and Persons Possessed of several Places in several Harbours there, shall make Election in which he or they will Abide, within Eight and forty Hours after Demand by any After-comer; And the Admiral of the respective Harbours shall determine all Differences touching that Matter. And it is thereby further Enacted, That all Inhabitants and others, who have Possessed themselves of any Stage, Cook-Room, Beech, or other Place in the said Harbours, which before that time belonged to Fishing-Ships, for the Taking Bait, Fishing, Drying, Curing and Husbanding of Fish, since the Year One thousand six hundred eighty five, should before the said Five and twentieth Day of March, leave the same for the Publick Use of the Fishing-Ships arriving there; and that no Fisherman or Inhabitant in Newfoundland, or other Person, should after the said Five and twentieth Day of March, Possess himself of any the Stages, Cook-Rooms, Beeches, or other Places which, since the Year One thousand six hundred eighty five, did, or thereafter should belong to any Fishing-Ship, before the Arrival of the Fishing-Ships from England, Wales or Berwick, and until such Ships be Provided with Stages, Cook-Rooms, Beeches, and other Places, for taking Bait and Fishing, and for Drying, Curing and Husbanding of Fish: Provided that such Persons, as since the Five and twentieth of March, One thousand six hundred eighty five, have or thereafter should Build any Houses, Stages, Cook-Rooms, Train-Fats, or other Conveniencies for Fishing there, that did not, since the Year One thousand six hundred eighty five, belong to Fishing-Ships, should peaceably enjoy the same. And it is thereby further Enacted, That no By-Boat-Keepers should meddle with any House, Stage, Cook-Room, Train-Fat or other Conveniency, that did, since the Year One thousand six hundred eighty five, belong to Fishing-Ships, or should be made by Ships after the Five and twentieth Day of March, One thousand seven hundred; and that every Master of a By-Boat should carry at least Two Fresh Men in Six, (viz.) One that has made but One Voyage, and One that never was at Sea before; and that every Inhabitant should be obliged to Imploy Two such Fresh Men, as the By-Boat-Keepers are obliged for every By-Boat kept by them; and the Master of every Fishing-Ship should Carry One such Fresh Man that never was at Sea before, in every Five Men they carry; and the Master of every By-Boat, or Fishing-Ship, should make Oath before the Collector, or Principal Officer of the Customs of the Port (which Officers are thereby Impowered to give the said Oath) whence such Ship intends to Sail, That they have such Fresh Men as the said Act directs, and should have a Certificate thereof gratis; And that the Master of any Fishing-Ship, going to Newfoundland, after the said Five and twentieth Day of March, should have One in every Five that is not a Seaman. And it is thereby further Enacted, That no Person should after the said Five and twentieth Day of March, Cut out, or Alter the Mark of any Boat or Train-Fat, to defraud the Owner, or remove the same whence they were left by the Owner, unless in case of necessity, and that upon Notice to the Admiral of the Place; and that no Person should Rind Trees in the Woods growing there, nor set on fire, or Damage the same, except for Fuel for the Ships and Inhabitants, or for Building or Repairs of Houses, Ships, Boats, and Train-Fats, and of the Stages, Cook-Rooms, Beeches, and other Places for taking Bait, Fishing, and Husbanding of Fish there, nor cast Anchor, or do any other Thing so as to Annoy the Haling of Sayns in the usual Baiting Places, or shoot their Sayns upon the Sayns of others, nor steal the Sayns of others, nor any Bait out of anothers Fishing-Boat or Net: And the Admirals of every Port or Harbour in Newfoundland, are required to see the Rules and Orders in the said Act for Regulating the Fishery duly put in Execution, and Yearly to keep a Journal of all Ships, Boats, Stages, Train-Fats, and Seamen in their respective Harbours, and Deliver a Copy thereof to the Privy-Council at their Return to England. And it is thereby further Enacted, That all Differences arising in Newfoundland, or any the Islands there, about the Right and Property of Fishing-Rooms, Stages, Flakes or other Conveniency for Fishing or Curing of Fish, shall be determined by the Fishing Admirals in the several Harbours; and an Appeal is given from such Judgment to the Commanders of the Men of War appointed Convoys for Newfoundland: And that the Inhabitants of Newfoundland, and the Islands adjacent, should strictly observe the Lords Day: And that no Publick-House should on that Day sell any Wine, Beer, Ale, Cyder, or other Strong-Waters, or Tobacco, or other Liquors. And whereas We have been informed of several Abuses by the Masters of Ships, and the Inhabitants, and others contrary to the said Act, (viz.) That the Inhabitants do Rind the Trees, and Ingross and Incroach upon Fishing Ship-Rooms, and destroy several of the Stages, Flakes and Cook-Rooms, and that the Fishing Admirals are negligent in their Duty of putting the said Act in Execution, and of keeping Journals of the Fishery, and that the said Fishing Admirals, being Traders themselves, are partial in their Determination of Differences, and that the Masters of Fishing-Ships, and of By-Boats, do neglect to produce Certificates of their Compliments of Green Men or Fresh Men, contrary to the said Act; Which Matters being lately taken Notice of in the Humble Address of the Knights, Citizens and Burgesses of the last Parliament, We have thought fit, by and with the Advice of Our Privy-Council, to Issue forth this Our Royal Proclamation; And We do hereby strictly Charge and Command all Our Loving Subjects, who may be any ways concerned in Putting the said Laws in Execution, that they take effectual Care to bring to Condign Punishment all manner of Persons who shall be found offending against such Act of Parliament.

Given at Our Court at Kensington, the Twenty sixth Day of June, in the Seventh Year of Our Reign.

GOD SAVE THE QUEEN.

London, Printed by Charles Bill, and the Executrix of Thomas Newcomb, deceas'd; Printers to the Queens most Excellent Majesty. 1708.   (Price Two Pence.)

1 p. folio. Copies in B. M., P. C., and P. R. O. Entered on Patent Rolls; entered in Privy Council Register, Anne, vol. 4, p. 120. Printed in "London Gazette," July 12, 1708.

1711, JUNE 23.

[ESTABLISHING POST OFFICE IN AMERICA.]

BY THE QUEEN.

A PROCLAMATION

For Enforcing the due Execution of the Act, Intituled, An Act for Establishing a General Post-Office for all Her Majesties Dominions, and for Settling a Weekly Sum out of the Revenues thereof, for the Service of the War, and other Her Majesties Occasions.

Anne R.

Whereas by an Act of Parliament made in the Last Session of Parliament, Intituled, An Act for Establishing a General Post-Office for all Her Majesties Dominions, and for Settling a Weekly Sum out of the Revenues thereof, for the Service of the War, and other Her Majesties Occasions,[66] It is Enacted, That from and after the First Day of this Instant June, there be One General Letter-Office and Post-Office Established in the City of London, from whence all Letters and Packets may be with speed and expedition sent into any Part of the Kingdom of Great Britain and Ireland, or to North-America, the West-Indies, or to any other of Our Dominions or Territories, or to any other Kingdom or Country beyond the Seas; at which said Office all Returns and Answers may be Received. And that One Master of the said General Letter-Office and Post-Office shall be appointed by Us, under Our Great Seal of Great Britain, by the Name and Stile of our Postmaster General: And that no Person or Persons whatsoever, in any Part of Our Kingdoms of Great Britain and Ireland, or other Our Plantations or Colonies in the West-Indies and America, other than Our Postmaster General for the time being, and his Deputies, Servants, and Assigns, shall presume to Receive, Take up, Order, Dispatch, Convey, Carry, Recarry, or Deliver any Letter or Letters, Packet or Packets of Letters, other than to and from any Town or Place to or from the next Post-Road or Stage appointed for that Purpose, above Six Miles from a General Office; and other than and except such Letters as shall respectively concern Goods sent by Common known Carriers of Goods, by Carts, Waggons, or Pack-Horses, and which shall be respectively Delivered with the Goods such Letters do concern, without Hire or Reward, or other Profit or Advantage for Receiving or Delivering such Letters; and except Letters of Merchants and Masters, Owners of any Ships, Barques, or Vessels of Merchandize, or any the Cargo or Lading therein, sent on Board such Ships,

---

[66] *Statutes of the Realm,* ix, 393 (9 Anne, ch. 11; ch. 10 in some editions of the Statutes).

Barques, or Vessels of Merchandize, whereof such Merchants or Masters are Owners, and Delivered by any Masters of any such Ships, Barques, or Vessels of Merchandize, or by any other Person Employed by them for the Carriage of such Letters, according to their respective Directions, so as such Letters be Delivered to the respective Persons to whom they shall be Directed, without Paying or Receiving any Hire or Reward, Advantage or Profit for the same in anywise; and except Commissions or the Returns thereof, Affidavits, Writs, Process or Proceeding, or Returns thereof, Issuing out of any Court; and also any Letter or Letters to be sent by any Private Friend or Friends in their way of Journey or Travel, or by any Messenger or Messengers sent on purpose, for or concerning the private Affair of any Person or Persons; or make any Collection of Letters, or Set up or Employ any Foot-Post, Horse-Post, or Packet-Boat, or other Vessel or Boat, or other Person or Persons, Conveyance or Conveyances whatsoever, for the Receiving, Taking up, Ordering, Dispatching, Conveying, Carrying, Recarrying, or Delivering any Letter or Letters, Packet or Packets of Letters, by Sea or by Land, or on any River within Our Dominions, or by means whereof any Letter or Letters, Packet or Packets of Letters, shall be Collected, Received, Taken up, Ordered, Dispatched, Conveyed, Carried, Recarried, or Delivered, by Sea or Land, or on any River within Our Dominions (other than as before Excepted;) or shall presume to Keep, Provide or Maintain Horses or Furniture, for the Horsing of any Person or Persons Riding Post, (that is to say) Riding several Stages upon a Post-Road, and Changing Horses, or shall Lett to Hire, or Furnish any Person or Persons whatsoever with Horses or Furniture for Riding Post, as aforesaid, on any of the Post-Roads or Stages now or hereafter to be Appointed, with or without a Guide or Horn, for Hire or Reward, or on any Agreement or Promise of Reward, or whereby he or they may have any Profit or Advantage, on pain of Forfeiting the Sum of Five Pounds of British Money for every several Offence against the Tenor of the said Act, and also of the Sum of One hundred Pounds of like British Money for every Week that every Offender against the same Act shall Collect, Receive, Take up, Order, Dispatch, Convey, Carry, Recarry, or Deliver any Letter or Letters, Packet or Packets of Letters, by Sea or Land, or on any River within Our Dominions (other than as before excepted;) or that shall presume to Set up, Continue, or Employ any Foot-Post, Horse-Post, or Packet-Boat, or other Vessel or Boat, or any other Person or Persons, Conveyance or Conveyances whatsoever, for the Receiving, Taking up, Ordering, Dispatching, Conveying, Carrying, Recarrying, or Delivering of any Letter or Letters, Packet or Packets of Letters, by Sea or Land, or on any River within Our Dominions, as aforesaid; which said Penalties and Forfeitures are to be Sued for, and Recovered in such Courts, and to be Received and Divided in such manner, and for such Uses, as in the said Act is for that purpose mentioned, together with full Costs of Suit. But it is by the said Act Provided, That if the Postmaster doth not or cannot Furnish any Person Riding in Post, with sufficient Horses, within one Half Hour after Demand, then such Person is at Liberty to Provide himself as he can to the next Stage, and so at every Stage where he shall not be Furnished, as aforesaid; and the Person who shall Furnish such Horses shall therefore by [be] liable to any Penalty by reason thereof. And by a Proviso contained in the said Act, it is Declared, That nothing in the Exception above mentioned contained, shall be construed to extend to give any Licence or Authority to any Common known Carriers of Goods, by Carts, Waggons, or Pack-Horses, their Servants or Agents, to Receive, Collect or Deliver, with or without Hire, any Letter or Letters, Packet or Packets of Letters whatsoever, that do not concern Goods in their Carts, Waggons, or on their Pack-Horses; nor to any Owners or Drivers of Stage-Coaches; nor to any Masters, Owners or Commanders of Boats called Passage-Boats, sailing between any Part of Great Britain or Ireland, and any Parts or Places beyond the Seas, or their Servants or Agents; nor to any Passenger or Passengers on Board such Boats or Vessels; nor to the Owners or Watermen on Board of any Boat, Barge, or Vessel, Passing or Repassing on any River or Rivers, to and from any Parts of Great Britain and Ireland, North-America, or the West-Indies, or other Our Dominions or Territories, although such Drivers of Stage-Coaches, Owners, Masters or Commanders of Boats called Passage-Boats, or Passengers therein, Owners or Watermen on Board of any such Boat, Barge, or Vessel, Passing or Repassing on any such River or Rivers, as aforesaid, do not receive any Hire or Reward, or other Advantage for the same; but that all such Carriers, Owners, and Drivers of Stage-Coaches, Owners, Masters or Commanders of Passage-Boats, and the Passengers therein, and all Owners and Watermen on Board of any Boat, Barge, or Vessel, Passing or Repassing on any River or Rivers, to or from any the Parts and Places aforesaid, Collecting and Delivering Letters, as aforesaid, though without Hire or Reward, shall be Deemed and Taken, and are thereby Declared to be Persons Offending against the said Act, and to Forfeit and Pay such Sum and Sums of Money, as Persons Collecting, Receiving, Taking up, Conveying, and Delivering of Letters for Hire, or Setting up, Employing and Maintaining any Posts contrary to the said Act, or that are or shall be concerned therein, are therein, as is herein before mentioned, Enacted to Forfeit and Pay. And by another Proviso in the said Act it is Declared, That nothing in the said Act contained should extend to give Licence to any Person or Persons whatsoever, to make Collection of Letters in or near the City of London, or Suburbs thereof, under Pretence of Conveying the same to any Part or Place in the said City or Suburbs, or to the General Post-Office of the said City, without the Licence and Leave of the Postmaster General for the time being; and that any Person or Persons Acting contrary thereunto, should Forfeit and Pay as Persons Collecting, Receiving, Carrying, Recarrying, and Delivering Letters contrary to the said Act, are thereby Enacted to Forfeit and Pay, and to be Recovered, as aforesaid, with full Costs of Suit. And by the said Act it is further Enacted, That all Letters and Packets, that by any Master of any Ship or Vessel, or any of his Company, or any Passengers therein, shall or may be brought to any Post-Town, or which shall arrive or touch at any Post belonging to any Post-Town within any of Our Dominions, or any the Members thereof, or which shall be on Board any Ship or Vessel that shall or doth touch or stay at any such Post-Town, (other than such Letters as are before excepted) shall by such Master, Passengers, or other Person or Persons, be forthwith delivered to the Deputy or Deputies only of such Postmaster General for the time being, by him appointed for such Place or Post-Town, and to be by such Deputy or Deputies sent Post unto the said General Post-Office, to be delivered according to the several and respective Directions of the same, upon pain of Forfeiting the Sum of Five Pounds of British Money for every several Offence against the Tenor of the said Act, to be Recovered in manner aforesaid, with full Costs of Suit. And for the Encouragement of all such Masters of Ships or Vessels, or such other Persons, on their Arrival at such Ports, as aforesaid, from any Parts beyond the Seas, to deliver unto the Deputy or Deputies of such Postmaster General for such Place or Post-Town at which they shall so touch or arrive, all such Letters and Packets as they shall respectively have on Board such Vessel or Vessels, every such Master or other Person, for every Letter or Packet of Letters he or they shall so deliver unto such Deputy or Deputies, shall receive the Sum of One Peny of such Deputy or Deputies, he or they Signing such Certificate as in the said Act is mentioned. And We being Willing and Desirous that Our Good Subjects should have Early and Sufficient Notice of the Penalties and Forfeitures before mentioned, to the end they may avoid Incurring the same, and that the Revenue granted by the said Act may be duly answered to Us, and all Frauds in Prejudice of the same prevented, have thought fit, and do by this Our Royal Proclamation (by and with the Advice of Our Privy Council) Notifie and Declare to all Our Loving Subjects the Purport and Tenor of the said several Parts of the said Act, hereby Requiring and Commanding all Persons concerned to conform themselves to the said Act.

Given at Our Court at Kensington, the Twenty third Day of June, 1711. In the Tenth Year of Our Reign.

God save the Queen.

London, Printed by the Assigns of Thomas Newcomb, and Henry Hills, deceas'd; Printers to the Queens most Excellent Majesty. 1711.   (Price Two Pence.)

1 p. folio. There are two issues varying in the cut of the royal arms. Copies in B. M. and P. R. O. Entered on Patent Rolls; entered in Privy Council Register, Anne, vol. 5, p. 260. Printed in "London Gazette," June 28, 1711.

1714, OCTOBER 4.

[CONCERNING PASSES FOR SHIPS.]

BY THE KING.

A PROCLAMATION

Requiring all Ships and Vessels, Trading from the Plantations in the way of the Algerines, to Furnish themselves with Passes.

George R.

Whereas pursuant to Treaties Concluded between Our Predecessors, and the Government of Algier,[67] several Passes have been Granted under the Hand and Seal of the High Admirals of Great Britain, or the Commissioners for Executing that Office of Our respective Dominions: And whereas Our Commissioners for Executing the Office of High Admiral, have humbly Represented unto Us, That they have reason to apprehend, that several of the said Passes of the Old Form have been Clandestinely altered, as well in their Dates as otherwise, which may be very Prejudicial to the Trading Ships of Our Subjects: For Preventing whereof We have thought fit, by the Advice of Our Privy Council, to Publish this Our Royal Proclamation, hereby Declaring, That all such Passes of the Old Form, which have been so Issued, shall not Continue in Force longer than the Thirtieth Day of July

---

[67] Since the proclamation of April 1, 1676 (see p. 129, with note) the question of ship passes had been given frequent attention, but seldom directly concerned the American trade. On February 9, 1677, the Privy Council drew up a long set of regulations regarding the form and issuing of passes, with direct reference to the Plantations trade (printed in *Acts of the Privy Council*, i, 692-700) but the proclamation then ordered to be issued to explain these regulations, if published, has not been found. The treaty with Algiers of April 10, 1682, required that all English merchants should have a pass under the seal of the Lord High Admiral or his commissioners and a proclamation was issued April 13, 1683, to that effect. Further proclamations, containing reference to the treaties of 1682 and April 5, 1686, were issued on March 17, 1692 and June 9, 1700, to reinforce these provisions. On February 17, 1698, the Privy Council took action allowing the granting of passes in the Plantations (*Acts of the Privy Council*, ii, 318). Since certain passes for the trade with Algiers had been clandestinely altered, a proclamation was published on January 17, 1714, canceling all passes held twelve months from that date and requiring new ones to be issued (these proclamations are calendared in Lord Crawford's *Tudor and Stuart Proclamations*). In connection with the issuing of the above printed proclamation concerning passes for the Plantations trade, the Privy Council proposed to send a certain number of passes over to the governors of the colonies, there to be issued by them, but to this the government of Algiers objected (*Acts of the Privy Council*, ii, 682).

next. And We do hereby strictly Charge and Command all Our Loving Subjects, who are or shall be possessed of any such Passes, That they do, as soon as may be, return the same into the Office of Admiralty of Great Britain, in order to their being Cancelled. And whereas, pursuant to the late Treaty with Algier, it is absolutely necessary, That all Ships and Vessels belonging to Our Loving Subjects of Great Britain and Ireland, as well as Our Foreign Governments and Plantations, which shall have occasion to Trade to Portugal, the Canaries, Guinea, the Indies, into the Mediterranean, or elsewhere, in the way of the Cruizers of the aforesaid Government of Algier, should be furnished with Passes of the New Form, by or before the said Thirtieth Day of July next, lest by their being met with by the Ships of Algier, unfurnished with such Passes, they be Brought up, and the Ships and Goods Confiscated; We do hereby strictly Charge and Require the Owners and Masters of all Ships and Vessels of Our Loving Subjects Trading, as aforesaid, to take particular Care that they do timely furnish themselves with such Passes of the New Form accordingly.

Given at Our Court at St. James's, the Fourth Day of October, 1714. In the First Year of Our Reign.

God save the King.

London, Printed by John Baskett, Printer to the Kings most Excellent Majesty, And by the Assigns of Thomas Newcomb, and Henry Hills, deceas'd. 1714.

1 p. folio. Copies in B. M., and Signet. Entered on Patent Rolls; entered in Privy Council Register, I Geo., vol. 1, p. 91. Printed in "London Gazette," October 4, 1714.

1714, NOVEMBER 22.

[CONTINUING OFFICERS IN THE COLONIES.]

BY THE KING.

A PROCLAMATION

DECLARING HIS MAJESTIES PLEASURE FOR CONTINUING THE OFFICERS IN
HIS MAJESTIES PLANTATIONS, TILL HIS MAJESTIES PLEASURE SHALL BE
FURTHER DECLARED.

GEORGE R.

Whereas by an Act of Parliament made in the Sixth Year of the Reign of the late Queen Anne, Our most Dear Sister, Intituled, An Act for the Security of Her Majesties Person and Government, and of the Succession to the Crown of Great Britain in the Protestant Line,[68] It was Enacted, amongst other Things, That no Office, Place, or Employment, Civil or Military, within any of Her said late Majesties Plantations, should become Void, by reason of the Demise or Death of Her said late Majesty, but that the Person and Persons in any of the said Offices, Places, or Employments, should Continue in the respective Offices, Places, and Employments for the Space of Six Months next after such Death or Demise, unless sooner Removed and Discharged by Us; And in regard it may happen, that Our Pleasure may not, within the said time, be Declared touching the said Offices, which will, at the end of the said Six Months, become Void: We, for the Preventing the Inconveniences that may happen thereby, in Our Princely Wisdom and Care of the State (reserving to Our Judgment hereafter the Reformation and Redress of any Abuses in Misgovernment, upon due Knowledge and Examination thereof) are Pleased, and do hereby Order, Signifie, and Declare, That all Persons that, at the time of the Decease of Her said late Majesty, were Duly and Lawfully Possessed of or Invested in any Office, Place or Employment, Civil or Military, in any of Our Plantations, and which have not been since Removed from such their Offices, Places, or Employments, shall be and shall hold themselves Continued in the said Offices, Places, or Employments, as formerly they Held and Enjoyed the same, until Our Pleasure be further known, or that other Provision be made, pursuant to Her late Majesties Commissions and Instructions to Her Governors and Officers of the Plantations aforesaid.[69] And that in the mean time for the Preservation of

[68] *Statutes of the Realm,* viii, 738; 6 Anne, ch. 41 (ch. 7 in other editions of the Statutes).

[69] The Privy Council, August 5, 1714, passed an order that all officers in Great Britain and the Plantations should be continued in office, and on August 10 drafted a form of proclamation for proclaiming the King in the Plantations (*Acts of Privy Council,* ii, 682). The

the Peace, and necessary Proceedings in Matters of Justice, and for the Safety and Service of the State, all the said Persons, of whatsoever Degree or Condition, do not fail every one severally, according to his Place, Office, or Charge, to proceed in the Performance and Execution of all Duties thereunto belonging, as formerly appertained unto them while the late Queen was Living. And further We do hereby Will and Command all and singular Our Subjects in the said Plantations, of what Estate or Degree they or any of them be, to be Aiding, Helping and Assisting, at the Commandment of the said Officers, in the Performance and Execution of the said Offices and Places, as they tender Our Displeasure, and will answer for the contrary at their utmost Perils.

Given at Our Court at St. James's, the Two and twentieth Day of November, 1714. In the First Year of Our Reign.

GOD SAVE THE KING.

London, Printed by John Baskett, Printer to the Kings most Excellent Majesty, And by the Assigns of Thomas Newcomb, and Henry Hills, deceas'd. 1714.

1 p. folio. Copies in B. M., Dalk., and P. C. Entered on Patent Rolls; entered in Privy Council Register, I Geo., vol. 1, p. 119. Printed in "London Gazette," November 27, 1714.

---

proclamation proceedings are printed in the records of several of the colonies.

1717, SEPTEMBER 5.

[FOR SUPPRESSING PIRATES IN WEST INDIES.]

BY THE KING.

A PROCLAMATION

For Suppressing of Pirates.

George R.

Whereas We have received Information, That several Persons, Subjects of Great Britain, have, since the Twenty fourth Day of June, in the Year of our Lord One thousand seven hundred and fifteen, committed divers Piracies and Robberies upon the High Seas in the West-Indies, or adjoyning to Our Plantations, which hath, and may Occasion great Damage to the Merchants of Great Britain, and others, Trading into those Parts; And though We have appointed such a Force as We Judge sufficient for Suppressing the said Piracies: Yet the more effectually to put an End to the same, We have thought fit, by and with the Advice of our Privy-Council, to Issue this Our Royal Proclamation; And We do hereby Promise and Declare, That in case any of the said Pirates shall, on or before the Fifth Day of September, in the Year of our Lord One thousand seven hundred and eighteen,[70] Surrender him or themselves to One of Our Principal Secretaries of State in Great Britain or Ireland, or to any Governor or Deputy-Governor of any of Our Plantations or Dominions beyond the Seas, every such Pirate and Pirates, so Surrendring him or themselves, as aforesaid, shall have Our Gracious Pardon of and for such his or their Piracy or Piracies, by him or them Committed before the Fifth Day of January next ensuing. And We do hereby strictly Charge and Command all Our Admirals, Captains, and other Officers at Sea, and all Our Governors and Commanders of any Forts, Castles, or other Places in Our Plantations, and all other Our Officers Civil and Military, to Seize and Take such of the Pirates who shall refuse or neglect to Surrender themselves accordingly. And We do hereby further Declare, That in case any Person or Persons, on or after the Sixth Day of September, One thousand seven hundred and eighteen, shall Discover or Seize, or cause or procure to be Discovered or Seized, any One or more of the said Pirates, so neglecting or refusing to Surrender themselves, as aforesaid, so as they may be brought to Justice, and Convicted of the said Offence, such Person or Persons, so making

---

[70] This date was extended to July 1, 1710, according to a proclamation of December 21, 1718, printed on p. 178. On February 9, 1718, the Attorney-General was requested to interpret the meaning of several clauses in the above proclamation, and the Queries and Answers are printed in full in the *Acts of the Privy Council*, ii, 723.

such Discovery or Seizure, or causing or procuring such Discovery or Seizure to be made, shall have and receive as a Reward for the same, viz. For every Commander of any Pirate-Ship or Vessel the Sum of One hundred Pounds; For every Lieutenant, Master, Boatswain, Carpenter, and Gunner, the Sum of Forty Pounds; For every Inferior Officer the Sum of Thirty Pounds; And for every Private Man the Sum of Twenty Pounds. And if any Person or Persons, belonging to, and being Part of the Crew of any such Pirate-Ship or Vessel, shall, on or after the said Sixth Day of September, One thousand seven hundred and eighteen, Seize and Deliver, or cause to be Seized or Delivered, any Commander or Commanders of such Pirate-Ship or Vessel, so as that he or they be brought to Justice, and convicted of the said Offence, such Person or Persons, as a Reward for the same, shall receive for every such Commander the Sum of Two hundred Pounds; which said Sums the Lord Treasurer, or the Commissioners of Our Treasury for the time being, are hereby required and directed to Pay accordingly.

Given at Our Court at Hampton-Court, the Fifth Day of September, 1717. In the Fourth Year of Our Reign.

God save the King.

London, Printed by John Baskett, Printer to the Kings most Excellent Majesty, And by the Assigns of Thomas Newcomb, and Henry Hills, deceas'd. 1717.

1 p. folio. Copies in Dalk., P. C., and P. R. O. Entered on Patent Rolls; entered in Privy Council Register, I Geo., vol. 2, p. 38. Printed in "London Gazette," September 17, 1717.

1718, DECEMBER 21.

[FOR SUPPRESSING PIRATES IN WEST INDIES.]

BY THE KING.

A PROCLAMATION

GEORGE R.

Whereas We did think fit, by and with the Advice of Our Privy-Council, to Issue Our Royal Proclamation, bearing Date the Fifth Day of September, One thousand seven hundred and seventeen, in the Fourth Year of Our Reign, therein taking Notice, That We had received Information, that several Persons, Subjects of Great Britain, had, since the Four and twentieth Day of June, in the Year of our Lord One thousand seven hundred and fifteen, committed divers Piracies and Robberies upon the High Seas in the West-Indies, or adjoyning to Our Plantations, which had and might Occasion great Damage to the Merchants of Great Britain, and others, Trading into those Parts: And We did thereby Promise and Declare, That in case any the said Pirates should, on or before the Fifth Day of September, One thousand seven hundred and eighteen, Surrender him or themselves in manner as therein is directed, every such Pirate and Pirates, so Surrendring him or themselves, as aforesaid, should have Our Gracious Pardon of and for such his or their Piracy or Piracies, by him or them committed before the Fifth Day of January then next ensuing: And whereas several of the said Pirates, not having had timely Notice of Our said Proclamation, may not have Surrendred themselves within the time therein appointed, and by reason thereof are uncapable of Receiving the Benefit of Our Royal Mercy and Clemency intended thereby: And though We have appointed such a Force, as We judge sufficient for Suppressing the said Piracies, yet the more effectually to put an end to the same, We have thought fit, by and with the Advice of Our Privy-Council, to Issue this Our Royal Proclamation; And We do hereby Promise and Declare, That in case any the said Pirates shall, on or before the First Day of July, in the Year of Our Lord One thousand seven hundred and nineteen, Surrender him or themselves to One of Our Principal Secretaries of State in Great Britain or Ireland, or to any Governor or Deputy-Governor of any of Our Plantations or Dominions beyond the Seas, every such Pirate and Pirates, so Surrendring him or themselves, as aforesaid, shall have Our Gracious Pardon of and for such his or their Piracy or Piracies, by him or them Committed before such time as they shall have received Notice of this Our Royal Proclamation; which Pardon or Pardons We have Authorized and Commanded Our respective Governors to Grant accordingly. And We do hereby strictly Charge and Command all Our

Admirals, Captains, and other Officers at Sea, and all Our Governors and Commanders of any Forts, Castles, or other Places in Our Plantations, and all others Our Officers Civil and Military, to Seize and Take such of the Pirates, who shall refuse or neglect to Surrender themselves accordingly. And We do hereby further Declare, That in case any Person or Persons, on or after the First Day of July, One thousand seven hundred and nineteen, shall Discover or Seize, or Cause or Procure to be Discovered or Seized, any One or more of the said Pirates, so Neglecting or Refusing to Surrender themselves, as aforesaid, so as they may be brought to Justice, and Convicted of the said Offence, such Person or Persons, so making such Discovery or Seizure, or Causing or Procuring such Discovery or Seizure to be made, shall Have and Receive as a Reward for the same, (viz.) For every Commander of any Pirate-Ship or Vessel the Sum of One hundred Pounds; For every Lieutenant, Master, Boatswain, Carpenter, and Gunner, the Sum of Forty Pounds; For every Inferior Officer the Sum of Thirty Pounds; And for every Private Man, the Sum of Twenty Pounds; And if any Person or Persons, belonging to, and being part of the Crew of any such Pirate-Ship or Vessel, shall, on or after the said First Day of July, One thousand seven hundred and nineteen, Seize and Deliver, or cause to be Seized and Delivered, any Commander or Commanders of such Pirate-Ship or Vessel, so as that he or they be brought to Justice, and Convicted of the said Offence, such Person or Persons, as a Reward for the same, shall Receive for every such Commander the Sum of Two hundred Pounds; which said Sums the Lord Treasurer, or the Commissioners of Our Treasury for the time being, are hereby Required and Directed to Pay accordingly.

Given at Our Court at St. James's, the Twenty first Day of December 1718. In the Fifth Year of Our Reign.

God Save The King.

London, Printed by John Baskett, Printer to the Kings most Excellent Majesty, And by the Assigns of Thomas Newcomb, and Henry Hills, deceas'd. 1718.

1 p. folio. Copies in P. C., and P. R. O. Entered on Patent Rolls; entered in Privy Council Register, I Geo., vol. 2, p. 206. Printed in "London Gazette," December 27, 1718.

1722, JULY 19.

[CONCERNING PASSES FOR SHIPS.]

BY THE KING.

A PROCLAMATION

REQUIRING PASSES FORMERLY GRANTED TO SHIPS AND VESSELS TRADING
IN THE WAY OF THE ALGERINE CRUIZERS, TO BE RETURNED INTO THE OFFICE OF
THE ADMIRALTY OF GREAT BRITAIN; AND OTHER PASSES TO BE ISSUED
OF A NEW FORM.

GEORGE R.

Whereas by Our Royal Proclamation bearing Date the Fourth Day of October,[71] in the First Year of Our Reign, We did Charge and Require, that the Owners and Masters of all Ships and Vessels belonging to Our loving Subjects of Great Britain and Ireland, as well as Our Foreign Governments and Plantations, which should have Occasion to trade to Portugal, the Canaries, Guinea, the Indies, into the Mediterranean, or elsewhere, in the Way of the Cruizers of the Government of Algier, should be furnished with Passes of the Form thereby directed, by or before the Thirtieth Day of July, in the Year of Our Lord One thousand seven hundred and fifteen. And whereas Our Commissioners for Executing the Office of High Admiral of Great Britain and Ireland, have humbly represented unto Us, That it may have happened, that when such Ships or Vessels have either been taken in Time of War, or disposed of by Sale in Remote Parts, the Passes issued to them, as aforesaid, may have fallen into the Hands of Foreigners, or have been sold to them with the Ships or Vessels, the latter being directly contrary to the Bonds entred into by the Masters of such Ships and Vessels to return the aforesaid Passes, that so they may be Cancelled at the Admiralty-Office: And Our said Commissioners for Executing the Office of High Admiral of Great Britain and Ireland, having further represented unto Us, That they have been informed, that several Ships and Vessels, belonging to Foreign Princes or States, have by some Indirect Means procured and carried on their Trade with such Passes, as aforesaid; which Indirect Proceedings are not only Prejudical to Our Trading Subjects, and Our Revenue, but may occasion Misunderstandings between Us and the aforesaid Government of Algier: For Preventing whereof We have thought fit, by the Advice of Our Privy-Council, to Publish this Our Royal Proclamation, hereby Declaring, that all such Passes of the Old Form, which have been issued before the Date of this Our Royal Proclama-

---

[71] See proclamation of October 4, 1714, printed on p. 172, with note.

tion, shall not continue in Force longer than for the Space of Twelve Months from the Date hereof (Excepting such as have been granted to such Ships or Vessels as are gone or going to the East-Indies, or to the South-Seas, or any other long Trading Voyages.) And We do hereby strictly Charge and Command all Our Loving Subjects, who are, or shall be possessed of any such Passes, that they do, within the Space of Twelve Months from the Date of this Our Royal Proclamation, as aforesaid, return the same (Excepting such as before excepted) into the Office of the Admiralty of Great Britain, in Order to their being Cancelled; and that they do furnish themselves with Passes of a New Form, under the Hands and Seals of Our Commissioners for Executing the Office of High Admiral of Great Britain and Ireland, in lieu thereof, for their several Ships and Vessels, according to the Treaties concluded between Us and the said Government of Algier, and Our Instructions given to Our said Commissioners for Executing the Office of High Admiral of Great Britain and Ireland touching the same.

Given at Our Court at Kensington the Nineteenth Day of July, in the Eighth Year of Our Reign.

GOD SAVE THE KING.

London, Printed by John Baskett, Printer to the Kings most Excellent Majesty, And by the Assigns of Thomas Newcomb, and Henry Hills, deceas'd. 1722.

1 p. folio. Copies in P. C., and P. R. O. Entered on Patent Rolls; entered in Privy Council Register, I Geo., vol. 4, p. 62. Printed in "London Gazette," July 24, 1722.

1727, JULY 5.

[CONTINUING OFFICERS IN THE COLONIES.]

BY THE KING.

A PROCLAMATION

DECLARING HIS MAJESTY'S PLEASURE FOR CONTINUING THE OFFICERS IN
HIS MAJESTY'S PLANTATIONS, TILL HIS MAJESTY'S PLEASURE SHALL
BE FURTHER SIGNIFIED.[72]

GEORGE R.

Whereas by an Act of Parliament, made in the Sixth Year of the late Queen Anne, of Blessed Memory, intituled, An Act for the Security of Her Majesty's Person and Government, and of the Succession to the Crown of Great Britain in the Protestant Line, it was enacted (amongst other things) That no Office, Place, or Employment, Civil or Military, within any of Her said late Majesty's Plantations, should become void by reason of the Demise, or Death of Her said late Majesty, Her Heirs, or Successors, Kings or Queens of this Realm; but that the Person and Persons in any of the Offices, Places, or Employments aforesaid, should continue in their respective Offices, Places, and Employments, for the Space of Six Months next after such Death or Demise, unless sooner removed and discharged by the next in Succession, to whom the Crown of this Realm should come, remain, and be, according to thé several Acts of Parliament for limiting and settling the Succession of the Crown, as by the said recited Act may appear; and in regard it may happen, that Our pleasure may not within the said time be declared, touching the said Offices, Places, and Employments in Our Foreign Plantations, which will at the End of the said Six Months become void; We, for preventing the Inconveniences that may happen thereby, in Our Princely Wisdom, and Care of the State (reserving to Our Judgment hereafter the Reformation and Redress of any Abuses in the Execution of any such Offices, Places, and Employments, upon due Knowledge and Examination thereof) have thought fit, with the Advice of Our Privy Council, to issue this Our Royal Proclamation, and do hereby order, signify, and declare, That all Persons, that at the Time of the Decease of Our late Royal Father King George the First, of Glorious Memory, were duly and lawfully possessed of, or invested in any Office, Place, or Employment, Civil or Military, in any of

[72] This proclamation, with a form of proclamation for proclaiming the new King, was sent over to each colony. In the state archives of some of the colonies, this correspondence is still preserved, and in some cases has been printed, i.e., in *Pennsylvania Archives*, ser. 1, vol. 1, p. 200.

Our Plantations, and which have not been since removed from such their Offices, Places, or Employments, shall be, and shall hold themselves continued in the said Offices, Places, and Employments, as formerly they held and enjoyed the same, until Our Pleasure be further known, or other Provision be made, pursuant to the Commissions and Instructions of Our said late Royal Father, to His Governors and Officers of the Plantations aforesaid; and that in the mean time, for the Preservation of the Peace, and necessary Proceedings in Matters of Justice, and for the Safety and Service of the State, all the said Persons, of whatsoever Degree or Condition, do not fail every one severally, according to his Place, Office, or Charge, to proceed in the Performance and Execution of all Duties thereunto belonging, as formerly appertained unto them, during the life of Our said late Royal Father; and further, We do hereby will and command all and singular Our Subjects in the said Plantations, of what Estate or Degree they, or any of them be, to be aiding, helping, and assisting, at the Commandment of the said Officers, in the Performance and Execution of the said Offices and Places, as they tender Our Displeasure, and will answer the contrary at their utmost Perils.

Given at Our Court at St. James's, the Fifth Day of July, 1727, and in the First Year of Our Reign.

GOD SAVE THE KING.

London, Printed by John Baskett, Printer to the King's most Excellent Majesty; and Thomas Norris, Assignee to George Hills, 1727.   Price Two Pence.

1 p. folio. Copy in P. C. Entered on Patent Rolls; entered in Privy Council Register, II Geo., vol. 1, p. 32. Printed in "American Weekly Mercury," September 28, 1727.

1729, DECEMBER 31.

[CONCERNING PASSES FOR SHIPS.]

BY THE KING.

A PROCLAMATION

REQUIRING PASSES FORMERLY GRANTED TO SHIPS AND VESSELS, TRADING IN THE WAY OF THE CRUIZERS BELONGING TO THE GOVERNMENTS ON THE COAST OF BARBARY, TO BE RETURNED INTO THE OFFICE OF THE ADMIRALTY OF GREAT BRITAIN, AND OTHER PASSES OF DIFFERENT FORMS TO BE ISSUED.

GEORGE R.

Whereas our Royal Father of Glorious Memory, by His Proclamation, bearing Date the Nineteenth Day of July, in the Eighth Year of His Reign[73], did charge and command all His loving Subjects, who then were, or should be possessed of any Passes, which before the said Nineteenth Day of July had been issued for Ships and Vessels belonging to His said late Majesty's Subjects trading to Portugal, the Canaries, Guinea, the Indies, into the Mediterranean, or elsewhere, in the Way of the Cruizers of the Government of Algiers (excepting such as had been granted to such Ships or Vessels as were gone or going to the East Indies, or the South Seas, or any other long Trading Voyages) to return the same, and furnish themselves with Passes of a new Form, under the Hands and Seals of the Commissioners for executing the Office of High Admiral of Great Britain and Ireland, in lieu thereof, for their several Ships and Vessels, in such Manner as by the said recited Proclamation was directed: And whereas it hath been humbly represented unto Us, That it may have happened that several Passes granted pursuant to the said recited Proclamation may, either by Accident, or undue Means, have fallen into the Hands of Foreigners, who by Colour of such Passes may carry on their Trade; We, taking the Premises into Our Royal Consideration, and judging it necessary to put a speedy Stop to all such indirect Practices, which do not only tend to the Prejudice of Our trading Subjects, but may occasion a Misunderstanding between Us and the Governments on the Coast of Barbary, for preventing thereof have thought fit, by the Advice of our Privy Council, to publish this Our Royal Proclamation, and do hereby declare, That all such Passes of the present Form now in being shall not continue in Force longer than Twelve Months, to be computed from the First Day of March next ensuing the Date hereof (except such Passes as have been granted to Ships gone or going to the East Indies, or other remote Voyages, where they can-

---

[73] See proclamation of July 19, 1722, printed on p. 180.

not be timely furnished with new Passes) and We do hereby strictly charge and command all Our loving Subjects, who are or shall be possessed of any such Passes, That they do within the Space of Twelve Months, to be computed from the said First Day of March next, return the same (except such as are before excepted) into the Office of the Admiralty of Great Britain, or to the respective Collectors of Our Customs at the Out-Ports of Great Britain and Ireland, or to the Governors of some of Our Foreign Plantations or Dominions, in order to their being cancelled; and that they do furnish themselves with Passes of a new Form, under the Hands and Seals of our Commissioners for executing the Office of High Admiral of Great Britain and Ireland, in lieu thereof, for their several Ships and Vessels, according to the Treaties subsisting between Us and the said Governments on the Coast of Barbary, and the Regulations made by Our said Royal Father, by Order in His Privy Council, on the Fourteenth Day of June, in the Year One thousand seven hundred and twenty two, and Our Instructions given to Our said Commissioners for executing the Office of High Admiral of Great Britain and Ireland, touching the same: And whereas many Ships and Vessels belonging to Our loving Subjects continue several Years trading from Port to Port in the Mediterranean without returning Home, whereby they cannot so conveniently procure their Passes to be exchanged, We do hereby, for the Ease of Our Trading Subjects, publish and declare Our Pleasure, That upon the Application of any Owner of any Ship or Vessel, or other substantial Merchant, to the Office of the Admiralty of Great Britain, and Oath made by him of the Property of such Ship or Vessel, and that Three Fourths of the Company are Our Subjects, according to an Act made in the Twelfth Year of the Reign of Our Royal Predecessor King Charles the Second [intituled, An Act for the Encouraging and Increasing of Shipping and Navigation] and upon entring into the usual Bond for the Return of such Pass at the End of the Voyage, it shall and may be lawful for Our Commissioners for executing the Office of High Admiral of Great Britain and Ireland, or Our High Admiral of Great Britain and Ireland for the time being, and they are respectively impowered to make out a new Pass for such Ship or Vessel, and send the same to such of His Majesty's Consuls in the Mediterranean, as the said Owner or Merchant shall desire, with Direction to such Consul, that upon Application to him from the Master of the Ship for which the Pass is made out, and surrendering up his old Pass, and entring into a like Bond for the Return of such new Pass, he shall deliver out the said new Pass to such Master, and transmit the old one, with the Bond, to the Office of the Admiralty of Great Britain. And in order more effectually to hinder for the future any Abuses that may be attempted by Foreigners relating to the new Passes to be issued as aforesaid, We do hereby further declare Our Royal Will and Pleasure, That all such new Passes to be hereafter issued for any Ships or Vessels whatsoever belonging to any of Our Subjects of the Island of Minorca or Gibraltar, shall be made out in a peculiar Form, different from the Form of the new Passes to be issued for Ships and Vessels belonging to any other Part of our Dominions, and that such new Passes shall be lodged with the respective Governors, Lieutenant Governors, or Commanders in Chief for the time being, of the said Island of Minorca and Gibraltar, and issued out only by them, according to the Regulations made by Our said Royal Father in Council, as aforesaid; and the said respective Governors, Lieutenant Governors, and Commanders in Chief are hereby charged and required not to issue or deliver out any such Passes to any Persons whatsoever, other than such as are really Our Subjects inhabiting in the said Island of Minorca or Gibraltar respectively, and strictly to conform themselves in all respects to the Regulations and Instructions made and given, as aforesaid. And We do hereby further publish and declare, That by Our Orders made in Our Privy Council on the Eighteenth Day of this instant December, We have ordered and directed, that the proper Officers of Our Customs in the several Ports of Our Kingdoms of Great Britain and Ireland do demand of the Masters of all Merchant Ships, so soon as they shall return into Port from a Foreign Voyage, all Passes granted as aforesaid, which shall be in their Possession, to be produced to the said respective Officers of Our Customs; and that if the same shall appear to be of an older Date than Twelve Months for Ships and Vessels trading on this side the Streights Mouth, or for Ships and Vessels trading to a greater Distance, in case the Voyages of such last mentioned Ships and Vessels shall be determined, then such Passes shall be delivered up to the said respective Officers of Our Customs, and be by them returned to the Office of the Admiralty of Great Britain; and in case the Master of any such Ship or Vessel shall refuse to produce or deliver up such Passes, according to the true Intent of Our said Order, then the said Officers shall certify the Name of every such Master, and of the Ship or Vessel, to Our Commissioners for executing the Office of High Admiral of Great Britain and Ireland, or to Our High Admiral of Great Britain and Ireland for the time being, to the end that Directions may be given for putting the Bond, entered into on the granting any such Pass, in Suit. And all Our Governors, Lieutenant Governors, and Commanders in Chief of any of Our Islands, Colonies, or Plantations, Consuls residing in Foreign Parts, and all other Our Officers and Ministers whatsoever, and all other Our loving Subjects whom it may concern, are hereby expressly required and commanded to yield due Obedience unto, and strictly to observe all the Orders, Instructions, Regulations, and Directions before mentioned, on Pain of Our high Displeasure.

Given at Our Court at St. James's the Thirty first Day of December, 1729. in the Third Year of Our Reign.

GOD SAVE THE KING.

London, Printed by the Assigns of His Majesty's Printer, and of Henry Hills, deceas'd. 1729.

1 p. folio. Copies in Dalk., and P. C. Entered in Privy Council Register, II Geo., vol. 2, p. 126. Printed in "London Gazette," January 3, 1730.

1740, APRIL 9.

[ENCOURAGING TRADE WITH AMERICA.]

BY THE KING.

A PROCLAMATION

GEORGE R.

Whereas by an Act passed this present Sessions of Parliament, intituled, An Act for the more effectual securing and encouraging the Trade of his Majesty's British Subjects to America, and for the Encouragement of Seamen to enter into his Majesty's Service;[74] it is, among other Things, enacted, for the encouraging his Majesty's Subjects to engage in joint and united, as well as separate Expences, Expeditions, and Adventures, That We, our Heirs, and Successors, be impowered, from time to time, during the Continuance of the present or any future War[75], to grant Charters or Commissions for the more effectual enabling any Societies, or particular Persons to join in Expeditions by Sea or Land, and to sail to, and in any of the Seas in America, for the attacking, taking, or destroying any Ships, Goods, Moveables or Immoveables, Settlements, Factories, Creeks, Harbours, Places of Strength, Lands, Forts, Castles, and Fortifications, now belonging, or hereafter to belong to, or to be possest by any Enemy, in any Part or Parts of America; and for the better making and carrying on any Preparations for such Purposes, and for the making and assuring to the Societies or Persons concerned, their Heirs, Successors, Executors, Administrators, and Assigns, full and undoubted Properties, Rights, and Titles, in and to the same, which such Societies or Persons shall take or cause to be taken from the Enemy, under such Regulations, and in such Manner and Form, as We, our Heirs and Successors, shall think fit, and at any Times hereafter, by any further Grants or Charters to confirm, and further assure the Premisses to them, so as to enable them to have and enjoy the full Benefit thereof, but so, as that nothing therein contained shall extend to exclude or restrain any of our Subjects from having a full and free Trade to and in any Part of America: And whereas We are desirous, that none of our loving Subjects should be ignorant of the said Encouragement, We have thought fit, with the Advice of our Privy Council, to publish the same, by this Our Royal Proclamation, to the End that all Officers, Seamen, Marines, Soldiers, and others, Our Subjects, may be fully informed of the Benefit thereby intended for such of them, as shall be willing to assist by their Endeavours in the vigorous Prosecution of the War, and the Annoyance of the Enemy.

----

[74] *"Statutes at Large"* (*Basket*, 1764), vi, 379.

[75] War with Spain was declared October 19, 1739.

Given at our Court at St. James's the Ninth Day of April, 1740, in the Thirteenth Year of our Reign.

GOD SAVE THE KING.

London, Printed by John Baskett, Printer to the King's most Excellent Majesty. 1740.

1 p. folio. Copies in Dalk., and P. C.; also in N. Y. Public Library. Entered on Patent Rolls; entered in Privy Council Register, II Geo., vol. 7, p. 9. Printed in "London Gazette," April 12, 1740.

1740, JUNE 19.

[PROVIDING FOR DISTRIBUTION OF PRIZE MONEY.]

BY THE LORDS JUSTICES.

A PROCLAMATION

APPOINTING THE DISTRIBUTION OF PRIZES TAKEN, AND THE BOUNTY FOR TAKING SHIPS OF WAR OF THE ENEMY.

Jo. Cant.	Hervey C. P. S.	Pembroke,
Hardwicke C.	Dorset,	Ilay,
Wilmington P.	Devonshire,	Holles Newcastle.[76]

Whereas by an Act of Parliament made in the last Session of Parliament, intituled, An Act for the more effectual securing and encouraging the Trade of His Majesty's British Subjects to America, and for the Encouragement of Seamen to enter into His Majesty's Service, it is, amongst other Things, enacted, That the Flag Officers, Commanders, and other Officers, Seamen, Marines, and Soldiers on Board every Ship and Vessel of War, in His Majesty's Pay, shall have the sole Interest and Property of and in all and every Ship, Vessel, Goods, and Merchandize which they shall take after the Fourth Day of January, in the Year of Our Lord One thousand seven hundred and thirty nine,[77] in Europe, and after the Twenty Fourth Day of June, in the Year of Our Lord One thousand seven hundred and forty, in any other Part of the World (being first adjudged lawful Prize, in any of His Majesty's Courts of Admiralty in Great Britain, or in His Plantations in America, or elsewhere) to be divided in such Proportions, and after such Manner, as His Majesty, His Heirs, and Successors shall think fit to order and direct by Proclamation, to be issued for that Purpose. And as a farther Encouragement to the Officers, Seamen, Marines, Soldiers, and others on Board His Majesty's Ships of War, as also of Privateers, to attack, take, and destroy any Ships of Force belonging to the Enemy, it is thereby also enacted, That there shall be paid by the Treasurer of His Majesty's Navy, upon Bills to be made forth by the Commissioners of the Navy, to be paid according to the Course thereof, without Fee or Reward, unto the Officers, Seamen, Marines, Soldiers, and others that shall have been actually on Board such

---

[76] This proclamation was issued by the Lords Justices in the absence of the King, who from May to October, 1740, was at Hanover endeavoring to secure the allegiance to England of Frederick the Great.

[77] 1739-40. War had been declared with Spain, October 19, 1739.

of His Majesty's Ship or Ships of War, or Privateer or Privateers, in any Action where any Ship or Ships of War, or Privateers shall have been taken from the Enemy, sunk, burnt, or otherwise destroyed, Five Pounds for every Man, which was living on Board any Ship or Ships so taken, sunk, burnt, or otherwise destroyed, at the Beginning of the Engagement between them, the Numbers of such Men to be proved by the Oaths of Three or more of the chief Officers or Men, which were belonging to the said Ship or Ships of War, or Privateers of the Enemy, at the Time of her or their being taken as Prize, sunk, burnt, or otherwise destroyed, before the Mayor, or other chief Magistrate of the Port, whereunto any Prize, or Officers, or Men of such Ships as were sunk, burnt, or otherwise destroyed, shall be brought; which Oaths the said Mayor, or other chief Magistrate of any such Port is hereby impowered and required to administer, and shall forthwith grant a Certificate thereof, without Fee or Reward, directed to the Commissioners of the Navy: Upon producing which Certificate to the Commissioners of the Navy, together with an authentick Copy of the Condemnation of such Ship so taken; or if such Ship be sunk, burnt, or otherwise destroyed, on producing only a Certificate from the Mayor, or other chief Magistrate, as aforesaid, the said Commissioners of His Majesty's Navy, or such Person or Persons as they shall appoint for that Purpose, shall, according to the Course of the Navy, within Fifteen Days, make out Bills for the Amount of such Bounty, directed to the Treasurer of the Navy, payable to, and to be divided amongst the Officers, Seamen, Marines, and Soldiers on Board His Majesty's Ships of War, in Manner, Form, and Proportion, as, by His Majesty's Proclamation, to be issued for that Purpose, shall be directed and appointed; and amongst the Owners, Officers, and Seamen of any private Vessel, or Ship of War, in such Manner and Proportion, as, by any Agreement in Writing, they shall have entered into for that Purpose, shall be directed; We taking the Premisses into Consideration, do, pursuant to the said Act of Parliament (with the Advice of His Majesty's Privy Council) by this Proclamation order, direct, and appoint, that the neat Produce of all Prizes taken by His Majesty's Ships of War, and Bounty Money for Prisoners taken in such Prizes, be divided into Eight equal Parts, whereof the Captain or Captains of any of His Majesty's Ships of War, who shall be actually on Board at the taking of any Prize, shall be allowed Three Eighth Parts; But in case any Prize shall be taken by any Ship or Ships of War, under the Command of a Flag or Flags, the Flag Officer or Officers being actually on Board, or directing and assisting in the Capture, to have One Eighth Part of the said Three Eighths; to the Captains of the Marines, and Land Forces, Sea Lieutenants, and Master on Board any such Ships, shall be allowed One Eighth Part, to be equally divided amongst them; to the Lieutenants and Quarter-masters of Marines, and Lieutenants, Ensigns, and Quarter-masters of Land Forces, Boatswain, Gunner, Purser, Carpenter, Masters, Mate, Chirurgeons, and Chaplain on Board any such Ship, One Eighth Part to be equally divided amongst them; to the Midshipmen, Carpenter's Mates, Boatswain's Mates, Gunner's Mates, Master at Arms, Corporals, Yeoman of the Sheets, Coxswain, Quarter-master, Quarter-master's Mates, Chirurgeon's Mates, Yeoman of the Powder Room, and Serjeants of Marines or Land Forces on Board any such Ships, One Eighth Part to be equally divided amongst them; to the Trumpeters, Quarter-gunners, Carpenter's Crew, Steward, Cook, Armourer, Steward's

Mate, Cook's Mate, Gunsmith, Cooper, Swabber, ordinary Trumpeter, Barber, able Seamen, ordinary Seamen, and Marine or other Soldiers, Two Eighth Parts, to be equally divided amongst them: And in case any Sea Captain, inferior Commission or Warrant Sea Officers, belonging to any Ship of War, for whom any Shares of Prizes are hereby allowed, be absent, and not on Board at the Time of the Capture of any Prize, the Share of such Sea Captain, inferior Commission, or Warrant Sea Officer, shall be cast into the Shares hereby allowed to the Trumpeter, Quarter-gunners, Carpenter's Crew, Steward, Cook, Armourer, Steward's Mate, Cook's Mate, Gunsmith, Cooper, Swabber, ordinary Trumpeter, Barber, able Seamen, ordinary Seamen, and Marine or other Soldiers, to be equally divided amongst them; provided that if any Officer or Officers on Board any of His Majesty's Ships of War, at the Time of taking any such Prizes, shall have more Commissions, or Offices, than one, he or they shall be intitled only to the Share or Shares of such Prizes, which, according to the above mentioned Distribution, shall belong to his or their respective superior Commissions or Offices. And We do hereby strictly enjoin all and every Commander and Commanders of any Ships of War, taking any Prize, as soon as may be, to transmit, or cause to be transmitted, to the Commissioners of His Majesty's Navy, a true List of the Names of all the Officers, Seamen, Marines, Soldiers, and others, who were actually on Board His Majesty's Ships of War, under his or their Command, at the taking such Prize; which List shall contain the Quality of the Service of each Person on Board and be subscribed by the Captain or commanding Officer and Three or more of the chief Officers on Board. And We do hereby require and direct the Commissioners of His Majesty's Navy, or any Three or more of them, after Condemnation of such Prize, to examine, or cause to be examined such List, by the Muster-book of such Ships of War, and Lists annex'd thereto, to see that such List doth agree with the said Muster-book and annex'd Lists, as to the Names, Qualities, or Ratings of the Officers, Seamen, Marines, Soldiers, and others, belonging to such Ship of War; and upon Request forthwith to grant a Certificate of the Truth of any List transmitted to them, to the Agents nominated and appointed by the Captors pursuant to the said Act, to take care or dispose of such Prize, and also upon Application to them, to give or cause to be given unto the Agents, who shall at any Time or Times be appointed, as aforesaid, by the Captors of any Prizes taken by any of the Ships of War of His Majesty, all such Lists, from the Muster-book of any such Ships of War, and annexed Lists, as the said Agents shall find requisite for their Direction, in paying the Produce of such Prizes, or the Bounty, in case any Bounty shall be due for taking the same, and to be otherwise aiding and assisting to the said Agents, as shall be necessary.

Given at Whitehall the Nineteenth Day of June, 1740, and in the Fourteenth Year of His Majesty's Reign.

GOD SAVE THE KING.

London, Printed by John Baskett, Printer to the King's most Excellent Majesty. 1740.

1 p. folio. Copies in Antiq., Dalk., and P. C. Entered in Privy Council Register, II Geo., vol. 7, p. 118. Printed in "London Gazette," June 24, 1740.

1741, JUNE 18.

[REGULATING DISTRIBUTION OF PRIZES.]

BY THE LORDS JUSTICES.

A DECLARATION

APPOINTING THE DISTRIBUTION OR PRIZES TAKEN BY WAY OF REPRIZAL
BEFORE HIS MAJESTY'S DECLARATION OF WAR.

Wilmington, P.	Devonshire,	Montagu,	Cha. Wager.[78]
Dorset,	Holles Newcastle,	Pembroke,	

His Majesty having, on the Tenth Day of July, One thousand seven hundred and thirty nine, taken into His serious Consideration the many and repeated Depredations which had been committed, and the many unjust Seizures which had been made in the West Indies, and elsewhere, by Spanish Guarda Costas, and Ships acting under the Commissions of the King of Spain, or his Governors, contrary to the Law of Nations, and in Violation of the Treaties subsisting between the Crown of Great Britain and Spain, whereby His Majesty's trading Subjects had sustained great Losses; and His Majesty having determined to take such Measures as were necessary for vindicating the Honour of His Crown, and for procuring Reparation and Satisfaction to His injured Subjects, was pleased, by and with the Advice of His Privy Council, upon the said Tenth Day of July, to order that General Reprizals should be granted against the Ships, Goods, and Subjects of the King of Spain; so that, as well His Majesty's Fleet and Ships, as also all other Ships and Vessels that should be commissionated by Letters of Marque or General Reprizals, or otherwise, by His Majesty's Commissioners for executing the Office of Lord High Admiral of Great Britain, should and might lawfully seize all Ships, Vessels, and Goods belonging to the King of Spain, or his Subjects, or others inhabiting within any the Territories of the King of Spain, and bring the same to Judgement in any of the Courts of Admiralty within His Majesty's Dominions:

> [The remainder of this proclamation, which has no further direct reference to the American plantations, provides for the distribution of the prize money arising from the sale of Spanish vessels seized between July 10 and the time of the declaration of war, October 19, 1739: namely, that one half should go to those who had suffered from unjust Spanish depredation according to such

---

[78] Issued by the Lords Justices, during the absence of the King at Hanover.

regulations as should later be determined, and one half should go to officers and sailors concerned in the capture according to the regulations of the Proclamation of June 19, 1740. Commanders who had taken prizes were to transmit to the Commissioners of the Navy true lists of all officers and seamen on board at the time of capture.]

Given at Whitehall the Eighteenth Day of June, 1741, in the Fifteenth Year of His Majesty's Reign.

GOD SAVE THE KING.

London, Printed by John Baskett, Printer to the King's most Excellent Majesty. 1741.

1 p. folio. Copies in Antiq., and P. C. Entered in Privy Council Register, II Geo., vol. 7, p. 490. Printed in the "London Gazette," June 20, 1741.

1741, JUNE 18.

[REGULATING DISTRIBUTION OF PRIZES.]

BY THE LORDS JUSTICES.

A DECLARATION

APPOINTING THE DISTRIBUTION OF PRIZES TAKEN SINCE THE DECLARATION OF
WAR, AND BEFORE THE COMMENCEMENT OF THE ACT OF PARLIAMENT
FOR GRANTING THE PRIZES TO THE CAPTORS.

Wilmington, P.	Devonshire,	Montagu,	Cha. Wager.
Dorset,	Holles Newcastle,	Pembroke,	

Whereas by an Act of Parliament made in the Thirteenth Year of His Majesty's
Reign, intituled, An Act for the more effectual securing and encouraging the Trade
of His Majesty's British Subjects to America, and for the Encouragement of Seamen to enter into His Majesty's Service, it is among other Things enacted, That the
Flag Officers, Commanders, and other Officers, Seamen, Marines, and Soldiers on
Board every Ship and Vessel of War in His Majesty's Pay, shall have the sole Interest
and Property of and in all and every Ship, Vessel, Goods, and Merchandize which
they shall take after the Fourth Day of January, in the Year of our Lord One thousand seven hundred and thirty-nine in Europe; and after the Twenty fourth Day of
June, in the Year of our Lord One thousand seven hundred and forty, in any other
Part of the World (being first adjudged lawful Prize in any of His Majesty's Courts
of Admiralty in Great Britain, or in His Plantations in America, or elsewhere) to
be divided in such Proportions, and after such Manner, as His Majesty, His Heirs,
and Successors shall think fit to order and direct, by Proclamation to be issued for
that Purpose, in Pursuance whereof a Proclamation was issued on the Nineteenth
of June, One thousand seven hundred and forty, directing in what Manner and
Proportion the said Prizes should be distributed among the Captors: And whereas
between the Time of His Majesty's Declaration of War against Spain, which was on
the Nineteenth of October, One thousand seven hundred and thirty-nine, and the
aforementioned Fourth of January, One thousand seven hundred and thirty nine,
His Majesty's Ships of War have seized and taken in Europe several Ships, Vessels,
and Goods belonging to the Enemy; and between the said Nineteenth of October
One thousand seven hundred and thirty-nine, and the said Twenty Fourth of June,
One thousand seven hundred and forty, His Majesty's Ships of War have taken
divers other Ships, Vessels, and Goods of the Enemy, in other Parts of the World,
the Property whereof became vested in His Majesty;

[The remainder of the proclamation provides for the distribution of prize money arising from the sale of the enemy's vessels seized within the specified intervals, among the officers and seamen of the ships concerned in the capture, according to the proclamation of June 19, 1740.]

Given at Whitehall the Eighteenth Day of June, One thousand seven hundred and forty one, in the Fifteenth Year of His Majesty's Reign.

GOD SAVE THE KING.

London, Printed by John Baskett, Printer to the King's most Excellent Majesty. 1741.

1 p. folio. Copy in P. C. Entered in Privy Council Register, II Geo., vol. 7, p. 493. Printed in "London Gazette," June 20, 1741.

1744, MARCH 29.

[DECLARATION OF WAR AGAINST FRANCE.]

HIS MAJESTY'S.

DECLARATION

Of War against the French King.

George R.

The Troubles, which broke out in Germany, on Account of the Succession of the late Emperor Charles the Sixth, having been begun, and carried on, by the Instigation, Assistance, and Support of the French King, with a View to overturn the Balance of Power in Europe, and to extend the dangerous Influence of that Crown, in direct Violation of the solemn Guaranty of the Pragmatic Sanction given by him in the Year One thousand seven hundred and thirty eight, in Consideration of the Cession of Lorraine; and We having, on Our Part, executed Our Engagements for maintaining the Pragmatic Sanction, with that good Faith, which is inseparable from Us; and having opposed the Attempts made against the Dominions of the Queen of Hungary; We are not surprised, that Our Conduct, in this Respect, should have drawn upon Us the Resentment of the French King, who has found his ambitious Views, in a great Measure, disappointed by the Assistance We have furnished to Our Ally, unjustly attacked by him; or that he should alledge it as a principal Reason for declaring War against Us.

From the Time, that We found Ourselves obliged, for the Maintenance of the just Rights of Our Subjects, to enter into a War with Spain, instead of observing a strict Neutrality, which We might have promised Ourselves on the Part of the French King, from whom We were even founded by Treaty to have demanded Assistance; he has given Encouragement and Support to Our Enemies, by conniving at his Subjects acting as Privateers under Spanish Commissions, both in Europe and America; and by sending in the Year One thousand seven hundred and forty, a strong Squadron into the American Seas, in order to prevent Us, from prosecuting the just War, which We were carrying on against Spain, in those Parts; And We have the most authentick Proof, that an Order was given to the Commander of the French Squadron, not only to act in a hostile Manner against Our Ships, either jointly with the Spaniards, or separately; but even to concert Measures with Our Enemies, for attacking one of Our principal Dominions in America; a Duplicate of that Order dated the Seventh of October, One thousand seven hundred and forty, having fallen into the Hands of the Commander in Chief of Our Squadron in the

West Indies. This injurious Proceeding was greatly aggravated by the French Minister at Our Court, having declared on Occasion of sending the said Squadron, that the French King was very far from having any Design, or Intention, of breaking with Us.

The same offensive Conduct was continued, on the Part of the French King, towards Us, by his Squadron in the Mediterranean, in the Year One thousand seven hundred and forty one, joining with, and protecting the Ships of Our Enemies, in Sight of Our Fleet, which was preparing to attack them.

These unwarrantable Proceedings; The notorious Breach of Treaties, by repairing the Fortifications, and erecting New Works at Dunkirk; the open Hostilities lately committed against Our Fleet in the Mediterranean; the Affront and Indignity offered to Us, by the Reception of the Son of the Pretender to Our Crown, in the French Dominions; the Embarkation actually made at Dunkirk, of a considerable Body of Troops, notoriously designed for an Invasion of this Kingdom, in Favour of the Pretender to Our Crown; and the sending a Squadron of French Ships of War into the Channel, to support the said Embarkation and Invasion; will be lasting Monuments of the little Regard had by the French Court, for the most solemn Engagements, when the Observance of them is inconsistent with Interest, Ambition, or Resentment.

We cannot omit taking Notice of the unjust Insinuations contained in the French King's Declaration of War against Us, with respect to the Convention made at Hanover, in October, One thousand seven hundred and forty one. That Convention, regarding Our Electorate only, had no Relation to Our Conduct as King of Great Britain: the Allegations concerning it, are groundless and injurious: Our Proceedings in that Respect, having been perfectly consistent with that good Faith which We have always made the Rule of Our Actions.

It is unnecessary to mention the Objections made to the Behaviour of Our Ministers in Foreign Courts; since it is notorious, that the principal View, and Object, of the Negotiations of the French Ministers in the several Courts of Europe, have been, either to stir up intestine Commotions in the Countries, where they resided; or to create Differences, and Misunderstandings, between them, and their respective Allies.

The Charge of Piracy, Cruelty, and Barbarity against Our Ships of War, is equally unjust and unbecoming; and We have all such Proceedings so much in Abhorrence, that, if any Practices of that Nature had been made appear to us, We should have taken effectual Care to put a Stop to them, and to have punished the Offenders in the severest Manner.

We being therefore indispensibly obliged to take up Arms, and entirely relying on the Help of Almighty God, who knows the Uprightness of Our Intentions, have thought fit to declare, and do hereby declare War against the French King; and We will, in pursuance of such Declaration, vigorously prosecute the same by Sea and Land; being assured of the ready Concurrence and Assistance, of all Our loving Subjects, in so just a Cause: And We do hereby will, and require, Our Generals and Commanders of Our Forces, Our Commissioners for Executing the Office of High

Admiral of Great Britain, Our Lieutenants of Our several Counties, Governors of Our Forts and Garrisons, and all other Officers under them, by Sea and Land, to do, and execute, all Acts of Hostility, in the Prosecution of this War against the said French King, his Vassals, and Subjects, and to oppose their Attempts; willing, and requiring, all Our Subjects to take Notice of the same, whom We henceforth strictly forbid to hold any Correspondence, or Communication, with the Subjects of the French King: And We do hereby command Our own Subjects, and advertise all other Persons of what Nation soever, not to transport or carry any Soldiers, Arms, Powder, Ammunition, or other Contraband Goods, to any of the Territories, Lands, Plantations, or Countries of the said French King; declaring, that whatsoever Ship or Vessel shall be met withal, transporting or carrying any Soldiers, Arms, Powder, Ammunition, or other Contraband Goods, to any of the Territories, Lands, Plantations, or Countries of the said French King, the same being taken, shall be condemned as good and lawful Prize. And whereas there are remaining in Our Kingdoms divers of the Subjects of the French King, We do hereby declare Our Royal Intention to be, that all the French Subjects, who shall demean themselves dutifully towards Us, shall be safe in their Persons and Estates.

Given at Our Court at St. James's, the Twenty ninth Day of March, 1744, in the Seventeenth Year of Our Reign.

GOD SAVE THE KING.

London, Printed by Thomas Baskett and Robert Baskett, Printers to the King's most Excellent Majesty. 1744.

1 p. folio. Copies in B. M., and P. C.; also in John Carter Brown Library. Entered on Patent Rolls; entered in Privy Council Register, II Geo., vol. 9, p. 269. Printed in "London Gazette," March 31, 1744. The declaration was reprinted in Boston by T. Fleet, 1744, as a broadside. Copies are in the American Antiquarian Society and the Boston Public Library.

1744, JUNE 14.

[REGARDING DISTRIBUTION OF PRIZES.]

BY THE KING.

A PROCLAMATION

George R.

Whereas Application has been made to Us, in order to prevent Disputes arising among the Flag Officers, who have been or may hereafter be employed in Our Service, upon the Construction of that Part of the Proclamation of Our Lords Justices, during Our Absence, on the Nineteenth Day of June, One thousand seven hundred and forty, appointing a Distribution of the Spanish Prizes and Bounty Money, which relates to the Shares granted to the Flag or Flag Officers, who shall be actually on Board at the taking any Prize, or shall be directing or assisting therein: And whereas We having taken the Opinion of Our Lords Commissioners of the Admiralty, do judge it expedient to make such a Regulation, as may explain and settle the Right of Flag Officers, and Commanders, in all Cases of Prizes taken from any of Our Enemies at Sea; We therefore, with the Advice of Our Privy Council, do by this Our Proclamation[79] publish, order, and declare, That the following Regulations be observed: First, That a Flag Officer commanding in Chief upon Service, shall have One Eighth Part of all Prizes taken by Ships under his Command: Secondly, That a Flag Officer sent to command at Jamaica, or elsewhere, shall have no Right to any Share of Prizes taken by Ships employed there before he arrives, within the Limits of his Command: Thirdly, That when an inferior Flag Officer, or Private Ships, are sent out to reinforce a superior Flag Officer at Jamaica, or elsewhere, the said superior Flag Officer shall have no Right to any Share in Prizes taken by them, before their Arrival within the Limits of his Command: Fourthly, That a Chief Flag Officer, returning home from Jamaica, or elsewhere, shall have no Share in Prizes taken by the Ships left at Jamaica, or elsewhere, after he has got out of the Limits of his Command: Fifthly, That if a Flag Officer is sent to command in the Out-ports of this Kingdom, he shall have no Share in Prizes taken by Ships that sail from that Port, by Order from the Admiralty: Sixthly, That when more Flag Officers than one serve together, the Eighth Part of all Prizes taken by any Ships of the Fleet or Squadron, shall be divided in the following Proportion, viz. If there

---

[79] A long proclamation was issued November 7, 1744, providing for the distribution of the bounty for destroying French ships, which is omitted from this volume since it contains no direct reference to America. It was printed in the *London Gazette* of November 10, 1744, and a copy of the original broadside is in the Privy Council Office.

be but Two Flag Officers, the Chief shall have Two Third Parts, and the other shall have the remaining Third Part; but if the Number of Flag Officers be more than Two, the Chief shall have only one half, and the other half shall be divided equally among the other Flag Officers: Seventhly, That Commodores, with Captains under them, shall be esteemed as Flag Officers, with respect to their Right to an Eighth Part of Prizes, whether commanding in Chief, or serving under Command.

Given at Our Court at Kensington, this Fourteenth Day of June, 1744, in the Eighteenth Year of Our Reign.

God save the King.

London, Printed by Thomas Baskett and Robert Baskett, Printers to the King's most Excellent Majesty. 1744.

1 p. folio. Copy in P. C. Entered on Patent Rolls; entered in Privy Council Register, II Geo., vol. 9, p. 355. Printed in "London Gazette," June 16, 1744.

1752, JUNE 25.

[CONTINUING OFFICERS IN GEORGIA.]

BY THE LORDS JUSTICES.

A PROCLAMATION.

Hardwicke,   C. Hartington,

Granville, P.   Holdernesse.[80]

Whereas by Letters Patent of his present Majesty, under his great Seal, which erected the Territories and Country of Georgia in America into One Free Province, under the Trustees for establishing the Colony of Georgia in America, the immediate Government thereof was, after the Determination of a Term of Twenty-one Years therein mentioned, to come to his said Majesty, his Heirs and Successors; which Term is not yet expired: And whereas the said Trustees having voluntarily made a Proposal to his Majesty, to make an absolute Surrender of all the Powers, Rights, and Trusts, vested in them by the said Charter; which his Majesty having been pleased graciously to accept, the said Trustees did, by their Indenture of Grant and Surrender, bearing Date the Twentieth Instant, grant and surrender to his Majesty, his Heirs, and Successors, the said Charter, and all Powers, Jurisdictions, Countries, and Territories, thereby granted to them; by which, the immediate Care of the said Province, and of his Majesty's Subjects there, is now devolved upon his Majesty;[81] We being desirious of making Provision for the present Government of the said Province, and securing the Peace and good Order thereof, until his Majesty shall establish such other Form and Order of Government therein, as to his Majesty, in his Royal Wisdom, shall seem most for the Honour of his State, and the Happiness of his Subjects there; have thought fit, with the Advice of his Majesty's Privy-Council, to issue this Proclamation; and do hereby order, signify, and declare his Majesty's Pleasure, That all Persons who now are, or, at the Time of the Publication of this Proclamation, shall be duly and lawfully possessed of, or invested in, any Offices or Places of Authority, Government, or Employment, Ecclesiastical, Civil, or Military, in his Majesty's said Colony of Georgia, and particularly all Governors, Lieutenants, or Deputy Governors, President, and Assistants, Council, Judges, Justices, Magistrates, Provost Marshals, Sheriffs, Justices of <u>the Peace, and all</u> others in any Place or Rank of Government, or concerned in the

---

[80] Issued by the Lords Justices, during the absence of the King at Hanover.

[81] The charter establishing the colony of Georgia, dated June 9, 1732, was formally surrendered by the Trustees, June 23, 1752, and the colony became a royal province (see C. C. Jones' *History of Georgia*, i, 450-459).

Administration of Government, either Inferior or Superior, and all other Officers and Ministers holding any Office, Place, or Employment there, shall hold under his Majesty, and be continued in their said several and respective Places, Offices, or Employments, and enjoy the same with the like Salaries, Fees, and Emoluments thereto belonging, which have hitherto been actually paid, until his Majesty's Pleasure be further known, or other Provision be made for the due Government and Ordering of his Majesty's said Colony: And that in the mean Time, for the Preservation of the publick Peace and Tranquillity of the said Province, We do strictly command all the said Persons, of whatsoever Rank, Degree, or Condition, to proceed in the Execution of their respective Offices, and to perform all the Duties thereunto belonging: And further, We do hereby will and command all and singular his Majesty's Subjects in the said Colony, of what Estate or Degree they, or any of them, be, to be obedient to, and aiding, helping, and assisting the said Officers and Ministers in the Performance and Execution of their said Offices, Places, and Employments, as they tender his Majesty's Displeasure, and will answer the contrary at their utmost Perils: All which Matters and Things, herein before commanded and directed, We do, by this Proclamation, order and direct to be done, performed, submitted to, and obeyed, until his Majesty shall further make known his Royal Will and Pleasure thereupon.

Given at Whitehall the Twenty-fifth Day of June, 1752, in the Twenty sixth Year of his Majesty's Reign.

GOD SAVE THE KING

Manuscript copy in P. C. No printed copy found. Entered on Patent Rolls, and in Crown Office Docquet Book, vol. 11; entered in Privy Council Register, II Geo., vol. 14, p. 105. Printed in "London Gazette," July 4, 1752, from which the above transcript was made.

1756, MAY 17.

[DECLARATION OF WAR AGAINST FRANCE.]

HIS MAJESTY'S

DECLARATION

OF WAR AGAINST THE FRENCH KING.

GEORGE R.

The unwarrantable Proceedings of the French in the West Indies, and North America, since the Conclusion of the Treaty of Aix la Chapelle, and the Usurpations and Encroachments made by them upon Our Territories, and the Settlements of Our Subjects in those Parts, particularly in Our Province of Nova Scotia, have been so notorious, and so frequent, that they cannot but be looked upon as a sufficient Evidence of a formed Design and Resolution in that Court, to pursue invariably such Measures, as should most effectually promote their ambitious Views, without any Regard to the most solemn Treaties and Engagements. We have not been wanting on Our Part, to make, from time to time, the most serious Representations to the French King, upon these repeated Acts of Violence, and to endeavour to obtain Redress and Satisfaction for the Injuries done to Our Subjects, and to prevent the like Causes of Complaint for the future: But though frequent Assurances have been given, that every thing should be settled agreeable to the Treaties subsisting between the Two Crowns, and particularly that the Evacuation of the Four Neutral Islands in the West Indies should be effected (which was expressly promised to Our Ambassadour in France) the Execution of these Assurances, and of the Treaties on which they were founded, has been evaded under the most frivolous Pretences; and the unjustifiable Practices of the French Governors, and of the Officers acting under their Authority, were still carried on, till, at length, in the Month of April, One thousand seven hundred and fifty four, they broke out in open Acts of Hostility, when, in Time of profound Peace, without any Declaration of War, and without any previous Notice given, or Application made, a Body of French Troops under the Command of an Officer bearing the French King's Commission, attacked in a hostile Manner, and possessed themselves of the English Fort on the Ohio in North America.

But notwithstanding this Act of Hostility, which could not but be looked upon as a Commencement of War, yet, from Our earnest Desire of Peace, and in Hopes the Court of France would disavow this Violence and Injustice, We contented Ourselves with sending such a Force to America, as was indispensably necessary for the immediate Defence and Protection of Our Subjects against fresh Attacks and Insults.

In the mean Time great Naval Armaments were preparing in the Ports of France, and a considerable Body of French Troops embarked for[82] North America; and though the French Ambassadour was sent back to England with specious Professions of a Desire to accommodate these Differences, yet it appeared, that their real Design was only to gain Time for the Passage of those Troops to America, which they hoped would secure the Superiority of the French Forces in those Parts, and enable them to carry their ambitions and oppressive Projects into Execution.

In these Circumstances We could not but think it incumbent upon Us, to endeavour to prevent the Success of so dangerous a Design, and to oppose the Landing of the French Troops in America; and in Consequence of the just and necessary Measures We had taken for that Purpose, the French Ambassadour was immediately recalled from Our Court, the Fortifications at Dunkirk, which had been repairing for some Time, were enlarged; great Bodies of Troops marched down to the Coast; and Our Kingdoms were threatened with an Invasion.

In order to prevent the Execution of these Designs, and to provide for the Security of Our Kingdoms, which were thus threatened, We could no longer forbear giving Orders for the seizing at Sea the Ships of the French King, and his Subjects. Notwithstanding which, as We were still unwilling to give up all Hopes that an Accommodation might be effected, We have contented Ourselves hitherto with detaining the said Ships, and preserving them, and (as far as was possible) their Cargoes intire, without proceeding to the Confiscation of them; but it being now evident, by the hostile Invasion actually made by the French King of Our Island of Minorca, that it is the determined Resolution of that Court to hearken to no Terms of Peace, but to carry on the War, which has been long begun on their Part, with the utmost Violence, We can no longer remain, consistently with what We owe to Our own Honour, and to the Welfare of Our Subjects, within those Bounds, which, from a Desire of Peace, We had hitherto observed.

We have therefore thought proper to declare War; and We do hereby Declare War against the French King, who hath so unjustly begun it, relying on the Help of Almighty God, in Our just Undertaking, and being assured of the hearty Concurrence and Assistance of Our Subjects, in Support of so good a Cause; hereby willing and requiring Our Captain General of Our Forces, Our Commissioners for executing the Office of Our High Admiral of Great Britain, Our Lieutenants of Our several Counties, Governors of Our Forts and Garrisons, and all other Officers and Soldiers under them, by Sea and Land, to do and execute all Acts of Hostility, in the Prosecution of this War against the French King, his Vassals and Subjects, and to oppose their Attempts: Willing and requiring all Our Subjects to take Notice

---

[82] In the copy in the British Museum, this word is printed *from,* but the word *for* is substituted in manuscript, and in a contemporaneous hand is appended the following note: "The above Error was not found out by either of the Clerks of the Secretaries of State, Offices, &c, but published and Publickly Stuck up at the 'Change, where a Country-fellow made his Remark on the Error, which occasion'd fresh Expresses to be dispatched to the [illegible] and Plantations abroad, at the additional Expense of £8000."

of the same; whom We henceforth strictly forbid to hold any Correspondence or Communication with the said French King, or his Subjects. And We do hereby command Our own Subjects, and advertise all other Persons, of what Nation soever, not to transport or carry any Soldiers, Arms, Powder, Ammunition, or other Contraband Goods, to any of the Territories, Lands, Plantations, or Countries of the said French King; Declaring, that whatsoever Ship or Vessel shall be met withal, transporting or carrying any Soldiers, Arms, Powder, Ammunition, or any other Contraband Goods, to any of the Territories, Lands, Plantations, or Countries of the said French King, the same, being taken, shall be condemned as good and lawful Prize.

And whereas there are remaining in Our Kingdom, divers of the Subjects of the French King, We do hereby Declare Our Royal Intention to be, That all the French Subjects who shall demean themselves dutifully towards Us, shall be safe in their Persons and Effects.

Given at our Court at Kensington, the Seventeenth Day of May, 1756, in the Twenty ninth Year of Our Reign.

GOD SAVE THE KING.

London: Printed by Thomas Baskett, Printer to the King's most Excellent Majesty; and by the Assigns of Robert Baskett. 1756.

1 p. folio. Copies in Antiq., B. M., and in Mass. Historical Society. Entered on Patent Rolls; entered in Privy Council Register, II Geo., vol. 16, p. 177. Printed in "London Gazette," May 18, 1756. Reprinted as a broadside by J. Parker, New York, 1756, of which a copy was in the N. Y. State Library.

1759, OCTOBER 23.

[THANKSGIVING IN ENGLAND FOR DEFEAT OF FRENCH.]

BY THE KING.

A PROCLAMATION

FOR A PUBLICK THANKSGIVING.

GEORGE R.

We do most devoutly and thankfully acknowledge the great Goodness and Mercy of Almighty God, who hath afforded Us his Protection and Assistance in the just War, in which, for the common Safety of Our Realms, and for disappointing the boundless Ambition of France, We are now engaged; and hath given such signal Successes to Our Arms, both by Sea and Land, particularly by the Defeat of the French Army in Canada, and the Taking of Quebec; and who hath most seasonably granted Us at this Time an uncommonly plentiful Harvest: And therefore, duly considering that such great and publick Blessings do call for publick and solemn Acknowledgments, We have thought fit, by and with the Advice of Our Privy Council, to issue this Our Royal Proclamation, hereby appointing and commanding, That a General Thanksgiving to Almighty God, for these His Mercies, be observed throughout Our Kingdom of England, Dominion of Wales, and Town of Berwick upon Tweed, upon Thursday the Twenty ninth Day of November next. And, for the better and more religious and orderly Solemnizing the same, We have given Directions to the most Reverend the Archbishops, and the Right Reverend the Bishops of England, to compose a Form of Prayer suitable to this Occasion, to be used in all Churches and Chapels, and other Places of Publick Worship, and to take Care for the timely dispersing thereof throughout their respective Dioceses. And We do strictly charge and command, That the said publick Day of Thanksgiving be religiously observed by all Our loving Subjects, as they tender the Favour of Almighty God, and upon Pain of suffering such Punishment as We may justly inflict upon all such as shall contemn or neglect the Performance of so religious and necessary a Duty.

Given at Our Court at Kensington, the Twenty third Day of October, One thousand seven hundred and fifty nine, in the Thirty third Year of our Reign.

GOD SAVE THE KING.

London: Printed by Thomas Baskett, Printer to the King's most Excellent Majesty; and by the Assigns of Robert Baskett. 1759.

1 p. folio. Only copy found in Mass. Historical Society. Entered on Patent Rolls; entered in Privy Council Register, II Geo., vol. 18, p. 170. Printed in "London Gazette," October 27, 1759. It was ordered by the Privy Council that the Thanksgiving should also be celebrated in Ireland, and a proclamation with practically the same wording was issued by the Lord Lieutenant and Council of Ireland, October 30, 1759. A printed copy of this latter proclamation is in the Dublin Public Record Office.

1759, OCTOBER 23.

[THANKSGIVING IN SCOTLAND FOR DEFEAT OF FRENCH.]

BY THE KING.

A PROCLAMATION

FOR A PUBLICK THANKSGIVING.

GEORGE R.

We do most devoutly and thankfully acknowledge the great Goodness and Mercy of Almighty God who hath afforded Us his Protection and Assistance in the just War in which for the common safety of Our Realms and for disappointing the boundless Ambition of France We are now engaged; and hath given such signal Successes to Our Arms both by Sea and Land particularly by the defeat of the French Army in Canada and the taking of Quebeck and who hath most seasonably granted Us at this time an uncommonly plentiful Harvest And therefore duly considering that such great and publick Blessings do call for publick and solemn Acknowledgments, We have thought fit by and with the Advice of Our Privy Council to issue this Our Royal Proclamation hereby appointing and commanding That a general Thanksgiving to Almighty God for these His Mercies be observed throughout that part of Our Kingdom of Great Britain called Scotland upon Thursday the Twenty Ninth day of November next. And we do strictly charge and command That the said Publick Thanksgiving be reverently and decently observed by all Our loving Subjects in Scotland on the said Twenty Ninth day of November next as they tender the favour of Almighty God and would avoid his Wrath and Indignation and upon pain of such Punishment as We may justly inflict upon all such as shall contemn or neglect the Performance of so religious a Duty. Our Will and Pleasure is therefore and We charge That incontinent this Our Proclamation seen Ye pass to the Market Cross of Edinburgh and all other Places needful and there in Our Name and Authority make Publication thereof that none pretend Ignorance And Our Will and Pleasure is That Our Sollicitor do cause printed Copies hereof to be sent to the Sherifs of the several Shires Stewarts of Stewarties and Baillies of Regalities and their Clerks whom We ordain to see the same published; And We appoint them to send Doubles thereof to the several Paroch Kirks within their Bounds that upon the Lords day immediately preceding the Day above mentioned the same may be published and read from the Pulpits immediately after Divine Service.

Given at Our Court at Kensington the twenty third day of October One Thousand Seven hundred and Fifty nine in the thirty third Year of Our Reign.

GOD SAVE THE KING.

1 p. folio. Only printed copy noted by the editor was advertised for sale by the Museum Book Store of London in 1909, priced at £27. 10s. Entered on Patent Rolls; entered in Privy Council Register, II Geo., vol. 18, p. 171, from which this transcript was made. Printed in "London Gazette," October 27, 1759.

1760, OCTOBER 27.

[CONTINUING OFFICERS IN THE COLONIES.]

BY THE KING.

A PROCLAMATION

Declaring His Majesty's Pleasure for continuing the Officers in His Majesty's Plantations till His Majesty's Pleasure shall be further signified.

George R.

Whereas by an Act of Parliament made in the Sixth Year of the late Queen Anne, of blessed Memory, intituled, "An Act for the Security of her Majesty's Person and Government, and of the Succession to the Crown of Great Britain in the Protestant Line," it was enacted (amongst other Things) That no Office, Place, or Employment, Civil or Military, within any of her said late Majesty's Plantations, should become void by Reason of the Demise or Death of her said late Majesty, her Heirs, or Successors, Kings or Queens of this Realm; but that the Person and Persons in any of the Offices, Places, or Employments aforesaid, should continue in their respective Offices, Places, and Employments, for the Space of Six Months next after such Death or Demise, unless sooner removed and discharged by the next in Succession to whom the Crown of this Realm should come, remain, and be, according to the several Acts of Parliament for limiting and settling the Succession of the Crown, as by the said recited Act may appear; And in regard it may happen, that Our Pleasure may not, within the said Time, be declared, touching the said Offices, Places, and Employments, in Our Foreign Plantations, which will, at the End of the said Six Months, become void; We, for preventing the Inconveniences that may happen thereby, in Our princely Wisdom and Care of the State (reserving to Our Judgement hereafter the Reformation and Redress of any Abuses in the Execution of any such Offices, Places, and Employments, upon due Knowledge and Examination thereof) have thought fit, with the Advice of Our Privy Council, to issue this Our Royal Proclamation, and do hereby order, signify, and declare, That all Persons that, at the Time of the Decease of Our late Royal Grandfather King George the Second, of glorious Memory, were duly and lawfully possessed of, or invested in, any Office, Place, or Employment, Civil or Military, in any of Our Plantations, and which have not been since removed from such their Offices, Places, or Employments, shall be, and shall hold themselves continued in the said Offices, Places, and Employments, as formerly they held and enjoyed the same, until Our Pleasure be further known, or other Provision be made, pursuant to the Commissions and Instructions of Our said late Royal Grandfather, to His Governors and Officers of the Plantations aforesaid; and that in the mean time, for the Preservation of the Peace, and necessary Proceedings in Matters of Justice, and for the Safety and Service of the State, all the said Persons, of whatsoever Degree or Condition, do not fail every one severally, according to his Place, Office, or Charge, to proceed in the Performance and Execution of all Duties thereunto belonging, as formerly appertained unto them, during the Life of Our said late Royal Grandfather: And further, We do hereby will and command all and singular Our Subjects in the said Plantations, of what Estate or Degree they, or any of them, be, to be aiding, helping, and assisting, at the Commandment of the said Officers, in the Performance and Execution of the said Offices and Places, as they tender Our Displeasure, and will answer the contrary at their utmost Perils.

Given at Our Court at Saville House, the Twenty Seventh Day of October, 1760, in the First Year of Our Reign.

GOD SAVE THE KING.

No printed copy found. Entered on Patent Rolls; in Crown Office Docquet Book, vol. II, where it is dated October 25; and in Privy Council Register, III Geo., vol. 1, p. 11. Printed in "London Gazette," October 13, 1761, from which this transcript was made.

1763, OCTOBER 7.

[ESTABLISHING NEW GOVERNMENTS IN AMERICA.]

BY THE KING.

A PROCLAMATION

GEORGE R.

Whereas We have taken into Our Royal Consideration the extensive and valuable Acquisitions in America, secured to Our Crown by the late Definitive Treaty of Peace, concluded at Paris the Tenth Day of February last;[83] and being desirous, that all Our loving Subjects, as well of Our Kingdoms as of Our Colonies in America, may avail themselves, with all convenient Speed, of the great Benefits and Advantages which must accrue therefrom to their Commerce, Manufactures, and Navigation; We have thought fit, with the Advice of Our Privy Council, to issue this Our Royal Proclamation,[84] hereby to publish and declare to all Our loving Subjects, that We have, with the Advice of Our said Privy Council, granted Our Letters Patent under Our Great Seal of Great Britain, to erect within the Countries and Islands ceded and confirmed to Us by the said Treaty, Four distinct and separate Governments, stiled and called by the Names of Quebec, East Florida, West Florida, and Grenada, and limited and bounded as follows; viz.

First. The Government of Quebec, bounded on the Labrador Coast by the River St. John, and from thence by a Line drawn from the Head of that River through the Lake St. John to the South End of the Lake nigh Pissin;[85] from whence the said Line crossing the River St. Lawrence and the Lake Champlain in Forty five Degrees of North Latitude, passes along the High Lands which divide the Rivers that empty themselves into the said River St. Lawrence, from those which fall into the Sea; and also along the North Coast of the Baye des Chaleurs, and the Coast of the Gulph of St. Lawrence to Cape Rosieres, and from thence crossing the Mouth of the River St. Lawrence by the West End of the Island of Anticosti, terminates at the aforesaid River of St. John.

[83] Text of treaty can be consulted in Chalmers' *Collection of Treaties*, i, 467.

[84] The events leading up to the issuing of this proclamation have been so thoroughly treated in C. W. Alvord's "Genesis of the Proclamation of 1763" in *Michigan Pioneer and Historical Collections*, vol. xxxvi, p. 20, and in C. E. Carter's *Great Britain and the Illinois Country* (Prize Essay of the Amer. Hist. Assoc., 1910) that any explanatory notes in this place seem unnecessary.

[85] *Nipissim* in proclamation as printed in the *London Gazette*.

Secondly. The Government of East Florida, bounded to the Westward by the Gulph of Mexico, and the Apalachicola River; to the Northward, by a Line drawn from that Part of the said River where the Chatahouchee and Flint Rivers meet, to the Source of St. Mary's River, and by the Course of the said River to the Atlantick Ocean; and to the Eastward and Southward, by the Atlantick Ocean, and the Gulph of Florida, including all Islands within Six Leagues of the Sea Coast.

Thirdly. The Government of West Florida, bounded to the Southward by the Gulph of Mexico, including all Islands within Six Leagues of the Coast from the River Apalachicola to Lake Pentchartrain; to the Westward, by the said Lake, the Lake Mauripas, and the River Mississippi; to the Northward, by a Line drawn due East from that Part of the River Mississippi which lies in Thirty one Degrees North Latitude, to the River Apalachicola or Chatahouchee; and to the Eastward by the said River.

Fourthly. The Government of Grenada, comprehending the Island of that Name, together with the Grenadines, and the Islands of Dominico, St. Vincents, and Tobago.

And, to the End that the open and free Fishery of Our Subjects may be extended to and carried on upon the Coast of Labrador and the adjacent Islands, We have thought fit, with the Advice of Our said Privy Council, to put all that Coast, from the River St. John's to Hudson's Streights, together with the Islands of Anticosti and Madelaine, and all other smaller Islands lying upon the said Coast, under the Care and Inspection of Our Governor of Newfoundland.

We have also, with the Advice of Our Privy Council, thought fit to annex the Islands of St. John's, and Cape Breton or Isle Royale, with the lesser Islands adjacent thereto, to Our Government of Nova Scotia.

We have also, with the Advice of Our Privy Council aforesaid, annexed to Our Province of Georgia all the Lands lying between the Rivers Altamaha and St. Mary's.

And whereas it will greatly contribute to the speedy settling Our said new Governments, that Our loving Subjects should be informed of Our Paternal Care for the Security of the Liberties and Properties of those who are and shall become Inhabitants thereof; We have thought fit to publish and declare, by this Our Proclamation, that We have, in the Letters Patent under Our Great Seal of Great Britain, by which the said Governments are constituted, given express Power and Direction to Our Governors of Our said Colonies respectively, that so soon as the State and Circumstances of the said Colonies will admit thereof, they shall, with the Advice and Consent of the Members of Our Council, summon and call General Assemblies within the said Governments respectively, in such Manner and Form as is used and directed in those Colonies and Provinces in America, which are under Our immediate Government; and We have also given Power to the said Governors, with the Consent of Our said Councils, and the Representatives of the People, so to be summoned as aforesaid, to make, constitute, and ordain Laws, Statutes, and Ordinances for the Publick Peace, Welfare, and Good Government of Our said Colonies, and of the People and Inhabitants thereof, as near as may be agreeable to the Laws of England, and under such Regulations and Restrictions as are used in other Colonies: And in the mean Time, and until such Assemblies can be called as aforesaid, all Persons inhabiting in, or resorting to Our said Colonies, may confide in Our Royal Protection for the Enjoyment of the Benefit of the Laws of Our Realm of England; for which Purpose, We have given Power under Our Great Seal to the Governors of Our said Colonies respectively, to erect and constitute, with the Advice of Our said Councils respectively, Courts of Judicature and Publick Justice, within Our said Colonies, for the hearing and determining all Causes, as well Criminal as Civil, according to Law and Equity, and as near as may be agreeable to the Laws of England, with Liberty to all Persons who may think themselves aggrieved by the Sentences of such Courts, in all Civil Cases, to appeal, under the usual Limitations and Restrictions, to Us in Our Privy Council.

We have also thought fit, with the Advice of Our Privy Council as aforesaid, to give unto the Governors and Councils of Our said Three New Colonies upon the Continent, full Power and Authority to settle and agree with the Inhabitants of Our said New Colonies, or with any other Persons who shall resort thereto, for such Lands, Tenements, and Hereditaments, as are now, or hereafter shall be in Our Power to dispose of, and them to grant to any such Person or Persons, upon such Terms, and under such moderate Quit-Rents, Services, and Acknowledgments as have been appointed and settled in Our other Colonies, and under such other Conditions as shall appear to Us to be necessary and expedient for the Advantage of the Grantees, and the Improvement and Settlement of our said Colonies.

And whereas We are desirous, upon all Occasions, to testify Our Royal Sense and Approbation of the Conduct and Bravery of the Officers and Soldiers of Our Armies, and to reward the same, We do hereby command and impower Our Governors of Our said Three New Colonies, and all other Our Governors of Our several Provinces on the Continent of North America, to grant, without Fee or Reward, to such Reduced Officers as have served in North America during the late War, and to such Private Soldiers as have been or shall be disbanded in America, and are actually residing there, and shall personally apply for the same, the following Quantities of Lands, subject at the Expiration of Ten Years to the same Quit-Rents as other Lands are subject to in the Province within which they are granted, as also subject to the same Conditions of Cultivation and Improvement; viz.

To every Person having the Rank of a Field Officer, Five thousand Acres.—To every Captain, Three thousand Acres.—To every Subaltern or Staff Officer, Two thousand Acres.—To every Non-Commission Officer, Two hundred Acres.—To every Private Man, Fifty Acres.

We do likewise authorize and require the Governors and Commanders in Chief of all Our said Colonies upon the Continent of North America, to grant the like Quantities of Land, and upon the same Conditions, to such Reduced Officers of Our Navy, of like Rank, as served on Board Our Ships of War in North America at the Times of the Reduction of Louisbourg and Quebec in the late War, and who shall personally apply to Our respective Governors for such Grants.

And whereas it is just and reasonable, and essential to Our Interest and the

Security of Our Colonies, that the several Nations or Tribes of Indians, with whom We are connected, and who live under Our Protection, should not be molested or disturbed in the Possession of such Parts of Our Dominions and Territories as, not having been ceded to, or purchased by Us, are reserved to them, or any of them, as their Hunting Grounds; We do therefore, with the Advice of Our Privy Council, declare it to be Our Royal Will and Pleasure, that no Governor or Commander in Chief in any of Our Colonies of Quebec, East Florida, or West Florida, do presume, upon any Pretence whatever, to grant Warrants of Survey, or pass any Patents for Lands beyond the Bounds of their respective Governments, as described in their Commissions; as also, that no Governor or Commander in Chief in any of Our other Colonies or Plantations in America, do presume, for the present, and until Our further Pleasure be known, to grant Warrants of Survey, or pass Patents for any Lands beyond the Heads or Sources of any of the Rivers which fall into the Atlantick Ocean from the West and North-West, or upon any Lands whatever, which, not having been ceded to, or purchased by Us as aforesaid, are reserved to the said Indians, or any of them.

And We do further declare it to be Our Royal Will and Pleasure, for the present as aforesaid, to reserve under Our Sovereignty, Protection, and Dominion, for the Use of the said Indians, all the Lands and Territories not included within the Limits of Our said Three New Governments, or within the Limits of the Territory granted to the Hudson's Bay Company, as also all the Lands and Territories lying to the Westward of the Sources of the Rivers which fall into the Sea from the West and North West, as aforesaid; and We do hereby strictly forbid, on Pain of Our Displeasure, all Our loving Subjects from making any Purchases or Settlements whatever, or taking Possession of any of the Lands above reserved, without Our especial Leave and Licence for that Purpose first obtained.

And We do further strictly enjoin and require all Persons whatever, who have either wilfully or inadvertently seated themselves upon any Lands within the Countries above described, or upon any other Lands, which, not having been ceded to, or purchased by Us, are still reserved to the said Indians as aforesaid, forthwith to remove themselves from such Settlements.

And whereas great Frauds and Abuses have been committed in the purchasing Lands of the Indians, to the great Prejudice of Our Interests, and to the great Dissatisfaction of the said Indians; in order therefore to prevent such Irregularities for the future, and to the End that the Indians may be convinced of Our Justice, and determined Resolution to remove all reasonable Cause of Discontent, We do, with the Advice of Our Privy Council, strictly enjoin and require, that no private Person do presume to make any Purchase from the said Indians of any Lands reserved to the said Indians, within those Parts of Our Colonies where We have thought proper to allow Settlement; but that if, at any Time, any of the said Indians should be inclined to dispose of the said Lands, the same shall be purchased only for Us, in Our Name, at some publick Meeting or Assembly of the said Indians to be held for that Purpose by the Governor or Commander in Chief of Our Colonies respectively, within which they shall lie: and in case they shall lie within the Limits of any Proprietary Government, they shall be purchased only for the Use and in the Name of such Proprietaries, conformable to such Directions and Instructions as We or they shall think proper to give for that Purpose: And We do, by the Advice of Our Privy Council, declare and enjoin, that the Trade with the said Indians shall be free and open to all our Subjects whatever; provided that every Person, who may incline to trade with the said Indians, do take out a Licence for carrying on such Trade from the Governor or Commander in Chief of any of Our Colonies respectively, where such Person shall reside; and also give Security to observe such Regulations as We shall at any Time think fit, by Ourselves or by Our Commissaries to be appointed for this Purpose, to direct and appoint for the Benefit of the said Trade; And We do hereby authorize, enjoin, and require the Governors and Commanders in Chief of all Our Colonies respectively, as well Those under Our immediate Government as those under the Government and Direction of Proprietaries, to grant such Licences without Fee or Reward, taking especial Care to insert therein a Condition, that such Licence shall be void, and the Security forfeited, in Case the Person, to whom the same is granted, shall refuse or neglect to observe such Regulations as We shall think proper to prescribe as aforesaid.

And We do further expressly enjoin and require all Officers whatever, as well Military as those employed in the Management and Direction of Indian Affairs within the Territories reserved as aforesaid for the Use of the said Indians, to seize and apprehend all Persons whatever, who, standing charged with Treasons, Misprisions of Treason, Murders, or other Felonies or Misdemeanors, shall fly from Justice, and take Refuge in the said Territory, and to send them under a proper Guard to the Colony where the Crime was committed of which they stand accused, in order to take their Tryal for the same.

Given at Our Court at St. James's, the Seventh Day of October, One thousand seven hundred and sixty three, in the Third Year of Our Reign.

GOD SAVE THE KING.

London: Printed by Mark Baskett, Printer to the King's most Excellent Majesty; and by the Assigns of Robert Baskett. 1763.

1 p. folio. Copies in Antiq., and P. C.; also in Mass. State Archives, and John Carter Brown Library. Entered on Patent Rolls; entered in Privy Council Register, III Geo., vol. 3, p. 102. Printed in "London Gazette," October 8, 1763, and in several of the colonial newspapers, as the "Providence Gazette," December 17, 1763; also in the "Annual Register," vi, 208, Knox, "New Collection of Voyages," 1767, ii, 265, and elsewhere.

1764, MARCH 26.

[COLONIZING GRANADA AND OTHER ISLANDS.]

BY THE KING.

A PROCLAMATION.

George R.

Whereas We have taken into Our Consideration, the great Benefit which will arise to the Commerce of Our Kingdoms and the Interests of Our Subjects, from the speedy Settlement of Our Islands of Grenada, the Grenadines, Dominica, St. Vincent, and Tobago. We do therefore think fit, with the Advice of Our Privy Council, to issue this Our Royal Proclamation to publish and declare to Our loving Subjects, that We have, with the Advice of Our said Privy Council, given the necessary Powers and Directions for an immediate Survey and Division into proper Parishes and Districts, of such of the said Islands as have not hitherto been so surveyed and divided, and for laying out such Lands in the said Islands, as are in Our Power to dispose of, into Allotments for Plantations of different Size and Extent, according as the Nature of the Land shall be more or less adapted to the Growth of Sugar, Coffee, Cocoa, Cotton, or other Articles of beneficial Culture, reserving to Us, Our Heirs, and Successors, such Parts of the said Islands as shall be necessary for erecting Fortifications thereon, and for all other military Purposes, for Glebes for Ministers, Allotments for Schoolmasters, for Woodlands, High Roads, and all other publick Purposes; and also reserving such Lands in Our Islands of Dominica and St. Vincent, as, at the Time of the Surrender of those Islands, were and still are in the Possession of the French Inhabitants of those Islands, which Lands, it is Our Will and Pleasure should be granted to such of the said Inhabitants as shall be inclined to accept the same, upon Leases for Terms absolute, or for renewable Terms, upon certain Conditions and under proper Restrictions. And We do hereby further publish and declare, that the Allotments for Plantations in Our Islands of Grenada, the Grenadines, Tobago, and St. Vincent, shall contain to Three Hundred Acres, with some few Allotments in each Island of Five Hundred Acres; and that the Allotments in Our Island of Dominica, which is represented to be not so well adapted to the Cultivation of Sugar, and which from its Situation requires in Policy to be well peopled with White Inhabitants, shall be in general from Fifty to One Hundred Acres.

And whereas We have thought fit to declare to Our Parliament at the Opening of the present Session, Our Gracious Intention of reserving for the publick Use, whatever Sums shall be produced by the Sale of any of the Lands belonging to Us in the Islands of the West Indies, which were ceded to Us by the late Treaty; We do further publish and declare, that when these Allotments, or a sufficient Part of them, shall have been laid out, the same shall be set up to Sale by Auction, at a Price per Acre, to be fixed thereon by Commissioners appointed for that Purpose, under Our Great Seal of Great Britain, who shall give publick Notice of the Time and Place of such Sale.

And We do hereby further publish and declare, that the Lands so set up to Sale by Auction, shall not be sold, but upon the following Terms, and under the following Conditions and Reservations, that is to say,

That each Purchaser shall immediately pay into the Hands of such Person as We shall appoint to receive the same, Twenty per Cent. of the whole Purchase-Money.

That the Remainder of the Purchase-Money shall be paid by different Install-ments, viz. Ten per Cent. within the First Year after the Purchase, Ten per Cent. more within the Second Year after such Purchase, and Twenty per Cent. within every successive Year, until the Whole is paid.

That each Purchaser of Lands which have been cleared and improved, shall, within the Space of Three Months from the Date of the Grant, settle and constantly keep upon the Lot purchased, One White Man or Two White Women for every Hundred Acres contained in the said Lot; and, in Default thereof, shall be subject to the Payment of Twenty Pounds per Annum for every White Woman, and Forty Pounds for every White Man, that shall be wanting to compleat the Number.

That the Purchaser of uncleared Lands shall clear and cultivate One Acre in every Twenty in each Year, until Half the Land so purchased shall be cleared; and, in Default thereof, shall pay Five Pounds per Annum for every Acre not cleared, pursuant to such Condition; and such Purchaser shall also be obliged to settle and constantly keep upon the Lot so purchased, One White Man or Two White Women for every Hundred Acres, as the same shall be cleared.

That each Purchaser shall, besides the Purchase-Money, be subject to the Pay-ment of an Annual Quit-Rent to Us, Our Heirs, and Successors, of Six-pence per Acre, under the Penalty of Five Pounds per Acre upon Non-payment thereof; such Quit-Rents, in the Case of the Purchase of cleared Lands, to commence from the Date of the Grant; and the first Payment to be made at the Expiration of the First Year; and in Case of the Purchase of the uncleared Lands, such Quit-Rents to com-mence at the Expiration of Twelve Months from the Time each Acre is cleared.

That in Case of Failure in the Payment of the Purchase-Money in the Manner above directed, the Purchaser shall forfeit all Right to the Lands purchased.

That no Person shall purchase at any publick Sale more than Five Hundred Acres of cleared or uncleared Lands, in the Islands of Grenada, and the Grena-dines, Tobago, and St. Vincent's, and in the Island of Dominica the Quantity shall be restrained to Three Hundred Acres; and in Order to enforce this necessary and essential Regulation, that a Condition shall be inserted in every Grant, to be made in Consequence of such Purchase, that in Case any Purchase shall be made contrary thereto, so that the Property of the Purchaser in the Islands where the Lands lie, shall thereby amount to more than the above Quantity respectively, the same shall be void, the Money paid thereon forfeited, and the consequential Grant of no Effect.

That all and every Purchaser of Lands, upon the foregoing Terms and Conditions, shall immediately, upon the Payment of the first Twenty per Cent. of the Purchase-Money, receive a Bill of Sale, signed by the said Commissioners, which shall entitle such Purchasers to a Grant of the said Lands, under the Seal of the Islands, containing the aforementioned Conditions and Reservations: Which said Purchase, and Grant in Consequence thereof, duly registered in the proper Offices, shall be good and valid in Law against Us, Our Heirs and Successors, unless the same shall be revoked: And We do hereby declare the same revocable by Our Commissioners of Our Treasury, or Our High Treasurer for the Time being, within Twelve Months from the Date thereof; in which Case such Purchase and Grant shall become void and of no Effect; and upon Notice of such Revocation, the said Commissioners shall return to such Purchaser the Money paid upon the Purchase, with legal Interest thereon, and reasonable Allowance for any Improvements made on the said Lands.

And whereas the Establishing Towns in proper Situations, within the said Islands, will conduce greatly to the Convenience of the Inhabitants, and the Benefit of Trade and Commerce; We have therefore thought fit, with the Advice of Our Privy Council, to direct a proper District in every Parish in each Island, to be laid out for that Purpose, into Lots for Tenements of different Size and Extent; and each Town-Lot to have a proportionate Allotment of Land contiguous to such Town, for a small Field or Pasture, allowing one Acre for every ten Foot in Front of the Town-Lot to which it is to be annexed; but no Field-Lot to exceed the Quantity of Six Acres.

And We do hereby further publish and declare, that such of these Town and Pasture-Lots, in each Island, as consist of Lands, which have been already cleared and improved, shall be set up to Sale by publick Auction, at a Price per Foot in Front of each Town-Lot, and a Price per Acre of the Field-Lot, to be fixed upon such Lot, by the said Commissioners, in like Manner as upon the Allotments for Plantations.

And We do further publish and declare, that the Lots, so set up to Sale by Auction, shall not be sold but upon the following Terms and Conditions; that is to say,

That the Purchase-Money, shall be paid in the same Proportion, by the like Installments and upon the same Conditions as are required in the Case of the Purchase of Allotments for Plantations.

That each Tenement shall be charged with the Payment of an Annual Ground-Rent to Us, Our Heirs, and Successors, of One Penny per Foot in Front, and Sixpence per Acre, for each Acre of the Field annexed to such Tenement; the said Rents to commence at the Expiration of one Year from the Date of the Purchase, and the Purchaser to be liable to the same Penalties, in Case of Failure of the Payment of the Purchase-Money, and the Ground-Rent and Quit-Rent, as We have already required in respect to the Purchase of Allotments for Plantations.

And We do further publish and declare, that the Reservations, which We have directed to be made for Town and Pasture-Lots of uncleared Lands, shall be granted in Fee Simple by Our Governor in Chief, under the Seal of the Islands, to any Persons, who will give such Security as Our Commissioners shall approve, for building on such Town-Lots within a reasonable Time, to be fixed by Our said Commissioners; and also for Inclosing, Fencing, and properly Clearing for Pasture, the Fields that shall be granted with such Tenement.

And We do further publish and declare, that We have directed that no more than one Town-Lot be granted to any one Person, and that no more than Six Acres of Pasture-Land be annexed to such Town-Lot, whatever Number of Feet in Front it shall consist of.

That each Grantee shall be obliged, under proper Penalties, to the Payment of an Annual Ground-Rent to Us, Our Heirs, and Successors, of One Penny per Foot in Front of the Town-Lot for a Tenement, and Sixpence per Acre for each Acre of the Pasture-Lot; the first Payment to be made within two Years from the Date of the Grant.

And in order the more effectually to conduce to the Peopling Our said Islands with industrious White Inhabitants, upon which their Strength and Security do essentially depend; We have thought fit, with the Advice of Our said Council, to direct a Quantity of Land, not exceeding Eight Hundred Acres, to be reserved in such Parts of every Parish in each Island respectively, as are not adapted for Sugar Plantations, for the Accommodation of poor Settlers, to be divided into Lots, of not less than Ten, not more than Thirty Acres each; And we do hereby further publish and declare, that the said Allotments are to be granted in Fee Simple, under the Seal of Our said Islands, to such poor Protestants as shall apply for the same, in Proportion to their respective Abilities to cultivate the said Lands; and subject to the following Conditions; that is to say,

That each Grantee shall, at the Expiration of four Years from the Date of the Grant, pay a Quit-Rent to Us, Our Heirs, and Successors, of Six-pence per Acre, for every Acre then cleared, and a Penalty of Two Shillings per Acre, for every Acre of Land uncleared; which said Penalty of Two Shillings per Acre shall be reduced to Six-pence per Acre, as the Land shall be cleared; and in Case of Failure of such Rent and Penalty, the Grantee shall be subject to the further Penalty of the Payment of Five Pounds for every Acre, for which such Quit-Rent shall not be paid.

That each Grantee shall enter upon and occupy the Land within Three Months from the Date of the Grant; and shall continue to occupy and improve the same, for Twelve successive Months, from the Time of such first Settlement.

That the Lands shall, for the Space of Seven Years, be unalienable by Sale, nor shall the same be let, set or assigned over during the same Term, otherwise than to the Use and Benefit of any Child or Children of such original Settler, without especial licence in Writing first had and obtained, from the Chief Governor or Commander in Chief of Our said Islands for the Time being; and in Case of Failure or Default in either of the two last mentioned Conditions, the Grant to be void.

And We do hereby further publish and declare, that all Grants made of the said Allotments for poor Settlers, as also all Grants made of Town and Pasture Lots of cleared and uncleared Lands, shall be absolute and final.

That in all Grants to be made of Allotments for Plantations and Town and Pasture Lots, and of Lands for poor Settlers, there shall be a Reservation to Us, Our Heirs, and Successors of all Mines of Gold and Silver.

And We do further publish and declare, that the first Sale of Lands shall be in the Month of June next, if the Surveys can be made so soon; due Notice of which, as also of the Place of Sale, will be given by Our Commissioners appointed as aforesaid, for the Disposal of the said Lands.

Given at Our Court at St. James's, the Twenty-sixth Day of March, One thousand seven hundred and sixty-four, in the Fourth Year of Our Reign.

God Save the King.

A printed copy is noted in Crawford's "Handlist of Proclamations" as being in the Society of Antiquaries, but it could not be found by the present editor, who used the "London Gazette" as the source of his transcript. Entered on Patent Rolls, and in Crown Office Docquet Book, vol. 12; entered in Privy Council Register, III Geo., vol. 3, p. 342. Printed in "London Gazette" March 27, 1764.

1772, AUGUST 26.

[FOR APPREHENDING DESTROYERS OF THE GASPEE.]

BY THE KING.

A PROCLAMATION:

For the discovering and apprehending the Persons who plundered and burnt the Gaspee Schooner; and barbarously wounded and ill treated Lieutenant William Dudingston, Commander of the said Schooner.

Whereas We have received Information, That upon the 10th Day of June last, between the Hours of Twelve and One in the Morning, in the Providence or Narrowganset River, in Our Colony of Rhode-Island and Providence Plantations, a great Number of Persons, armed with Guns and other offensive Weapons and led by Two Persons, who were called the Captain and Head-Sheriff, in several armed Boats, attacked and Boarded Our Vessel called the Gaspee[86] Schooner, then lying at single Anchor in the said River, commanded by Our Lieutenant William Dudingston, under the Orders of Our Rear-Admiral John Montagu, and having dangerously wounded and barbarously treated the said William Dudingston, took, plundered and burnt the said Schooner: We, to the Intent that such outrageous and heinous Offenders may be discovered, and brought to condign Punishment, have thought fit, with the Advice of Our Privy Council, to issue this Our Royal Proclamation: And We are hereby graciously pleased to promise, that if any Person or Persons shall discover any other Person or Persons concerned in the said daring and heinous Offences, above mentioned, so that he or they may be apprehended and brought to Justice, such Discoverer shall have and receive, as a Reward for such Discovery, upon Conviction of each of the said Offenders, the Sum of Five Hundred Pounds. And if any Person or Persons shall discover either of the said Persons who acted as, or called themselves, or were called by their said Accomplices, the Head-Sheriff or the Captain, so that they, or either of them, may be apprehended and brought to Punishment, such Discoverer shall have and receive, as a Reward for such Discovery, upon Conviction of either of the said Persons, the further Sum of Five Hundred pounds, over and above the Sum of Five Hundred Pounds herein before promised, for the discovery and apprehending any

[86] The numerous documents relating to the burning of the Gaspee are printed in *R. I. Colonial Records*, vol. 7, pp. 55-192; also in R. I. Historical Society *Proceedings*, 1890-91, pp. 80-92, and *Publications*, vol. 7, pp. 238-244.

of the other common Offenders, abovementioned; and if any Person or Persons concerned therein, except the Two Persons who were called the Head-Sheriff, and Captain, and the Person or Persons who wounded Our said Lieutenant William Dudingston, shall discover any one or more of the said Accomplices, so that he or they may be apprehended and brought to Punishment, such Discoverer shall have and receive the said Reward or Rewards of Five Hundred Pounds, or One Thousand Pounds, as the Case may be, and also Our gracious Pardon for his said Offence. And the Commissioners for executing the Office of Treasurer of Our Exchequer, are hereby required to make Payment accordingly of the said Rewards. And We do hereby strictly charge and command all Our Governors, Deputy-Governors, Magistrates, Officers, and all other Our Loving Subjects, that they do use their utmost Diligence in their several Places and Capacities, to find out, discover and apprehend the said Offenders, in Order to their being brought to Justice. And We do hereby command that this Our Proclamation be printed and published in the usual Form,[87] and affixed in the principal Places of Our Town of Newport, and other Towns in Our said Colony, that none may pretend Ignorance.

Given at Our Court at St. James's, the Twenty-Sixth Day of August, 1772, in the Twelfth Year of Our Reign.

GOD SAVE THE KING.

Printed by Solomon Southwick, Printer to the Honorable the Governor and Company of the Colony of Rhode-Island and Providence-Plantations, in New-England.

1 p. folio. Copy in R. I. Historical Society. Entered in Privy Council Register, III Geo., vol. 9, p. 428. Printed in "R. I. Colonial Records," vii, 107.

---

[87] This is the only proclamation of which the editor finds record that was printed outside of Great Britain. A marginal note appended to the entry of the proclamation in the Privy Council Register (III Geo., vol. 9, p. 428) reads: "N. B. The original proclamation under the Great Seal was sent over to Rhode Island with the Commission &c by the Secretary of State." In the *London Gazette* of September 8, 1772, an article dated at Whitehall, August 29, and evidently officially inspired, recites the circumstances of the attack upon the Gaspee, the appointment of a commission of inquiry, and the issuance of a Proclamation which was "to be printed and published within the said Colony of Rhode Island." Under date of December 22, 1772, Governor Wanton of Rhode Island wrote to the Sheriffs of the several counties: "In obedience to the King's command, signified to me, by the Right Honorable the Earl of Dartmouth, one of his principal secretaries of state, I have caused to be printed His Majesty's proclamation for discovering and apprehending the persons who plundered and burnt the Gaspee schooner; copies of which, I send you by express, which you are forthwith to affix in the most public places of the several towns within your colony" (*R. I. Colonial Records*, vii, 117). John Howland relates that the proclamation was posted near the Market house in Providence, but was struck down by a patriotic citizen and "mingled with the filth of the street" (Stone's *Life of Howland*, p. 37).

The editor could find no printed copy of this proclamation in England, but a few days after returning to America had the good fortune to discover one of the original broadsides, which was purchased for the R. I. Historical Society.

1774, DECEMBER 16.

[PROVIDING COPPER CURRENCY FOR VIRGINIA.]

BY THE KING.

A PROCLAMATION

GEORGE R.

Whereas it hath been humbly represented to Us on the part and behalf of Our Colony of Virginia that a Currency of Copper Money within the same Colony would be highly beneficial to Our good Subjects the Inhabitants thereof for the more easy and convenient making of small Payments; And Whereas the Treasurer of Our said Colony being thereunto authorized by an Act of Our Governor Council and Assembly of Our said Colony passed in the tenth Year of Our Reign[88] hath delivered to the Master and Worker of Our Mint in Our Tower of London a sufficient quantity of Fine Copper in Barrs nealed for the Coinage of five Tons of the Pieces hereinafter mentioned after making the just and usual Allowances to the Officers of Our Mint; And Whereas Our said Master and Worker of Our Mint hath in pursuance of Our Warrant for that purpose issued Coined thereout five Tons of Pieces of Copper Coin of such Weight that Sixty Pieces thereof are equal to one Pound Weight averdupois without erring either in excess or defect above one thirtieth part and are of the value of two shillings and sixpence according to the Currency of Money in Our said Colony of Virginia And each Piece is Stamped on one side with Our effigies with the Inscription Georgius III Rex and on the reverse with the Virginia Arms with the St. Georges Cross leaving out the escutcheon of Crowns except one Crown at the Top as on the Guinea without Crest Supporters or Motto except the word Virginia round the Arms with the date of the Year which are now ready to be exported to Our said Colony of Virginia.[89] We have thereupon with the Advice of Our Privy Council thought fit to issue this Our Royal Proclamation And We do accordingly hereby Ordain declare and Command that the said Pieces of Copper Money so Coined Stamped and impressed as aforesaid <u>shall be current</u> and lawful Money of and in Our said Colony of Virginia and of

[88] The Virginia Assembly, in November, 1769, authorized the treasurer to purchase copper in Great Britain for the purpose of importing copper money to the colony (Hening's *Statutes*, viii, 343).

[89] There are many of these Virginia copper half-pennies, dated 1773, preserved in coin collections. They answer perfectly in appearance to the above description (see Dickeson, *American Numismatical Manual*, p. 84, and cut on plate viii). Although dated in 1773, it was apparently not until the following year that they were ready to be exported and the proclamation enforcing their acceptance issued.

and within the Districts and precincts of the same and shall pass and be received therein after the rate following that is to say Twenty four of the said Pieces shall pass and be received for the Sum of one shilling according to the Currency of Our said Province of Virginia and at and after such rate shall be computed accepted and taken accordingly in all Bargains Rates Payments and other Transactions of Money; Provided always and We do hereby further declare that no person shall be obliged to take more than one shilling of such Copper Money in any one Payment of any Sum of Money under twenty Shillings nor more than two shillings and sixpence thereof in any one payment of a larger Sum of Money than twenty shillings;

Given at Our Court at St. James's the Sixteenth day of December 1774 in the Fifteenth Year of Our Reign.

GOD SAVE THE KING.

No printed copy found. Entered in Privy Council Register, III Geo., vol. 11, p. 267, from which this transcript was taken.

1775, AUGUST 23.

[FOR SUPPRESSION OF REBELLION IN AMERICA.]

BY THE KING.

A PROCLAMATION

For suppressing Rebellion and Sedition.

George R.

Whereas many of Our Subjects in divers Parts of Our Colonies and Plantations in North America, misled by dangerous and ill-designing Men, and forgetting the Allegiance which they owe to the Power that has protected and sustained them, after various disorderly Acts committed in Disturbance of the Publick Peace, to the Obstruction of lawful Commerce, and to the Oppression of Our loyal Subjects carrying on the same, have at length proceeded to an open and avowed Rebellion, by arraying themselves in hostile Manner to withstand the Execution of the Law, and traitorously preparing, ordering, and levying War against Us; And whereas there is Reason to apprehend that such Rebellion hath been much promoted and encouraged by the traitorous Correspondence, Counsels, and Comfort of divers wicked and desperate Persons within this Realm: To the End therefore that none of Our Subjects may neglect or violate their Duty through Ignorance thereof, or through any Doubt of the Protection which the Law will afford to their Loyalty and Zeal; We have thought fit, by and with the Advice of Our Privy Council, to issue this Our Royal Proclamation, hereby declaring that not only all Our Officers Civil and Military are obliged to exert their utmost Endeavours to suppress such Rebellion, and to bring the Traitors to Justice; but that all Our Subjects of this Realm and the Dominions thereunto belonging are bound by Law to be aiding and assisting in the Suppression of such Rebellion, and to disclose and make known all traitorous Conspiracies and Attempts against Us, Our Crown and Dignity; And We do accordingly strictly charge and command all Our Officers as well Civil as Military, and all other Our obedient and loyal Subjects, to use their utmost Endeavours to withstand and suppress such Rebellion, and to disclose and make known all Treasons and traitorous Conspiracies which they shall know to be against Us, Our Crown and Dignity; and for that Purpose, that they transmit to One of Our Principal Secretaries of State, or other proper Officer, due and full Information of all Persons who shall be found carrying on Correspondence with, or in any Manner or Degree aiding or abetting the Persons now in open Arms and Rebellion against Our Government within any of Our Colonies and Plantations in North America, in order to bring to condign Punishment the Authors, Perpetrators, and Abettors of such traitorous Designs.

Given at Our Court at St. James's the Twenty-third Day of August, One thousand seven hundred and seventy-five, in the Fifteenth Year of Our Reign.

God save the King.

London: Printed by Charles Eyre and William Strahan, Printers to the King's most Excellent Majesty. 1775.

1 p. folio. Copies in Mass. State Archives, Boston Public Library, and N. Y. Public Library. Entered on Patent Rolls, and in Crown Office Docquet Book, vol. 12; entered in Privy Council Register, III Geo., vol. 12, p. 83. Printed in "London Gazette," August 26, 1775, and in most of the colonial newspapers. It was reprinted in broadside form in Boston (copies in N. Y. Public Library, Mass. Historical Society, and Mass. State Archives), and in New York (copy in Library of Congress); for the full titles, see Evans' "American Bibliography," nos. 14077 and 14078. The original English issue has been printed in facsimile form in the Boston Public Library "Bulletin" for October, 1892, and as an artotype by Bierstadt of New York, about 1890.

1775, DECEMBER 22.

[APPOINTING THE DISTRIBUTION OF PRIZES.]

BY THE KING.

A PROCLAMATION

APPOINTING THE DISTRIBUTION OF PRIZES TAKEN DURING THE CONTINUANCE
OF THE REBELLION NOW SUBSISTING IN DIVERS PARTS OF THE CONTINENT
OF NORTH AMERICA.

GEORGE R.

Whereas by an Act, made in this present Session of Parliament, intituled, An Act to prohibit all Trade and Intercourse with the Colonies of New Hampshire, Massachuset's Bay, Rhode Island, Connecticut, New York, New Jersey, Pensylvania, the Three Lower Counties on Delaware, Maryland, Virginia, North Carolina, South Carolina, and Georgia, during the Continuance of the present Rebellion within the said Colonies respectively; for repealing an Act, made in the Fourteenth Year of the Reign of His present Majesty, to discontinue the Landing and Discharging, Lading or Shipping, of Goods, Wares, and Merchandize, at the Town and within the Harbour of Boston, in the Province of Massachuset's Bay; and also Two Acts, made in the last Session of Parliament, for restraining the Trade and Commerce of the Colonies in the said Acts respectively mentioned; and to enable any Person or Persons, appointed and authorized by His Majesty to grant Pardons, to issue Proclamations, in the Cases, and for the Purposes therein mentioned; It is, amongst other Things, enacted, That all Ships and Vessels of or belonging to the Inhabitants of the said Colonies, together with their Cargoes, Apparel, and Furniture, except as in the said Act are excepted, and all other Ships and Vessels whatsoever, together with their Cargoes, Apparel, and Furniture, which shall be found trading in any Port or Place of the said Colonies, or going to trade, or coming from trading, in any such Port or Place, except as are therein also excepted, shall become forfeited to His Majesty, as if the same were the Ships and Effects of Open Enemies, and shall be so adjudged, deemed, and taken, in all Courts of Admiralty, and in all other Courts whatsoever: And, for the Encouragement of the Officers and Seamen of His Majesty's Ships of War, it is thereby also further enacted, That the Flag Officers, Captains, Commanders, and other commissioned Officers in His Majesty's Pay, and also the Seamen, Marines, and Soldiers on Board, shall have the sole Interest and Property of and in all and every such Ship, Vessel, Goods, and Merchandize, which they shall seize and take, (being first adjudged lawful Prize in any of His Majesty's Courts of Admiralty) to be divided in such Proportions, and after such Manner, as His Majesty shall think fit to order and direct by Proclamation or Proclamations hereafter to be issued for those Purposes: We, taking the Premises into Consideration, do, pursuant to the said Act of Parliament, (with the Advice of Our Privy Council), by this Our Proclamation, order, direct, and appoint, That the neat Produce of all Prizes taken, in Pursuance of the said Act, by Our Ships of War, be divided into Eight equal Parts, and be distributed in Manner following; that is to say, To the Captain or Captains of any of Our Ships of War, who shall be actually on Board at the Taking of any Prize, Three Eighth Parts; but in case any such Prize shall be taken by any of Our Ship or Ships of War, under the Command of a Flag or Flags, the Flag Officer or Officers, being actually on Board, or directing and assisting in the Capture, shall have One of the said Three Eighth Parts, the said One Eighth Part to be paid to such Flag or Flag Officers, in such Proportions, and subject to such Regulations, as are herein-after for that Purpose mentioned: To the Captains of Marines and Land Forces, Sea Lieutenants and Master, on Board any such Ships, One Eighth Part, to be equally divided amongst them: To the Lieutenants and Quarter Masters of Marines, and Lieutenants, Ensigns, and Quarter Masters of Land Forces, Boatswain, Gunner, Purser, Carpenter, Master's Mate, Chirurgeon, Pilot, and Chaplain, on Board any such Ship, One Eighth Part, to be equally divided amongst them: To the Midshipmen, Secretary to Flag Officers, Captain's Clerk, Master Sail Maker, Carpenter's Mates, Boatswain's Mates, Gunner's Mates, Master at Arms, Corporals, Yeomen of the Sheets, Coxswain, Quarter Masters, Quarter Master's Mates, Chirurgeon's Mates, Yeomen of the Powder Room, and Serjeants of Marines or Land Forces, on Board any such Ships, One Eighth Part, to be equally divided amongst them; To the Trumpeters, Quarter Gunners, Carpenter's Crew, Steward, Cook, Armourer, Steward's Mate, Cook's Mate, Gunsmith, Cooper, Swabber, Ordinary Trumpeter, Barber, Able Seamen, Ordinary Seamen, and Marine or other Soldiers, and all other Persons doing Duty, or assisting on Board any such Ships, Two Eighth Parts, to be equally divided amongst them. And in case any Sea Captain, inferior Commission or Warrant Sea Officers, belonging to any Ship of War, for whom any Shares of Prizes are hereby allowed, be absent at the Time of the Capture of any Prize, the Share of such Sea Captain, inferior Commission or Warrant Sea Officer, shall be cast into the Shares hereby allowed to the Trumpeters, Quarter Gunners, Carpenter's Crew, Steward, Cook, Armourer, Steward's Mate, Cook's Mate, Gunsmith, Cooper, Swabber, Ordinary Trumpeter, Barber, Able Seamen, Ordinary Seamen, and Marine or other Soldiers, and other Persons doing Duty, or assisting on Board any such Ships, to be equally divided amongst them. Provided, That if any Officer or Officers on Board any of Our Ships of War, at the Time of taking any such Prizes, shall have more Commissions or Offices than one, he or they shall be intitled only to the Share or Shares of the said Prizes which, according to the above-mentioned Distribution, shall belong to his or their respective superior Commissions or Offices. And We do hereby strictly enjoin all and every Commander and Commanders of any Ships of War, taking any Prize, as soon as may be, to transmit, or cause to be transmitted, to the Commissioners of Our Navy, a true List of the Names of all the Officers, Seamen, Marines, Soldiers, or others, who were actually on Board

Our Ships of War, under his or their Command, at the taking such Prize; which List shall contain the Quality of the Service of each Person on Board, and be subscribed by the Captain or Commanding Officer, and Three or more of the Chief Officers on Board. And We do hereby require and direct the Commissioners of Our Navy, or any Three or more of them, to examine, or cause to be examined, such Lists by the Muster Books of such Ships of War, and Lists annexed thereto, to see that such Lists do agree with the said Muster Book, and annexed Lists, as to the Names, Qualities, or Ratings of the Officers, Seamen, Marines, Soldiers, and others belonging to such Ship of War; and, upon Request, forthwith to grant a Certificate of the Truth of any List transmitted to them, to the Agents nominated and appointed by the Captors, pursuant to the said Act, to take care or dispose of such Prize; and also, upon Application to them, to give, or cause to be given, unto the Agents who shall, at any Time or Times, be appointed as aforesaid by the Captors, all such Lists from the Muster Books of any such Ships of War, and annexed Lists, as the said Agents shall find requisite for their Direction in paying the Produce of such Prizes, and to be otherwise aiding and assisting to the said Agents, as shall be necessary. And as touching the said One Eighth Part, herein before mentioned to be granted to the Flag or Flag Officers, who shall be actually on Board at the taking of any Prize, or shall be directing and assisting therein, We have thought fit, and do, by these Presents, publish, order, and declare, That the following Regulations be observed; First, That a Flag Officer commanding in Chief, where there is but One Flag Officer upon Service, shall have to his own Use the said One Eighth Part of the Prizes taken by Ships under his Command: Secondly, That a Flag Officer sent to command at Jamaica, or elsewhere, shall have no Right to any Share of the Prizes taken, by Ships employed there, before he arrives at the Place to which he is sent, and actually takes upon him the Command: Thirdly, That when an inferior Flag Officer is sent out to reinforce a superior Flag Officer at Jamaica, or elsewhere, the said superior Flag Officer shall have no Right to any Share in the Prizes taken by them before they arrive within the Limits of his Command, and actually receive some Orders from him: Fourthly, That a Chief Flag Officer returning home from Jamaica, or elsewhere, shall have no Share of the Prizes taken by the Ships left behind to act under another Command: Fifthly, That if a Flag Officer is sent to command in the Out-ports of this Kingdom, he shall have no Share of the Prizes taken by Ships that sailed from that Port, by Order from the Admiralty: Sixthly, That when more Flag Officers than One serve together, the Eighth Part of the Prizes taken by any Ships of the Fleet, or Squadron, shall be divided in the following Proportions; videlicet, If there be but Two Flag Officers, the Chief shall have Two Third Parts of the said One Eighth Part, and the other shall have the remaining Third Part; but if the Number of Flag Officers be more than Two, the Chief shall have only One Half, and the other Half shall be divided equally among the other Flag Officers: Seventhly, That Commodores, with Captains under them, shall be esteemed as Flag Officers, with respect to their Right to an Eighth Part of Prizes taken, whether commanding in Chief, or serving under Command.

Given at our Court at St. James's, the Twenty-second Day of December, One thousand seven hundred and seventy-five, in the Sixteenth Year of Our Reign.

God save the King.

London: Printed by Charles Eyre and William Strahan, Printers to the King's most Excellent Majesty. 1775.

1 p. folio. Copies in Antiq., and P. C. Entered on Patent Rolls, and in Crown Office Docquet Book, vol. 12; entered in Privy Council Register, III Geo., vol. 12, p. 267. Printed in "London Gazette," December 23, 1775.

1776, OCTOBER 30.

[FAST DAY IN ENGLAND.]

BY THE KING.

A PROCLAMATION

For a general Fast.

George R.

We, taking into Our most serious Consideration the just and necessary Measures of Force which We are obliged to use against Our rebellious Subjects in Our Colonies and Provinces in North America; and putting Our Trust in Almighty God, that he will vouchsafe a Special Blessing on Our Arms, both by Sea and Land, have resolved, and do, by and with the Advice of Our Privy Council, hereby command, That a Publick Fast and Humiliation be observed throughout that Part of Our Kingdom of Great Britain called England, Our Dominion of Wales, and Town of Berwick upon Tweed, upon Friday the Thirteenth Day of December next; that so both We and Our People may humble Ourselves before Almighty God, in order to obtain Pardon of Our Sins; and may, in the most devout and solemn Manner, send up Our Prayers and Supplications to the Divine Majesty, for averting those heavy Judgements, which Our manifold Sins and Provocations have most justly deserved, and for imploring his Intervention and Blessing speedily to deliver Our loyal Subjects within Our Colonies and Provinces in North America from the Violence, Injustice, and Tyranny of those daring Rebels who have assumed to themselves the Exercise of Arbitrary Power, to open the Eyes of those who have been deluded by specious Falshoods, into Acts of Treason and Rebellion, to turn the Hearts of the Authors of these Calamities, and finally to restore Our People in those distracted Provinces and Colonies to the happy Condition of being free Subjects of a free State; under which heretofore they flourished so long and prospered so much: And We do strictly charge and command, that the said Publick Fast be reverently and devoutly observed by all Our loving Subjects in England, Our Dominion of Wales, and Town of Berwick upon Tweed, as they tender the Favour of Almighty God, and would avoid his Wrath and Indignation; and upon Pain of such Punishment, as We may justly inflict upon all such as contemn and neglect the Performance of so religious a Duty. And for the better and more orderly solemnizing the same, We have given Directions to the most Reverend the Archbishops, and the Right Reverend the Bishops of England to compose a Form of Prayer suitable to this Occasion, to be used in all Churches, Chapels, and Places of Publick Worship; and to take Care the same be timely dispersed throughout their respective Dioceses.

Given at Our Court at St. James's, the Thirtieth Day of October, One thousand seven hundred and seventy-six, in the Seventeenth Year of Our Reign.

GOD SAVE THE KING.

London: Printed by Charles Eyre and William Strahan, Printers to the King's most Excellent Majesty. MDCCLXXVI.

1 p. folio. Copy in B. M. Entered on Patent Rolls; entered in Privy Council Register, III Geo., vol. 13, p. 172. Printed in "London Gazette," November 2, 1776. A proclamation with practically the same wording was issued by the Lord Lieutenant and Council of Ireland, November 7, 1776 (copy in Dublin P. R. O.), in consequence of an order of the Privy Council (Privy Council Register, III Geo., vol. 13, p. 174).

1776, OCTOBER 30.

[FAST DAY IN SCOTLAND.]

BY THE KING.

A PROCLAMATION

For a general Fast.

George R.

We taking into Our most serious Consideration the just and necessary Measures of Force, which We are obliged to use against Our rebellious Subjects in Our Colonies and Provinces in North America, and putting Our Trust in Almighty God that he will vouchsafe a special Blessing on Our Arms both by Sea and Land, have resolved, and do, by and with the Advice of Our Privy Council, hereby command, That a Publick Fast and Humiliation be observed throughout that Part of Our Kingdom of Great Britain called Scotland, upon Thursday the Twelfth Day of December next, that so both We and Our People may humble Ourselves before Almighty God, in order to obtain Pardon of Our Sins, and may, in the most devout and solemn Manner, send up Our Prayers and Supplications to the Divine Majesty, for averting those heavy Judgments which Our manifold Sins and Provocations have most justly deserved, and for imploring His Intervention and Blessing speedily to deliver Our Loyal Subjects within Our Colonies and Provinces in North America, from the Violence, Injustice, and Tyranny of those daring Rebels, who have assumed to themselves the Exercise of Arbitrary Power; to open the Eyes of those who have been deluded by specious Falsehoods into Acts of Treason and Rebellion; to turn the Hearts of the Authors of these Calamities; and finally to restore Our People, in those distracted Provinces and Colonies, to the happy Condition of being Free Subjects of a Free State, under which heretofore they flourished so long, and prospered so much. And We do strictly charge and command, that the said Publick Fast be reverently and devoutly observed by all Our loving Subjects in Scotland, as they tender the Favour of Almighty God, and would avoid His Wrath and Indignation, and upon Pain of such Punishment as we may justly inflict on all such as contemn and neglect the Performance of so Religious a Duty. Our Will is therefore, and We charge, That incontinent this Our Proclamation seen, ye pass to the Market Cross of Edinburgh, and all other Places needful, and there, in Our Name and Authority, make Publication hereof, that none pretend Ignorance. And Our Will and Pleasure is, That Our Solicitor do cause printed Copies hereof to be sent to the Sheriffs of the several Shires, Stewarts of

Stewarties, and Bailiffs of Regalities, and their Clerks, whom We ordain to see the same published: And We appoint them to send Doubles hereof to the several Paroch Kirks within their Bounds, that upon the Lord's Day immediately preceding the Day abovementioned, the same may be published and read from the Pulpits, immediately after Divine Service.

Given at Our Court at St. James's the Thirtieth Day of October, One thousand seven hundred and seventy-six, in the Seventeenth Year of Our Reign.

GOD SAVE THE KING.

No printed copy found. Entered on Patent Rolls; entered in Privy Council Register, III Geo., vol. 13, p. 173. Printed in "London Gazette," November 2, 1776.

1778, JANUARY 23.

[FAST DAY IN ENGLAND.]

BY THE KING.

A PROCLAMATION

For a general Fast.

George R.

We, taking into Our most serious Consideration the just and necessary Measures of Force which We are obliged to use against Our Rebellious Subjects in Our Colonies and Provinces in North America; and putting Our Trust in Almighty God, that He will vouchsafe a special Blessing on Our Arms, both by Sea and Land, have resolved, and do, by and with the Advice of Our Privy Council, hereby command, That a Publick Fast and Humiliation be observed throughout that Part of Our Kingdom of Great Britain called England, Our Dominion of Wales, and Town of Berwick upon Tweed, upon Friday the Twenty-seventh Day of February next; that so both We and Our People may humble Ourselves before Almighty God, in order to obtain Pardon of Our Sins; and may, in the most devout and solemn Manner, send up Our Prayers and Supplications to the Divine Majesty for averting those heavy Judgements, which Our manifold Sins and Provocations have most justly deserved, and for imploring his Intervention and Blessing speedily to deliver Our loyal Subjects within Our Colonies and Provinces in North America from the Violence, Injustice, and Tyranny of those daring Rebels who have assumed to themselves the Exercise of Arbitrary Power, to open the Eyes of those who have been deluded by specious Falsehoods into Acts of Treason and Rebellion, to turn the Hearts of the Authors of these Calamities, and finally to restore Our People in those distracted Provinces and Colonies to the happy Condition of being free Subjects of a free State, under which heretofore they flourished so long and prospered so much: And We do strictly charge and command, That the said Publick Fast be reverently and devoutly observed by all Our loving Subjects in England, Our Dominion of Wales, and Town of Berwick upon Tweed, as they tender the Favour of Almighty God, and would avoid his Wrath and Indignation; and upon Pain of such Punishment as We may justly inflict on all such as contemn and neglect the Performance of so religious a Duty. And for the better and more orderly solemnizing the same, We have given Directions to the Most Reverend the Archbishops, and the Right Reverend the Bishops of England, to compose a Form of Prayer suitable to this Occasion, to be used in all Churches, Chapels, and Places of Publick Worship; and to take Care the same be timely dispersed throughout their respective Dioceses.

Given at Our Court at St. James's, the Twenty-third Day of January, One thousand seven hundred and seventy-eight, in the Eighteenth Year of Our Reign.

God save the King.

London: Printed by Charles Eyre and William Strahan, Printers to the King's most Excellent Majesty. MDCCLXXVIII.

1 p. folio. Copy in P. C. Entered on Patent Rolls, and in Crown Office Docquet Book, vol. 12, entered in Privy Council Register, III Geo., vol. 14, p. 458. Printed in "London Gazette," January 24, 1778. A proclamation with practically the same wording was issued by the Lord Lieutenant and Council of Ireland, January 31, 1775 (copy in Dublin P. R. O.), in consequence of an order of the Privy Council (Privy Council Register, III Geo., vol. 14, p. 461).

1778, JANUARY 23.

[FAST DAY IN SCOTLAND.]

BY THE KING.

A PROCLAMATION

For a general Fast.

George R.

We, taking into Our most serious Consideration the just and necessary Measures of Force which We are obliged to use against Our Rebellious Subjects in Our Colonies and Provinces in North America; and putting Our Trust in Almighty God, that He will vouchsafe a special Blessing on Our Arms, both by Sea and Land, have resolved, and do, by and with the Advice of Our Privy Council, hereby command, That a Publick Fast and Humiliation be observed throughout that Part of Our Kingdom of Great Britain called Scotland, upon Thursday the Twenty sixth Day of February next; that so both We and Our People may humble Ourselves before Almighty God, in order to obtain Pardon of Our Sins; and may, in the most devout and solemn Manner, send up Our Prayers and Supplications to the Divine Majesty, for averting those heavy Judgments, which Our manifold Sins and Provocations have most justly deserved, and for imploring His Intervention and Blessing, speedily to deliver Our loyal Subjects, within Our Colonies and Provinces in North America, from the Violence, Injustice and Tyranny of those daring Rebels, who have assumed to themselves the Exercise of Arbitrary Power; to open the Eyes of those who have been deluded by specious Falsehoods into Acts of Treason and Rebellion; to turn the Hearts of the Authors of these Calamities; and finally to restore Our People in those distracted Provinces and Colonies to the happy Condition of being Free Subjects of a Free State, under which heretofore they flourished so long and prospered so much. And We do strictly charge and command, That the said Publick Fast be reverently and devoutly observed by all Our loving Subjects in Scotland, as they tender the Favour of Almighty God, and would avoid His Wrath and Indignation; and upon Pain of such Punishment as We may justly inflict on all such as contemn and neglect the Performance of so religious a Duty. Our Will is therefore, and We charge, That incontinent this Our Proclamation seen, ye pass to the Market Cross of Edinburgh, and all other Places needful, and there, in Our Name and Authority, make Publication hereof, that none pretend Ignorance. And Our Will and Pleasure is, That Our Solicitor do cause printed Copies hereof to be sent to the Sheriffs of the several Shires, Stewarts of Stewarties, and

Bailif's of Regalities, and their Clerks, whom We ordain to see the same published; and We appoint them to send Doubles hereof to the several Paroch Kirks within their Bounds, that upon the Lord's Day immediately preceding the Day above mentioned, the same may be published and read from the Pulpits immediately after Divine Service.

Given at Our Court at St. James's, the Twenty-third Day of January, One thousand seven hundred and seventy-eight, in the Eighteenth Year of Our Reign.

GOD SAVE THE KING.

No printed copy found. Entered on Patent Rolls, and in Crown Office Docquet Book, vol. 12; entered in Privy Council Register, III Geo., vol. 14, p. 460. Printed in "London Gazette," January 24, 1778.

1778, SEPTEMBER 16.

[REGARDING THE DISTRIBUTION OF PRIZES.]

BY THE KING.

A PROCLAMATION

For granting the Distribution of Prizes
during the present Hostilities.

George R.

Whereas, by Our Order in Council dated the Twenty-ninth Day of July last, We have ordered that general Reprisals be granted against the Ships, Goods, and Subjects of the French King, and that as well Our Fleets and Ships, as also all other Ships and Vessels that shall be commissionated by Letters of Marque, or general Reprisals, or otherwise, by Our Commissioners for executing Our Office of Lord High Admiral of Great Britain, shall and may lawfully seize all Ships, Vessels and Goods, belonging to the French King, and bring the same to Judgement in any of Our Courts of Admiralty within Our Dominions: We, being desirous to give due Encouragement to all Our faithful Subjects who shall lawfully seize the same, and having declared in Council, by Our Order of the Seventh of last Month, Our Intentions concerning the Distribution of all Manner of Captures, Seizures, Prizes and Reprisals, of all Ships and Goods, during the present Hostilities, do now make known to all Our loving Subjects, and all others whom it may concern, by this Our Proclamation, by and with the Advice of Our Privy Council, that Our Will and Pleasure is, That the Neat Produce of all Prizes taken, the Right whereof is inherent in Us, and Our Crown, be given to the Takers in the Proportion and Manner of Proceeding herein-after set forth: that is to say, That all Prizes taken by Ships and Vessels having Commissions of Letters of Marque and Reprisals, may be sold and disposed of by the Merchants, Owners, Fitters, and others to whom such Letters of Marque and Reprisals are granted, for their own Use and Benefit, after final Adjudication, and not before. And We do hereby further Order and direct, that the Neat Produce of all Prizes which are or shall be taken by any of Our Ships or Vessels of War, shall be for the entire Benefit and Encouragement of Our Flag Officers, Captains, Commanders, and other Commissioned Officers in Our Pay, and of the Seamen, Marines, and Soldiers, on Board Our said Ships and Vessels at the Time of the Capture; and that such Prizes may be lawfully sold and disposed of by them and their Agents, after the same shall have been to Us finally adjudged lawful Prize, and not otherwise. The Distribution shall be made as follows; the Whole of the Neat Produce being first divided into Eight equal Parts;

The Captain or Captains of any of Our said Ships and Vessels of War, who shall be actually on Board at the Taking of any Prize, shall have Three Eighth Parts; but in case any such Prize shall be taken by any of Our Ships or Vessels of War, under the Command of a Flag or Flags, the Flag Officer or Officers being actually on Board or directing and assisting in the Capture, shall have One of the said Three Eighth Parts; the said One Eighth Part to be paid to such Flag or Flag Officers in such Proportions, and subject to such Regulations, as are herein-after mentioned:

The Captains of Marines and Land Forces, Sea Lieutenants, and Master on Board, shall have One Eighth Part, to be equally divided amongst them:

The Lieutenants and Quarter Masters of Marines, and Lieutenants, Ensigns, and Quarter Masters of Land Forces, Secretaries of Admirals or of Commodores, with Captains under them, Boatswains, Gunners, Purser, Carpenter, Master's Mates, Chirurgeon, Pilot, and Chaplain on Board, shall have One Eighth Part, to be equally divided amongst them:

The Midshipmen, Captain's Clerk, Master Sailmaker, Carpenter's Mates, Boatswain's Mates, Gunner's Mates, Master at Arms, Corporals, Yeomen of the Sheets, Cockswain, Quarter Masters, Quarter Masters Mates, Chirurgeon's Mates, Yeomen of the Powder Room, Serjeants of Marines, and Land Forces on Board, shall have One Eighth Part, to be equally divided amongst them:

The Trumpeters, Quarter Gunners, Carpenter's Crew, Stewards, Cook, Armourer, Steward's Mate, Cook's Mate, Gunsmith, Cooper, Swabber, Ordinary Trumpeter, Barber, Able Seamen, Ordinary Seamen, and Marines, and other Soldiers, and all other Persons doing Duty and assisting on Board, shall have Two Eighth Parts, to be equally divided amongst them:

Provided, That if any Officer being on Board any of Our Ships of War, at the Time of taking any Prize, shall have more Commissions or Offices than One, such Officer shall be intitled only to the Share or Shares of the Prizes which, according to the above-mentioned Distribution, shall belong to his superior Commission or Office. And We do hereby strictly enjoin all Commanders of Our Ships and Vessels of War taking any Prize, as soon as may be, to transmit, or cause to be transmitted, to the Commissioners of Our Navy, a true List of the Names of all the Officers, Seamen, Marines, Soldiers, and others, who were actually on Board Our Ships and Vessels of War under their Command at the Time of the Capture; which List shall contain the Quality of the Service of each Person on Board, and be subscribed by the Captain or Commanding Officer, and Three or more of the Chief Officers on Board. And we do hereby require and direct the Commissioners of Our Navy, or any Three or more of them, to examine, or cause to be examined, such Lists by the Muster Books of such Ships and Vessels of War, and Lists annexed thereto, to see that such Lists do agree with the said Muster Books and annexed Lists, as to the Names, Qualities, or Ratings of the Officers, Seamen, Marines, Soldiers, and others belonging to such Ships and Vessels of War, and upon Request forthwith to grant a Certificate of the Truth of any List transmitted to them, to the Agents nominated and appointed by the Captors, to take care and dispose of such Prize; and also upon Application to them (the said Commissioners) they shall give, or cause to be given, to the said Agents, all such Lists from the Muster Books of any such Ships of War, and annexed Lists, as the said Agents shall find requisite for their Direction in paying the Produce of such Prizes, and otherwise shall be aiding and assisting to the said Agents in all such Matters as shall be necessary. We do hereby further will and direct, that the following Regulations shall be observed concerning the One Eighth Part herein-before mentioned to be granted to the Flag, or Flag Officers, who shall actually be on Board at the taking of any Prize, or shall be directing or assisting therein: First, That a Flag Officer, Commander in Chief, when there is but One Flag Officer upon Service, shall have to his own Use the said One Eighth Part of the Prizes taken by Ships and Vessels under his Command: Secondly, That a Flag Officer, sent to command at Jamaica, or elsewhere, shall have no Right to any Share of Prizes taken by Ships or Vessels employed there, before he arrives at the Place to which he is sent, and actually takes upon him the Command: Thirdly, That when an inferior Flag Officer is sent out to reinforce a superior Flag Officer at Jamaica, or elsewhere, the superior Flag Officer shall have no Right to any Share or Prizes taken by the inferior Flag Officer, before the inferior Flag Officer shall arrive within the Limits of the Command of the superior Flag Officer, and actually receive some Order from him: Fourthly, That a Chief Flag Officer returning home from Jamaica, or elsewhere, shall have no Share of the Prizes taken by the Ships or Vessels left behind to act under another Command: Fifthly, That if a Flag Officer is sent to command in the Out-ports of this Kingdom, he shall have no Share of the Prizes taken by Ships or Vessels which have sailed from that Port by Order from the Admiralty: Sixthly, That when more Flag Officers than One serve together, the Eighth Part of the Prizes taken by any Ships or Vessels of the Fleet or Squadron, shall be divided in the following Proportions; viz. If there be but Two Flag Officers, the Chief shall have Two Third Parts of the said One Eighth Part, and the other shall have the remaining Third Part; but if the Number of Flag Officers be more than Two, the Chief shall have only One Half, and the other Half shall be equally divided amongst the other Flag Officers: Seventhly, That Commodores with Captains under them shall be esteemed as Flag Officers with respect to the Eighth Part of Prizes taken, whether commanding in Chief or serving under Command. And We do hereby further order, That in the Case of Cutters, Schooners, and other armed Vessels commanded by Lieutenants, the Share of such Lieutenants shall be Three Eighth Parts of the Prize, unless such Lieutenants shall be under the Command of a Flag Officer or Officers; in which Case the Flag Officer or Officers shall have One of the said Three Eighths, to be divided among such Flag Officer or Flag Officers in the Manner herein-before directed in the Case of Captains serving under Flag Officers: Secondly, We direct that the Share of the Master or other Person acting as Second in Command, and the Pilot, (if there happens to be One on Board) shall be One Eighth Part, to be divided into Three equal Parts; of which Two Thirds shall go to the Master, or other Person acting as Second in Command, and the remaining One Third to the Pilot; but if there is no Pilot, then such Eighth Part to go wholly to the Master or Person acting as Second in Command: That the Share of the Chirurgeon, or Chirurgeon's Mate, (where there is no Chirurgeon) Midshipmen, and Clerk and Steward, shall be One Eighth; That the Share of the

Boatswain's, Gunner's, and Carpenter's Mates, Yeomen of the Sheets, Sailmaker, Quarter Master, and Quarter Master's Mate, shall be One Eighth; and the Share of the Seamen, Marines, and other Persons on Board, assisting in the Capture, shall be Two Eighth Parts. But it is Our Intention nevertheless, that the above Distribution shall only extend to such Captures as shall be made by any Cutter, Schooner, or armed Vessel, without any of His Majesty's Ships or Vessels of War being present or within Sight of, and adding to the Encouragement of the Captors, and Terror of the Enemy: But in Case any of His Majesty's Ships or Vessels of War shall be present, or in Sight, that then the Officers, Pilots, Petty Officers, and Men on Board such Cutters and Schooners, or armed Vessels, shall share in the same Proportion as is allowed to Persons of the like Rank and Denomination on Board His Majesty's Ships and Vessels of War. Lastly, it is Our Will and Pleasure, That this Our Declaration, and Order in Council thereupon, shall extend not only to Captures from the French King, his Subjects, and others inhabiting his Countries, but also shall extend in the like Manner to all Ships and Goods now taken, and not finally adjudged and condemned, and divided, or to be taken hereafter, under the Act of Parliament of the Sixteenth Year of Our Reign, whereby it is enacted, That, for the Encouragement of Our Officers of Our Ships of War, the Flag Officers, Captains, Commanders, and other Commissioned Officers in Our Pay, and the Seamen, Marines, and Soldiers on Board, shall have the sole Interest and Property of and in all and every such Ships and Goods as therein are recited, which they shall seize and take; but being first adjudged, that is to say, finally adjudged lawful Prize, and which are by the said Act declared forfeited to Us, and to be divided and disposed of in such Proportion and after such Manner as We, Our Heirs and Successors, shall by Proclamation or Proclamations order and direct.

Given at Our Court at St. James's, the Sixteenth Day of September, One thousand seven hundred and seventy-eight, in the Eighteenth Year of Our Reign.

GOD SAVE THE KING.

London: Printed by Charles Eyre and William Strahan, Printers to the King's most Excellent Majesty. 1778.

1 p. folio. Copies in Antiq., and P. C.; also in John Carter Brown Library. Entered on Patent Rolls, and in Crown Office Docquet Book, vol. 12; entered in Privy Council Register, III Geo., vol. 15, p. 515. Printed in "London Gazette," September 19, 1778.

1779, JANUARY 1.

[FAST DAY IN ENGLAND.]

BY THE KING.

A PROCLAMATION

For a General Fast.

George R.

We, taking into Our most serious Consideration the just and necessary Hostilities in which We are engaged with the French King, and the unnatural Rebellion carrying on in some of Our Provinces and Colonies in North America, and putting Our Trust in Almighty God, that he will vouchsafe a special Blessing on Our Arms both by Sea and Land, have resolved, and do, by and with the Advice of Our Privy Council, hereby Command, That a Public Fast and Humiliation be observed throughout that Part of Great Britain called England, Our Dominion of Wales, and Town of Berwick upon Tweed, upon Wednesday the Tenth Day of February next; that so both We and Our People may humble Ourselves before Almighty God, in order to obtain Pardon of Our Sins; and may, in the most devout and solemn Manner, send up Our Prayers and Supplications to the Divine Majesty, for averting those heavy Judgments which Our manifold Sins and Provocations have most justly deserved; and imploring His Blessing and Assistance on Our Arms; and for restoring and perpetuating Peace, Safety, and Prosperity, to Us and Our Kingdoms: And We do strictly Charge and Command, That the said Public Fast be reverently and devoutly observed by all Our loving Subjects in England, Our Dominion of Wales, and Town of Berwick upon Tweed, as they tender the Favour of Almighty God, and would avoid His Wrath and Indignation; and upon Pain of such Punishment as We may justly inflict on all such as contemn and neglect the Performance of so religious and necessary a Duty. And, for the better and more orderly solemnizing the same, We have given Directions to the Most Reverend the Archbishops, and the Right Reverend the Bishops of England, to compose a Form of Prayer suitable to this Occasion, to be used in all Churches, Chapels, and Places of Public Worship; and to take Care the same be timely dispersed throughout their respective Dioceses.

Given at Our Court at St. James's, the First Day of January, One thousand seven hundred and seventy-nine, in the Nineteenth Year of Our Reign.

God save the King.

No printed copy found. Entered on Patent Rolls, and in Crown Office Docquet Book, vol. 12; entered in Privy Council Register, III Geo., vol. 16, p. 181. Printed in "London Gazette," January 2, 1779. A proclamation with practically the same wording was issued by the Lord Lieutenant and Council of Ireland, January 11, 1779 (copy in Dublin P. R. O.), in consequence of an order of the Privy Council (Privy Council Register, III Geo., vol. 16, p. 184).

1779, JANUARY 1.

[FAST DAY IN SCOTLAND.]

BY THE KING.

A PROCLAMATION

For a General Fast.

George R.

We, taking into Our most serious Consideration the just and necessary Hostilities in which We are engaged with the French King, and the unnatural Rebellion carrying on in some of Our Provinces and Colonies in North America, and putting Our Trust in Almighty God, that he will vouchsafe a special Blessing on Our Arms both by Sea and Land, have resolved, and do, by and with the Advice of Our Privy Council, hereby command, That a Publick Fast and Humiliation be observed, throughout that Part of Our Kingdom of Great Britain called Scotland, on Tuesday the Ninth Day of February next; that so both We and Our People may humble Ourselves before Almighty God, in order to obtain Pardon of Our Sins; and may, in the most devout and solemn Manner, send up Our Prayers and Supplications to the Divine Majesty, for averting those heavy Judgements which Our manifold Sins and Provocations have most justly deserved, and imploring his Blessing and Assistance on Our Arms, and for restoring and perpetuating Peace, Safety, and Prosperity, to Us and Our Kingdoms: And We do strictly Charge and Command, That the said Publick Fast be reverently and devoutly observed by all Our loving Subjects in Scotland, as they tender the Favour of Almighty God, and would avoid his Wrath and Indignation; and upon Pain of such Punishment as We may justly inflict on all such as contemn and neglect the Performance of so religious and necessary a Duty. Our Will is therefore, and We charge, That incontinent this Our Proclamation seen, ye pass to the Market Cross of Edinburgh, and all other Places needful, and there, in Our Name and Authority, make Publication hereof, that none pretend Ignorance. And Our Will and Pleasure is, That Our Solicitor do cause printed Copies hereof to be sent to the Sheriffs of the several Shires, Stewarts of Stewarties, and Bailiffs of Regalities, and their Clerks, whom We ordain to see the same published; and We appoint them to send Doubles hereof to the several Paroch Kirks within their Bounds, that upon the Lord's Day immediately preceding the Day above-mentioned, the same may be published and read from the Pulpits, immediately after Divine Service.

Given at Our Court at St. James's, the First Day of January, One thousand seven hundred and seventy-nine, in the Nineteenth Year of Our Reign.

GOD SAVE THE KING.

London: Printed by Charles Eyre and William Strahan, Printers to the King's most Excellent Majesty. MDCCLXXIX.

1 p. folio. Copy in P. C. Entered on Patent Rolls, and in Crown Office Docquet Book, vol. 12; entered in Privy Council Register, III Geo., vol. 16, p. 182. Printed in "London Gazette," January 2, 1779.

1779, DECEMBER 13.

[FAST DAY IN ENGLAND.]

BY THE KING.

A PROCLAMATION

For a General Fast.

George R.

We, taking into Our most serious Consideration the just and necessary Hostilities in which We are engaged, and the unnatural Rebellion carrying on in some of Our Provinces and Colonies in North America, and putting Our Trust in Almighty God, that he will vouchsafe a Special Blessing on Our Arms both by Sea and Land, have resolved, and do, by and with the Advice of Our Privy Council, hereby command, That a Publick Fast and Humiliation be observed throughout that Part of Our Kingdom of Great Britain called England, Our Dominion of Wales, and Town of Berwick upon Tweed, upon Friday the Fourth Day of February next; that so both We and Our People may humble Ourselves before Almighty God, in order to obtain Pardon of Our Sins; and may, in the most devout and solemn Manner, send up Our Prayers and Supplications to the Divine Majesty, for averting those heavy Judgements which Our manifold Sins and Provocations have most justly deserved, and imploring his Blessing and Assistance on Our Arms, and for restoring and perpetuating Peace, Safety, and Prosperity, to Us and Our Kingdoms: And We do strictly charge and command, That the said Publick Fast be reverently and devoutly observed by all Our loving Subjects in England, our Dominion of Wales, and Town of Berwick upon Tweed, as they tender the Favour of Almighty God, and would avoid his Wrath and Indignation; and upon Pain of such Punishment as We may justly inflict on all such as contemn and neglect the Performance of so religious and necessary a Duty. And for the better and more orderly solemnizing the same, We have given Directions to the Most Reverend the Archbishops, and the Right Reverend the Bishops of England, to compose a Form of Prayer suitable to this Occasion, to be used in all Churches, Chapels, and Places of Publick Worship, and to take care the same be timely dispersed throughout their respective Dioceses.

Given at Our Court at St. James's, the Thirteenth of December, One thousand seven hundred and seventy-nine, in the Twentieth Year of Our Reign.

God save the King.

London: Printed by Charles Eyre and William Strahan, Printers to the King's most Excellent Majesty. MDCCLXXIX.

1 p. folio. Copy in P. R. O. Entered on Patent Rolls, and in Crown Office Docquet Book, vol. 12; entered in Privy Council Register, III Geo., vol. 17, p. 453. Printed in "London Gazette," December 14, 1779. A proclamation with practically the same wording was issued by the Lord Lieutenant and Council of Ireland, December 24, 1779 (copy in Dublin P. R. O.), in consequence of an order of the Privy Council (Privy Council Register, III Geo., vol. 17, p. 455).

1779, DECEMBER 13.

[FAST DAY IN SCOTLAND.]

BY THE KING.

A PROCLAMATION

For a General Fast.

George R.

We, taking into Our most serious Consideration the just and necessary Hostilities in which We are engaged, and the unnatural Rebellion carrying on in some of Our Provinces and Colonies in North America, and putting Our Trust in Almighty God, that he will vouchsafe a special Blessing on Our Arms both by Sea and Land, have resolved, and do, by and with the Advice of Our Privy Council, hereby command, That a Publick Fast and Humiliation be observed throughout that Part of Our Kingdom of Great Britain called Scotland, on Thursday the Third Day of February next; that so both We and Our People may humble Ourselves before Almighty God, in order to obtain Pardon of Our Sins; and may, in the most devout and solemn Manner, send up Our Prayers and Supplications to the Divine Majesty, for averting those heavy Judgments which Our manifold Sins and Provocations have most justly deserved, and imploring His Blessing and Assistance on Our Arms, and for restoring and perpetuating Peace, Safety, and Prosperity, to Us and Our Kingdoms: And We do strictly charge and command, That the said Publick Fast be reverently and devoutly observed by all Our loving Subjects in Scotland, as they tender the Favour of Almighty God, and would avoid His Wrath and Indignation; and upon Pain of such Punishment as We may justly inflict on all such as contemn and neglect the Performance of so religious and necessary a Duty. Our Will is therefore, and We charge, That incontinent this Our Proclamation seen, ye pass to the Market Cross of Edinburgh, and all other Places needful, and there, in Our Name and Authority, make Publication hereof, that none pretend Ignorance. And Our Will and Pleasure is, That Our Solicitor do cause printed Copies hereof to be sent to the Sheriffs of the several Shires, Stewarts of Stewarties, and Bailiffs of Regalities, and their Clerks, whom We ordain to see the same published: and We appoint them to send Doubles hereof to the several Paroch Kirks within their Bounds, that upon the Lord's Day immediately preceding the Day above mentioned the same may be published and read from the Pulpits, immediately after Divine Service.

Given at Our Court at St. James's, the Thirteenth Day of December, One thousand seven hundred and seventy-nine, in the Twentieth Year of Our Reign.

God Save the King.

No printed copy found. Entered on Patent Rolls, and in Crown Office Docquet Book, vol. 12; entered in Privy Council Register, III Geo., vol. 17, p. 454. Printed in "London Gazette," December 14, 1779.

1780, DECEMBER 20.

[RELATIONS OF ENGLAND TO HOLLAND.]

MANIFESTO.

GEORGE R.

Through the whole Course of Our Reign, Our Conduct towards the States General of the United Provinces has been that of a sincere Friend and faithful Ally. Had they adhered to those wise Principles which used to govern the Republic, they must have shewn themselves equally sollicitous to maintain the Friendship which has so long subsisted between the two Nations, and which is essential to the Interests of both: But from the Prevalence of a Faction devoted to France, and following the Dictates of that Court, a very different Policy has prevailed. The Return made to Our Friendship, for some Time past, has been an open Contempt of the most solemn Engagements, and a repeated Violation of Public Faith.

On the Commencement of the Defensive War, in which We found Ourselves engaged by the Aggression of France, We shewed a tender Regard for the Interests of the States General, and a Desire of securing to their Subjects every Advantage of Trade, consistent with the great and just Principle of Our own Defence. Our Ambassador was instructed to offer a friendly Negotiation, to obviate every Thing that might lead to disagreeable Discussion; and to this Offer, solemnly made by him to the States General, the 2d of November, 1778, no Attention was paid.

After the Number of Our Enemies increased by the Aggression of Spain, equally unprovoked with that of France, We found it necessary to call upon the States General for the Performance of their Engagements. The Fifth Article of the perpetual Defensive Alliance between Our Crown and the States General, concluded at Westminster the 3d of March, 1678, besides the general Engagement for Succours, expressly stipulates, "That that Party of the two Allies that is not attacked, shall be obliged to break with the Aggressor in two Months after the Party attacked shall require it." Yet two Years have passed, without the least Assistance given to Us, without a single Syllable in Answer to Our repeated Demands.

So totally regardless have the States been of their Treaties with Us, that they readily promised Our Enemies to observe a Neutrality, in direct Contradiction to those Engagements; and whilst they have withheld from Us the Succours they were bound to furnish, every secret Assistance has been given the Enemy; and Inland Duties have been taken off, for the sole Purpose of facilitating the Carriage of Naval Stores to France.

In direct and open Violation of Treaty, they suffered an American Pirate to remain several Weeks in one of their Ports; and even permitted a Part of his Crew to mount Guard in a Fort in the Texel.

In the East-Indies, the Subjects of the States General, in Concert with France, have endeavoured to raise up Enemies against Us.

In the West-Indies, particularly at St. Eustatius, every Protection and Assistance has been given to Our Rebellious Subjects. Their Privateers are openly received in the Dutch Harbours; allowed to refit there; supplied with Arms and Ammunition; their Crews recruited; their Prizes brought in and sold; and all this in direct Violation of as clear and solemn Stipulations as can be made.

This Conduct, so inconsistent with all good Faith, so repugnant to the Sense of the wisest Part of the Dutch Nation, is chiefly to be ascribed to the Prevalence of the leading Magistrates of Amsterdam, whose secret Correspondence with Our Rebellious Subjects was suspected, long before it was made known by the fortunate Discovery of a Treaty, the first Article of which is:

"There shall be a firm, inviolable and universal Peace, and sincere Friendship, between their High Mightinesses the Estates of the Seven United Provinces of Holland, and the United States of North America, and the Subjects and People of the said Parties; and between the Countries, Islands, Cities, and Towns, situated under the Jurisdiction of the said United States of Holland, and the said United States of America, and the People and Inhabitants thereof, of every Degree, without Exception of Persons or Places."

This Treaty was signed in September, 1778, by the express Order of the Pensionary of Amsterdam, and other principal Magistrates of that City. They now not only avow the whole Transaction, but glory in it, and expressly say, even to the States General, that what they did "was what their indispensable Duty required."

In the mean Time, the States General declined to give any Answer to the Memorial presented by Our Ambassador; and this Refusal was aggravated by their proceeding upon other Business, nay upon the Consideration of this very Subject to internal Purposes; and while they found it impossible to approve the Conduct of their Subjects, they still industriously avoided to give Us the Satisfaction so manifestly due.

We had every Right to expect, that such a Discovery would have roused them to a just Indignation at the Insult offered to Us, and to themselves; and that they would have been eager to give Us full and ample Satisfaction for the Offence, and to inflict the severest Punishment upon the Offenders. The Urgency of the Business made an instant Answer essential to the Honour and Safety of this Country.[90]

---

[90] The Privy Council, by an order of April 17, 1780, declared that whereas the United Provinces had not lived up to the terms of their alliance with Great Britain, they should henceforth be considered a neutral power not privileged by treaty. On the same date as the publication of the Manifesto, December 20, 1780, the Council ordered that general reprisals should be granted against the ships of the United Provinces (Privy Council Register, III Geo., vol. 18). On December 27, 1780, the King issued a proclamation providing for the distribution of the prizes during the hostilities with the United Provinces, which is not here

The Demand was accordingly pressed by Our Ambassador in repeated Conferences with the Ministers, and in a Second Memorial: It was pressed with all the Earnestness which could proceed from Our ancient Friendship, and the Sense of recent Injuries; and the Answer now given to a Memorial on such a Subject, delivered about Five Weeks ago, is, *That the States have taken it ad referendum*. Such an Answer, upon such an Occasion, could only be dictated by the fixt Purpose of Hostility meditated, and already resolved, by the States, induced by the offensive Councils of Amsterdam thus to countenance the hostile Aggression, which the Magistrates of that City have made in the Name of the Republic.

There is an End of the Faith of all Treaties with Them, if Amsterdam may usurp the Sovereign Power, may violate those Treaties with Impunity, by pledging the States to Engagements directly contrary, and leaguing the Republic with the Rebels of a Sovereign to whom she is bound by the closest Ties. An Infraction of the Law of Nations, by the meanest Member of any Country, gives the injured State a Right to demand Satisfaction and Punishment: How much more so, when the Injury complained of is a flagrant Violation of Public Faith, committed by leading and predominant Members in the State? Since then the Satisfaction we have demanded is not given, We must, though most reluctantly, do Ourselves that Justice which We cannot otherwise obtain: We must consider the States General as Parties in the Injury which they will not repair, as Sharers in the Aggression which they refuse to punish, and must act accordingly. We have therefore ordered Our Ambassador to withdraw from the Hague, and shall immediately pursue such vigorous Measures as the Occasion fully justifies, and Our Dignity and the essential Interests of Our People require.

From a Regard to the Dutch Nation at large, We wish it were possible to direct those Measures wholly against Amsterdam; but this cannot be, unless the States General will immediately declare, that Amsterdam shall, upon this Occasion, receive no Assistance from them, but be left to abide the Consequences of it's Aggression.

Whilst Amsterdam is suffered to prevail in the general Councils, and is backed by the Strength of the State, it is impossible to resist the Aggression of so considerable a Part, without contending with the Whole. But We are too sensible of the common Interests of both Countries not to remember, in the Midst of such a Contest, that the only Point to be aimed at by Us, is to raise a Disposition in the Councils of the Republic to return to our ancient Union, by giving Us that Satisfaction for the past, and Security for the future, which We shall be as ready to receive as They can be to offer, and to the Attainment of which We shall direct all Our Operations. We mean only to provide for Our own Security, by defeating the dangerous Designs that have been formed against Us. We shall ever be disposed to return to Friendship with the States General, when they sincerely revert to that System which the Wisdom of their Ancestors formed, and which has now been subverted by a powerful Faction, conspiring with France against the true Interests of the Republic, no less than against those of Great Britain.

St. James's, December 20, 1780.

printed since it remotely concerns America.

G. R.

*No printed copy found, except as published in the "London Gazette Extraordinary,"
December 21, 1780, from which this transcript was taken.*

1781, JANUARY 12.

[FAST DAY IN ENGLAND.]

BY THE KING.

A PROCLAMATION

FOR A GENERAL FAST.

GEORGE R.

We, taking into Our most serious Consideration the just and necessary Hostilities in which We are engaged, and the unnatural Rebellion carrying on in some of Our Provinces and Colonies in North America, and putting Our Trust in Almighty God, that he will vouchsafe a Special Blessing on Our Arms both by Sea and Land, have resolved, and do, by and with the Advice of Our Privy Council, hereby command, That a Publick Fast and Humiliation be observed throughout that Part of Our Kingdom of Great Britain called England, Our Dominion of Wales, and Town of Berwick upon Tweed, upon Wednesday the Twenty-first Day of February next; that so both We and Our People may humble Ourselves before Almighty God, in order to obtain Pardon of Our Sins; and may, in the most devout and solemn Manner, send up Our Prayers and Supplications to the Divine Majesty, for averting those heavy Judgements which Our manifold Sins and Provocations have most justly deserved, and imploring His Blessing and Assistance on Our Arms, and for restoring and perpetuating Peace, Safety, and Prosperity to Us and Our Kingdoms. And We do strictly charge and command, That the said Publick Fast be reverently and devoutly observed by all Our loving Subjects in England, our Dominion of Wales, and Town of Berwick upon Tweed, as they tender the Favour of Almighty God, and would avoid His Wrath and Indignation; and upon Pain of such Punishment as We may justly inflict on all such as contemn and neglect the Performance of so religious and necessary a Duty. And for the better and more orderly solemnizing the same, We have given Directions to the Most Reverend the Archbishops, and the Right Reverend the Bishops of England, to compose a Form of Prayer suitable to this Occasion, to be used in all Churches, Chapels, and Places of Publick Worship, and to take care the same be timely dispersed throughout their respective Dioceses.

Given at Our Court at St. James's, the Twelfth of January, One thousand seven hundred and eighty-one, in the Twenty-first Year of Our Reign.

GOD SAVE THE KING.

London: Printed by Charles Eyre and William Strahan, Printers to the King's most Excellent Majesty. MDCCLXXXI.

1 p. folio. Copies in P. C., and P. R. O. Entered on Patent Rolls, and in Crown Office Docquet Book, vol. 12; entered in Privy Council Register, III Geo., vol. 19, p. 31. Printed in "London Gazette," January 13, 1781. A proclamation with practically the same wording was issued by the Lord Lieutenant and Council of Ireland, January 22, 1781 (copy in Dublin P. R. O.), in consequence of an order of the Privy Council (Privy Council Register, III Geo., vol. 19, p. 34).

1781, JANUARY 12.

[FAST DAY IN SCOTLAND.]

BY THE KING.

A PROCLAMATION

For a General Fast.

George R.

We, taking into Our most serious Consideration the just and necessary Hostilities in which We are engaged, and the unnatural Rebellion carrying on in some of Our Provinces and Colonies in North America, and putting our Trust in Almighty God, that he will vouchsafe a special Blessing on Our Arms both by Sea and Land, have resolved, and do, by and with the Advice of our Privy Council, hereby command, That a Publick Fast and Humiliation be observed, throughout that Part of Our Kingdom of Great Britain called Scotland, on Thursday the Twenty-second Day of February next; that so both We and Our People may humble Ourselves before Almighty God, in order to obtain Pardon of Our Sins; and may, in the most devout and solemn Manner, send up Our Prayers and Supplications to the Divine Majesty, for averting those heavy Judgements which Our manifold Sins and Provocations have most justly deserved, and imploring his Blessing and Assistance on Our Arms, and for restoring and perpetuating Peace, Safety, and Prosperity, to Us and Our Kingdoms: And We do stricly charge and command, That the said Publick Fast be reverently and devoutly observed by all Our loving Subjects in Scotland, as they tender the Favour of Almighty God, and would avoid His Wrath and Indignation; and upon Pain of such Punishment as We may justly inflict on all such as contemn and neglect the Performance of so religious and necessary a Duty. Our Will is therefore, and We charge, That incontinent this Our Proclamation seen, ye pass to the Market Cross of Edinburgh, and all other Places needful, and there, in Our Name and Authority, make Publication hereof, that none pretend Ignorance. And Our Will and Pleasure is, That Our Solicitor do cause printed Copies hereof to be sent to the Sheriffs of the several Shires, Stewarts of Stewarties, and Bailiffs of Regalities, and their Clerks, whom we ordain to see the same published; and We appoint them to send Doubles hereof to the several Paroch Kirks within their Bounds, that upon the Lord's Day immediately preceding the Day above-mentioned, the same may be published and read from the Pulpits, immediately after Divine Service.

Given at Our Court at St. James's, the Twelfth Day of January, One thousand seven hundred and eighty-one, in the Twenty-first Year of Our Reign.

God save the King.

London: Printed by Charles Eyre and William Strahan, Printers to the King's most Excellent Majesty. MDCCLXXXI.

1 p. folio. Copy in P. R. O. Entered on Patent Rolls, and in Crown Office Docquet Book, vol. 12; entered in Privy Council Register, III Geo., vol. 19, p. 33. Printed in "London Gazette," January 13, 1781.

1782, JANUARY 9.

[FAST DAY IN ENGLAND.]

BY THE KING.

A PROCLAMATION

For a General Fast.

George R.

We, taking into Our most serious Consideration the just and necessary Hostilities in which We are engaged, and the unnatural Rebellion carrying on in some of Our Provinces and Colonies in North America, and putting Our Trust in Almighty God, that he will vouchsafe a special Blessing on Our Arms both by Sea and Land, have resolved, and do, by and with the Advice of Our Privy Council, hereby command, That a Publick Fast and Humiliation be observed throughout that Part of Our Kingdom of Great Britain called England, Our Dominion of Wales, and Town of Berwick upon Tweed, upon Friday the Eighth Day of February next; that so both We and Our People may humble Ourselves before Almighty God, in order to obtain Pardon of Our Sins; and may, in the most devout and solemn Manner, send up Our Prayers and Supplications to the Divine Majesty, for averting those heavy Judgements which Our manifold Sins and Provocations have most justly deserved, and imploring His Blessing and Assistance on Our Arms, and for restoring and perpetuating Peace, Safety, and Prosperity to Us and Our Kingdoms: And We do strictly charge and command, That the said Publick Fast be reverently and devoutly observed by all Our loving Subjects in England, Our Dominion of Wales, and Town of Berwick upon Tweed, as they tender the Favour of Almighty God, and would avoid His Wrath and Indignation; and upon Pain of such Punishment as We may justly inflict on all such as contemn and neglect the performance of so religious and necessary a Duty. And for the better and more orderly solemnizing the same, We have given Directions to the Most Reverend the Archbishops, and the Right Reverend the Bishops of England, to compose a Form of Prayer suitable to this Occasion, to be used in all Churches, Chapels, and Places of Publick Worship, and to take Care the same be timely dispersed throughout their respective Dioceses.

Given at Our Court at St. James's, the Ninth Day of January, One thousand seven hundred and eighty-two, in the Twenty-second Year of Our Reign.

God save the King.

London: Printed by Charles Eyre and William Strahan, Printers to the King's most Excellent Majesty. MDCCLXXXII.

1 p. folio. Copies in P. C., and P. R. O. Entered on Patent Rolls, and in Crown Office Docquet Book, vol. 12; entered in Privy Council Register, III Geo., vol. 20, p. 124. Printed in "London Gazette," January 12, 1782. A proclamation with practically the same wording was issued by the Lord Lieutenant and Council of Ireland, January 17, 1782 (copy in Dublin P. R. O.), in consequence of an order of the Privy Council (Privy Council Register, III Geo., vol. 20, p. 126).

1782, JANUARY 9.

[FAST DAY IN SCOTLAND.]

BY THE KING.

A PROCLAMATION

For a General Fast.

George R.

We, taking into Our most serious Consideration the just and necessary Hostilities in which We are engaged, and the unnatural Rebellion carrying on in some of Our Provinces and Colonies in North America, and putting Our Trust in Almighty God, that he will vouchsafe a special Blessing on Our Arms both by Sea and Land, have resolved, and do, by and with the Advice of Our Privy Council, hereby command, That a Publick Fast and Humiliation be observed, throughout that Part of Our Kingdom of Great Britain called Scotland, on Thursday the Seventh Day of February next; that so both We and Our People may humble Ourselves before Almighty God, in order to obtain Pardon of Our Sins; and may, in the most devout and solemn Manner, send up Our Prayers and Supplications to the Divine Majesty, for averting those heavy Judgements which Our Manifold Sins and Provocations have most justly deserved, and imploring His Blessing and Assistance on Our Arms, and for restoring and perpetuating Peace, Safety, and Prosperity, to Us and Our Kingdoms: And We do strictly charge and command, That the said Publick Fast be reverently and devoutly observed by all Our loving Subjects in Scotland, as they tender the Favour of Almighty God, and would avoid His Wrath and Indignation; and upon Pain of such Punishment as We may justly inflict on all such as contemn and neglect the Performance of so religious and necessary a Duty. Our Will is therefore, and We charge, That incontinent this Our Proclamation seen, ye pass to the Market Cross of Edinburgh, and all other Places needful, and there, in Our Name and Authority, make Publication hereof, that none pretend Ignorance. And Our Will and Pleasure is, That Our Solicitor do cause printed Copies hereof to be sent to the Sheriffs of the several Shires, Stewarts of Stewarties, and Bailiffs of Regalities, and their Clerks, whom We ordain to see the same published; and We appoint them to send Doubles hereof to the several Paroch Kirks within their Bounds, that upon the Lord's Day immediately preceding the Day above-mentioned, the same may be published and read from the Pulpits, immediately after Divine Service.

Given at Our Court at St. James's, the Ninth Day of January, One thousand seven hundred and eighty-two, in the Twenty-second Year of Our Reign.

GOD SAVE THE KING.

London: Printed by Charles Eyre and William Strahan, Printers to the King's most Excellent Majesty. MDCCLXXXII.

1 p. folio. Copy in P. R. O. Entered on Patent Rolls, and in Crown Office Docquet Book, vol. 12; entered in Privy Council Register, III Geo., vol. 20, p. 125. Printed in "London Gazette," January 12, 1782.

1783, FEBRUARY 14.

[DECLARING CESSATION OF ARMS.]

BY THE KING.

A PROCLAMATION

DECLARING THE CESSATION OF ARMS, AS WELL BY SEA AS LAND, AGREED UPON BETWEEN HIS MAJESTY, THE MOST CHRISTIAN KING, THE KING OF SPAIN, THE STATES GENERAL OF THE UNITED PROVINCES, AND THE UNITED STATES OF AMERICA, AND ENJOINING THE OBSERVANCE THEREOF.

GEORGE R.

Whereas Provisional Articles were signed at Paris, on the Thirtieth Day of November last, between Our Commissioner for treating of Peace with the Commissioners of the United States of America and the Commissioners of the said States, to be inserted in and to constitute the Treaty of Peace proposed to be concluded between Us and the said United States, when Terms of Peace should be agreed upon between Us and his Most Christian Majesty:[91] And whereas Preliminaries for restoring Peace between Us and His Most Christian Majesty were signed at Versailles on the Twentieth Day of January last, by the Ministers of Us and the Most Christian King: And whereas Preliminaries for restoring Peace between Us and the King of Spain were also signed at Versailles on the Twentieth Day of January last, between the Ministers of Us and the King of Spain: And whereas, for putting an End to the Calamity of War as soon and as far as may be possible, it hath been agreed between Us, his Most Christian Majesty, the King of Spain, the States General of the United Provinces, and the United States of America, as follows; that is to say,

That such Vessels and Effects as should be taken in the Channel and in the North Seas, after the Space of Twelve Days, to be computed from the Ratification of the said Preliminary Articles, should be restored on all Sides; That the Term should be One Month from the Channel and the North Seas as far as the Canary Islands inclusively, whether in the Ocean or in the Mediterranean; Two Months from the said Canary Islands as far as the Equinoctial Line or Equator; and lastly, Five Months in all other Parts of the World, without any Exception, or any other more particular Description of Time or Place.

And whereas the Ratifications of the said Preliminary Articles between Us

[91] The text of the Provisional Articles of November 30, 1782, can be found in *Treaties and Conventions* (1889), p. 370.

and the Most Christian King, in due Form, were exchanged by the Ministers of Us and of the Most Christian King, on the Third Day of this instant February; and the Ratifications of the said Preliminary Articles between Us and the King of Spain were exchanged between the Ministers of Us and of the King of Spain, on the Ninth Day of this instant February; from which Days respectively the several Terms above-mentioned, of Twelve Days, of One Month, of Two Months, and of Five Months, are to be computed: And whereas it is Our Royal Will and Pleasure that the Cessation of Hostilities between Us and the States General of the United Provinces, and the United States of America, should be agreeable to the Epochs fixed between Us and the Most Christian King:

We have thought fit, by and with the Advice of Our Privy Council, to notify the same to all Our loving Subjects; and We do declare, that Our Royal Will and Pleasure is, and We do hereby strictly charge and command all Our Officers, both at Sea and Land, and all other Our Subjects whatsoever, to forbear all Acts of Hostility, either by Sea or Land, against His Most Christian Majesty, the King of Spain, the States General of the United Provinces, and the United States of America, their Vassals or Subjects, from and after the respective Times above-mentioned, and under the Penalty of incurring Our highest Displeasure.

Given at Our Court at St. James's, the Fourteenth Day of February, in the Twenty-third Year of Our Reign, and in the Year of Our Lord One thousand seven hundred and eighty-three.

GOD SAVE THE KING.

London: Printed by Charles Eyre and William Strahan, Printers to the King's most Excellent Majesty. 1783.

1 p. folio. Copies in P. C., and P. R. O. Entered on Patent Rolls, and in Crown Office Docquet Book, vol. 12; entered in Privy Council Register, III Geo., vol. 21, p. 181. Printed in "London Gazette," February 15, 1783, and in many of the American newspapers. Reprinted by James Rivington at New York, 1783, as a broadside, a copy of which is in the N. Y. Public Library. There is also a lithographic facsimile in the Emmet Collection in the N. Y. Public Library.

INDEX.

Lector House believes that a society develops through a two-fold approach of continuous learning and adaptation, which is derived from the study of classic literary works spread across the historic timeline of literature records. Therefore, we aim at reviving, repairing and redeveloping all those inaccessible or damaged but historically as well as culturally important literature across subjects so that the future generations may have an opportunity to study and learn from past works to embark upon a journey of creating a better future.

This book is a result of an effort made by Lector House towards making a contribution to the preservation and repair of original ancient works which might hold historical significance to the approach of continuous learning across subjects.

HAPPY READING & LEARNING!

LECTOR HOUSE LLP
E-MAIL: lectorpublishing@gmail.com